Comparative Politics

A Theoretical Framework

SECOND EDITION

Gabriel A. Almond

Stanford University

G. Bingham Powell, Jr.

University of Rochester

Robert J. Mundt

University of North Carolina at Charlotte

 HarperCollins*CollegePublishers*

Acquisitions Editor: Leo A. W. Wiegman
Project Coordination and Text Design: York Production Services
Cover Illustration/Photograph: Melissa Hayden/Photonica
Cover Designer: Kay Petronio
Electronic Production Manager: Mike Kemper
Electronic Page Makeup: York Production Services
Manufacturing Manager: Helen G. Landers
Printer and Binder: R.R. Donnelley & Sons Company
Cover Printer: Phoenix Color Corp.

Comparative Politics A Theoretical Framework

Library of Congress Cataloging-in-Publication Data

Almond, Gabriel Abraham, 1911–
   Comparative politics: a theoretical framework / Gabriel A. Almond, G. Bingham Powell, Jr., Robert J. Mundt.
      p.   cm.
   Includes bibliographical references and index.
   ISBN 0-673-52480-9
   1. Comparative government.   I. Powell, G. Bingham. II. Mundt, Robert J.   III. Title.
JF51.A575   1995
320.3–dc20   95-45451
                                                                 CIP

98 9 8 7 6 5 4 3

Contents

Preface   vii

Part One
INTRODUCTION   1

Gabriel A. Almond and G. Bingham Powell, Jr.

Chapter 1
ISSUES IN COMPARATIVE POLITICS   3
The Actors in Comparative Politics: Old and New States   3
Big and Small States   5
Rich and Poor Countries   6
Economic Inequality Within Countries   10
Dilemmas: Population Growth, Economic Development,
   and Environment   11
Ethnic and Religious Differences   14
World Trends and Political Problems   20
Key Terms   24
Suggested Readings   25

Chapter 2
CONCEPTS IN COMPARATIVE POLITICS   26
Why We Compare   26
How We Compare   27
A Few Definitions   28
Comparative Systems: Structure and Function   28
Political Structures or Institutions   31
An Illustrative Comparison: Russia in 1987 and 1994   35
The Policy Level: Performance, Outcome, and Evaluation   38
Key Terms   39
Suggested Readings   40

Part Two
SYSTEM, PROCESS, AND POLICY   41
Gabriel A. Almond and G. Bingham Powell, Jr.

Chapter 3
POLITICAL CULTURE AND POLITICAL SOCIALIZATION   43
Political Culture   43
Mapping the Three Levels of Political Culture   44
Political Socialization   50
Agents of Political Socialization   51
Trends in Contemporary Political Cultures   57
Key Terms   60
Suggested Readings   62

Chapter 4
POLITICAL STRUCTURE AND POLITICAL RECRUITMENT   63
Elections: An Example   63
Democratic and Authoritarian Political Structures   66
The Recruitment of Citizens   68
How Much Participation?   75
The Recruitment of Elites   76
Control of Elites   80
Key Terms   81
Suggested Readings   82

Chapter 5
INTEREST GROUPS AND INTEREST ARTICULATION   84
Types of Interest Groups   85
Access to the Influential   91
Policy Perspectives on Interest Articulation   96
Interest Group Development   98
Key Terms   100
Suggested Readings   102

Chapter 6
INTEREST AGGREGATION AND POLITICAL PARTIES   104

Interest Groups and Interest Aggregation   105
Competitive Party Systems and Interest Aggregation   107
Authoritarian Party Systems   116
Military Forces and Interest Aggregation   119
Trends in Interest Aggregations   121
Significance of Interest Aggregation   123
Key Terms   124
Suggested Readings   127

Chapter 7
GOVERNMENT AND POLICYMAKING   129

Decision Rules for Policymaking   130
Assemblies   138
Political Executives   142
The Bureaucracy   146
Key Terms   150
Suggested Readings   152

Chapter 8
PUBLIC POLICY   153

Extractive Performance   154
Distributive Performance   157
Regulative Performance   161
Symbolic Performance   163
Outcomes of Political Performance   164
Domestic Welfare Outcomes   164
Domestic Security Outcomes   171
Outputs and Outcomes in the International Arena   173
Political Goods and Political Productivity: A System, Process,
    and Policy Approach   176
Strategies for Producing Political Goods   179
Trade-offs and Opportunity Costs   186
Key Terms   187
Suggested Readings   189

Index   191

Preface

Comparative Politics: A Theoretical Framework, Second Edition, presents in the form of a separate book, the revised and updated chapters of Parts One and Two of Comparative Politics Today: A World View, Sixth Edition. Our purpose is to make our theoretical approach readily available to teachers of comparative politics who prefer to make their own selections of reading materials from the HarperCollins Comparative Politics Series and from the larger literature of country and analytical studies. In publishing this book HarperCollins continues the tradition of Comparative Politics: A Developmental Approach (1966), and the later edition of this work which was published under the title of Comparative Politics: System, Process, and Policy (1978).

As the second edition of Comparative Politics: A Theoretical Framework appears in the post Soviet world of the late 1990s democratization and liberal economic reforms continue as world wide trends, but some of the hoped for democratic transitions have already been aborted, while other appear fragile. The freeing of markets also continues, but the costs of economic transitions have been larger than expected and the anticipated benefits have often been slow to arrive. Many countries are divided by violent ethnic conflicts, and torn by fundamentalist religious movements. Some countries appear to be losing their coherence, and falling into chaos. Population growth and economic development impose intolerable burdens on the environment, challenging our capacity to cope and avoid disaster. A completely revised first chapter deals with these critical issues of contemporary politics.

The functional approach to comparative politics, pioneered in the earlier editions of this book is presented in summary in Chapter 2, and then in detail in Chapters 3—8. In these chapters we introduce the three levels of system, process, and policy. Understanding politics requires that we spell out how different kinds of political systems are formed, maintained, and changed through the cultural and structural processes of socialization and recruitment. These processes are treated in detail in Chapters 3 and 4.

The processes of policymaking, and the structures which dominate them, are treated in Chapters 5, 6, and 7, dealing with interest articulation and interest groups, interest aggregation and political parties, governmental institutions and policymaking processes. Chapter 8 deals with policy in the substantive sense, showing how the system and process functions affect the ways in which different kinds of political systems cope with the internal problems of welfare, security, and liberty, and the external ones of international security, welfare, and equity.

This threefold analytic structure enables the reader to move easily and logically from institution to institution, and from process to process without losing the essential thread of connection and meaning. In a discussion of political parties, for example, the reader is not simply confronted with descriptive detail but is led back to the socioeconomic and political phenomena which help explain the characteristics of a particular party system on the one hand, and led forward to some of the policy consequences of that party system on the other. In our approach we have avoided reductionism which seeks to explain politics as a consequence of social structure, or psychological and cultural characteristics. Governmental agencies and institutions as often become the independent variables—the initiators of socioeconomic and economic change—and the social and international environment the dependent ones. From a methodological point of view, Comparative Politics: A Theoretical Framework provides an interface for politics and public policy with the analytic approaches of sociology, psychology, and anthropology on the one hand and economics and philosophy on the other. Only this full range of interdisciplinary analysis makes it possible to capture the significance of the realm of politics, that which shapes and constrains it, but more important the choices and potentialities which it holds out to humanity.

Over the years we have had reason to be grateful to many colleagues for their suggestions for changes and improvements in this book as it has moved from edition to edition. For this edition we are particularly grateful to Thomas Remington for his help on Chapter 2, to Russell Dalton for his advice and suggestions particularly on Chapters 1 and 8; and to Frances Hagopian and Anne Lesch for their comments on our treatment of developing countries. We also wish to record our appreciation for the thoughtful and imaginative work of Leo Wiegman and Christopher Korintus of the Political Science section of HarperCollins who supervised and monitored the editing and production of this book. Tom Kulesa made important contributions to the visual aid program and the production of text supplements. Suzanne Daghlian has ably handled marketing for the prior and current edition.

In addition, a number of reviewers provided useful suggestions: David Mednicoff of Emory University, Suzanne Fiederlein of Virginia Commonwealth University, Mark A. Cichock of the University of Texas at Arlington, M. M. Eskandari-Qajar of Santa Barbara City College, Kaare Strom of the University of California at San Diego, William R. Garner of Southern Illinois University at Carbondale, Louis D. Hayes of the University of Montana, and Arend Lijphart of the University of California at San Diego.

Gabriel A. Almond
G. Bingham Powell, Jr.
Robert J. Mundt

PART
One

INTRODUCTION

Gabriel A. Almond
G. Bingham Powell, Jr.

Chapter *1*

Issues in Comparative Politics

THE ACTORS IN COMPARATIVE POLITICS: OLD AND NEW STATES

We begin our book by describing in a very general way what we compare in the study of comparative politics. Just about the entire surface of the world today is covered by independent countries. We call them *states* or *nations* or *nation-states*, and refer to their institutions as *governments*. When we speak of a "state," we have in mind an independent legal authority over a population in a particular territory. In America we confuse things a bit by calling the 50 constituent units that make up the United States "states," reflecting the "federal" or divided character of the American government (see Chapter 7). The states of the United States share the power and authority of the "state" with the central government.

When we speak of a "nation," we refer to the self-identification of a people, based on the language they speak and the values, allegiances, and historical memories they share. Some countries are nation-states in the sense that national identification and scope of legal authority largely coincide. But with recent trends in migration such previously uni-national states as France, Japan, and Germany, have become more multinational. Other countries such as the United States, Great Britain, and Canada, and others have long been multinational and have become even more so in recent decades. Whether a country is a uni-national state or a multinational state makes a lot of difference for its politics. And we will have something to say about this later in this chapter.

There were some 185 "member-states" of the United Nations (UN) in the spring of 1994.[1] The actual numbers of independent countries is greater than the total membership of the UN, and what with secessionary movements in today's world our figures may quickly get out of date. A little over two centuries ago, at the time the United States was gaining its independence, most of the independent states were in Europe (see Figure 1.1). Much of the rest of the world had been parcelled out as colonies to one or another of the European empires. Column two of Figure 1.1 shows the increase in the number of nations that took place in the nineteenth and early twentieth centuries, principally in Latin America when the Spanish and Portuguese empires broke up into 20 independent nations. Europe also experienced some of this movement toward national separation and independence as the Turkish Empire gave up Greece, Bulgaria, and Albania; and Scandinavia and the Low Countries divided into their present form. During the period between the two world wars (Figure 1.1, column 3) national proliferation extended to North Africa and the Middle East; and Europe continued to fragment as the Russian and Austro-Hungarian empires gave up Poland, Finland, Czechoslovakia, and Yugoslavia. There was a brief period of inde-

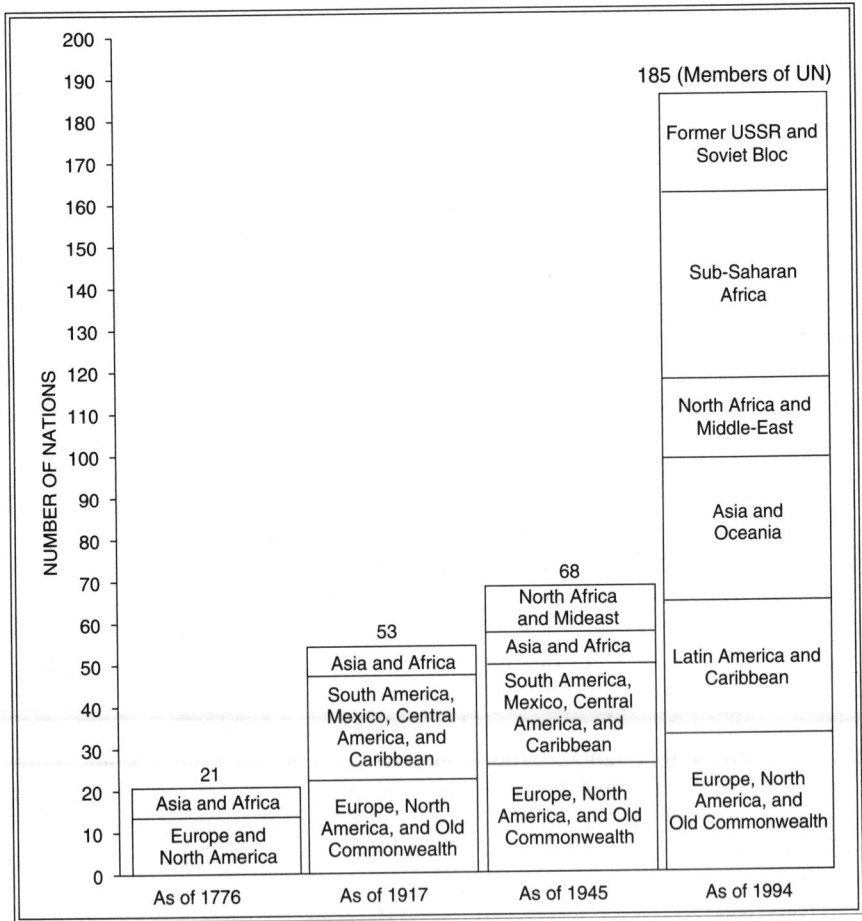

Figure 1.1 Formation of nations since 1776. (*Source:* For contemporary (to 1994) members, Information Office, United Nations. Data to 1945 from Charles Taylor and Michael Hudson, *World Handbook of Political and Social Indicators*. New Haven, CT: Yale Univ. Press, 1972, pp. 26 ff.)

pendence for the three Baltic countries—Lithuania, Latvia, and Estonia—between the wars, but they lost their independence in World War II and regained it in 1991.

In the period since World War II the development of new nations has really taken off. By 1994 117 new countries had joined the 68 countries that were in existence as of 1945. Forty-five (24 percent) out of the total number were in Sub-Saharan Africa; 34 (18 percent) were in Latin America and the Caribbean; 32 (17 percent) were in Asia and Oceania; 27 (15 percent) were in Europe, North America, and the countries of the Old Commonwealth; and the same number were in the former USSR and Eastern Europe. In the 1990s alone more than 20 new nations—mostly the successor states of the Soviet Union, Yugoslavia, and Czechoslovakia—have come into separate existence.

All these countries—new as well as old—share certain characteristics. They have legal authority over their territories and people; they have armies, air forces in most cases, and in some cases navies; they collect taxes and spend money; they regulate their economies, maintain public order, and pursue their general welfare. They send and receive ambassadors; they belong to the United Nations; and they do all these things through parliaments, cabinets, ministries, departments, courts, police, and prisons. But they also vary in many ways. Their physical size, histories, institutions, cultures, religions, economies, social structures—all of the factors that shape their politics—differ, often profoundly.

BIG AND SMALL STATES

Even without the rest of the former Soviet Union, Russia is still the largest country in area with more than 17 million square kilometers. China has the most people, with more than a billion. There are many countries at the other extreme, but the smallest legally independent political entity in both respects is Vatican City, the headquarters of the Catholic Church, with an area of less than half a square kilometer and under a thousand residents.

Table 1.1 reports the *population* and area of the 12 countries included in this book. China and India are clearly the population behemoths; Russia, China, the United States, and Brazil are the area giants. The population growth rate of the so-called Third World countries—Nigeria, Egypt, India, and Brazil—is double that of the advanced industrial countries. The political implications of these striking contrasts in population size and geographic area are not obvious or easily evaluated. It does not follow that only big countries are important and influential. Cuba challenged the United States for more than 30 years; Israel stands off the Arab world; and tiny Vatican City has great power and influence.

Nor does it follow that area and population size determine a country's political system. Both Luxembourg and the United States are democracies. Authoritarian regimes can be found in countries that are small, medium, or large. These enormous contrasts in size show only that the countries now making up the world differ greatly in their range of physical and human resources. Although area and population do not determine politics, economics, or culture, they are important factors affecting economic development, foreign policy and defense problems, and many other issues of political significance. The growth rates of populations have impor-

Table 1.1   AREA AND POPULATION OF SELECTED COUNTRIES

	Population (millions in 1992)	Average Annual Growth of Population (percent 1980–92)	Area (thousands of km)
China	1,162	1.4	9,561
India	884	2.1	3,288
United States	255	1.0	9,373
Brazil	154	2.0	8,512
Russia	149	0.6	17,075
Japan	125	0.5	378
Nigeria	102	3.0	924
Mexico	85	2.0	1,958
Germany	81	0.2	357
United Kingdom	58	0.2	245
France	57	0.5	552
Egypt	55	2.4	1,001

Source: World Bank, *World Development Report 1994* (New York: Oxford Univ. Press, 1994), Tables 1 and 25, pp. 162, 210.

tant implications for economic development. With population growth rates double those of the advanced countries, the Third World countries have to grow economically twice as fast just to keep from falling further behind.

The geographic location of nations has strategic implications that have been of great importance in their development. A nation located in the center of Europe in the sixteenth through nineteenth centuries could not avoid building a large land army to protect itself from the predatory threats of its neighbors. Such a nation would have difficulty developing free political institutions, since it would have to extract resources on a large scale and keep its population under control through *centralization*. England in the course of its development was protected by the English Channel; it could defend itself through its navy. It could do with a smaller army, lower taxation, and less centralization of power. The United States was a similar case. The Atlantic Ocean and the relatively open continent were of crucial importance in shaping U.S. political institutions. Far removed from the centers of Western development, the peoples of Asia, Africa, and Latin America were dominated, and in most cases colonized, by the more powerful Western nations. Only in recent decades, having won their freedom, are these nations seeking to develop their economies and modernize their societies, catching up in the cases of South Korea, Taiwan, and Singapore; and in the case of Japan, passing the Western pacesetters.

RICH AND POOR COUNTRIES

As significant as physical size, population, and location may be, such factors as the availability of natural resources, the level of economic and social development, and the rate of economic growth and social change are of equal, if not greater, importance. Economic development implies new resources that create possibilities for public welfare, as well as leading to challenges to master its often devastating impact on nature. The social changes that result from economic development transform the political processes of developing countries, and these processes are tested and strained by the difficult policy challenges confronting them.

Figure 1.2 gives the gross national product per capita for the twelve nations that we include in this book. We provide two measures of the national income of the twelve countries included in our book. *Gross National Product (GNP)* which is computed according to the exchange rate of the national currency is the standard measure which has been used over the years. *Purchasing Power Parity (PPP)* is a newer measure introduced by the International Monetary Fund which takes into account differences in price levels.[2] Figure 1.2 shows that when these differences are taken into account the income of Third World countries turns out to be substantially higher than has been previously reported. Thus Brazilian PPP per capita is almost twice its GNP per capita; China's and India's are almost four times as high. At the opposite end of the scale, the measure of Japan's per capita product is reduced from $28,190 to a $20,160, Germany's from $23,030 to $20,610, when we shift from the exchange rate measure to the purchasing power measure. Thus the income ratios in purchasing power while large as between the rich and the poor countries, are not as great as we have reported in earlier editions of this book. The Brazilian economy is about one-fourth that of the Japanese economy according to the purchasing power measure, and not one-ninth which would be the case if we used the exchange rate measure. The Chinese per capita product turns out to be about one-tenth that of Japan, and not less than a fiftieth according to the exchange rate measure.

The degree of inequality of income among nations has been somewhat exaggerated in other respects. Our statistics tend to underestimate goods and services produced and consumed by individuals themselves when they are engaged in sub-

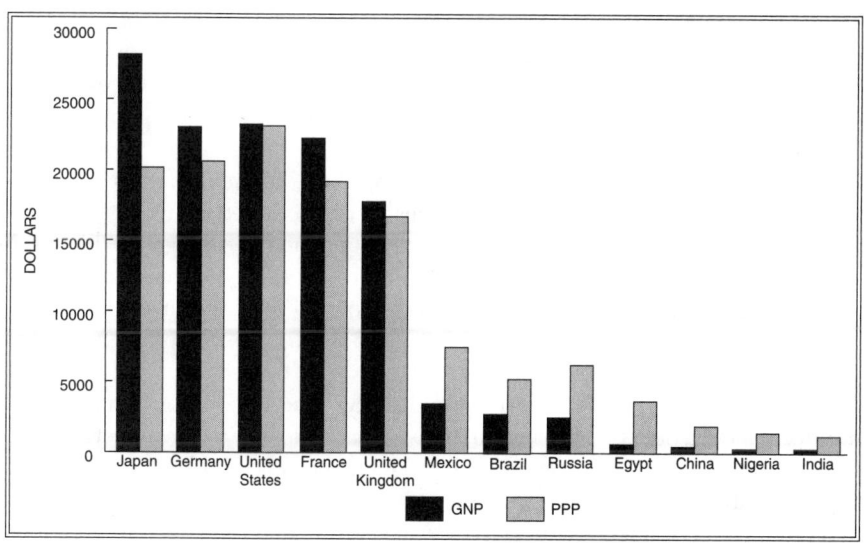

Figure 1.2 Per capita GNP and PPP for selected nations (in U.S. dollars, 1992). (*Source:* World Bank, *World Development Report.* New York: Oxford Univ. Press, 1994, Table 1, pp. 162–63; Table 30, pp. 220–21.)

sistence agriculture, or in household production for family use. Similarly national product estimates are not corrected for differences in the "cost of living" under different environmental conditions. As the *World Development Report* points out ". . . GNP is higher in colder countries, where people spend more money on heating and warm clothing, than in balmy climates, where people are comfortable wearing light clothing in the open air."[3]

These corrections in our numbers, and our interpretations of them, should not be permitted to conceal the great inequalities in the conditions of life in the developed, developing, and underdeveloped parts of the world. The implications of these differences are treated in detail in Chapter 8.

In Figure 1.3 we compare the percentages of the economically active populations employed in agriculture for our 12 selected countries. The first conclusion we draw after comparing Figures 1.2 and 1.3 is that the smaller the per capita GNP (or PPP) the larger is the proportion of the *labor force* used in agriculture. At the right side of the figure, the five advanced industrial countries—Japan, Germany, France, the United States, and the United Kingdom—all have agricultural labor forces in the single digits, the United States and the Great Britain at 2 percent each. At the left side of Figure 1.3 the three poorest countries—China, India, and Nigeria—have more than two-thirds of their labor forces employed in agriculture. The middle-income countries—Mexico and Brazil—have around a third to a fifth of their labor forces in agriculture.

Thus we have a picture of the economies of the rich countries as predominantly industrial, commercial, and professional, while the economies of the poor countries are predominantly agricultural. To be rich and industrialized, with a large professional service sector, also means to be healthy, literate, and educated (see Chapter 8) and to have access to the larger world of complex events, activities, and values. In highly industrialized countries such as Japan, Germany, the United States, France, and Britain practically everyone over the age of 15 can read and write. In India, Nigeria, and Egypt only one-half the adult population or less has this minimal degree of education. Moreover, the countries with the fewest literate citizens also have the fewest radios and television sets—devices that do not require literacy.

Industrialization, education, and exposure to the communications media are associated with better nutrition and medical care. In the economically advanced countries, fewer children die in infancy, and people on the average live longer. In recent years the average citizen of Britain, France, Germany, Japan, and the United States has had a life expectancy at birth of about 75 years. The average Mexican has a life expectancy of 66 years; the Indian, 61 years; the Egyptian, around 60 years; and the Nigerian little more than 50 years (see Table 8.3).

These characteristics—material productivity, education, exposure to communications media, longer and healthier lives—are closely interconnected. Only when a country becomes economically productive can it afford better education, communications media, and good nutrition and health care. In order to become more productive, it needs the resources to develop a skilled and healthy labor force and build the factories, productive farms, and transportation systems that material welfare requires. Preindustrial nations face most urgently the issues of economic

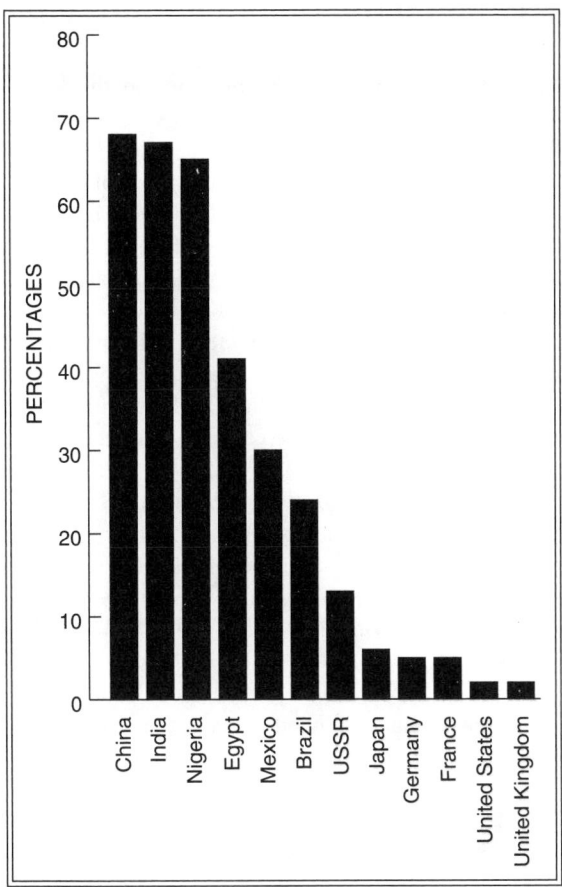

Figure 1.3 Percentage of economically active population in agriculture for selected nations (1990). (*Source:* FAO, United Nations, FAO Production Yearbook 1990 Rome: UN, 1991.)

development: how to improve the immediate welfare of their citizens, yet also build and invest for the future. Typically, these are also newer nations, and hence they also face the challenge of creating national awareness and building effective political institutions.

While the goal of economic growth for the lower-income economies of the world is generally accepted and fostered by such international agencies as the United Nations, the World Bank, and the International Development Fund, as well as the development aid programs of individual advanced industrial nations—it is now recognized as having an ominous "downside." The advanced economies have only begun to pay for the environmental costs of their industrial development. Questions of despoiled forests, depleted soils and fisheries, polluted air and bodies of water, endangered species, and a threatened ozone layer, now burden the legislative dockets of the economically advanced world. And these nations have not as yet solved the problem of what to do about the waste produced by nuclear power.

ECONOMIC INEQUALITY WITHIN COUNTRIES

It is misleading to distinguish among nations only on the basis of total mineral resources, gross national production, and averages such as per capita income, and the like. Wealth, income, and opportunity are not evenly distributed within nations, and these *inequalities* are among the most serious causes of political conflict. A large gross national product may conceal significant differences in the distribution of economic and social amenities and opportunities. A high rate of national growth may benefit only particular regions or social groups, leaving large areas or parts of the population unrewarded or even less well off than before. The "inner cities" of the United States; the older parts of such Indian cities as Delhi, Calcutta, and Bombay; the Barrios around the cities of Latin America; such regions as Appalachia in the United States, the Mezzogiorno (south) of Italy, and the arid north of Brazil—all suffer from poverty and hopelessness, while other parts of their countries experience growth and improved welfare.

The political processes of a country may be affected sharply by internal divisions of income, wealth, and occupation. Table 1.2 compares income distribution for most of the countries included in this book. Data on income distribution are not available for all of our 12 countries. We have substituted Poland for Russia, and Algeria and Ghana for Egypt and Nigeria, since the *World Bank Development Report* provides information on income distributions in these comparable countries. The table makes the point that there is a positive association between economic development and equality of income, at least past a certain stage in economic growth. Wealthy nations like Japan, the United States, and European countries tend to have more equitable income distributions than middle-income countries such as Brazil and Mexico. In the advanced industrial nations, the wealthiest 10 percent of the households receive about one-quarter of the national income, while the

Table 1.2   INCOME DISTRIBUTION FOR SELECTED NATIONS

Country	Year	Wealthiest 10%	Poorest 40%	GNP per Capita (1992)
Japan	1979	22.4	21.9	28,190
Germany	1988	24.4	18.8	23,030
United States	1985	25.0	15.7	23,240
France	1979	26.1	17.4	22,260
United Kingdom	1979	27.8	14.6	17,790
Mexico	1984	39.5	11.9	3,470
Brazil	1989	51.3	7.0	2,770
Poland	1989	21.6	23.0	1,910
Algeria	1988	31.7	17.9	1,840
China	1990	24.6	17.4	470
India	1989	27.1	21.3	31.0
Ghana	1989	29.0	18.3	450

Source: World Bank, *World Development Report, 1994* (New York: Oxford Univ. Press, 1994), Table 30, pp. 220–22.

poorest 40 percent receive about one-fifth. In the United States in 1985, the poorest 40 percent got less than one-eighth of the national income. Poorer nations, represented in Table 1.2 by India and Ghana, distributed around 30 percent of their income to the wealthiest one-tenth of their households and around 20 percent to their poorest two-fifths. In middle-income Brazil, the wealthiest 10 percent got more than one-half of the national income, and the poorest 40 percent got less than one-tenth. In a developed country such as Japan, the rich receive a little over four times the income going to the poor. In Mexico, a middle-income country, the ratio is closer to 10 to 1; and in Brazil it is more than 20 to 1. Yet the table also suggests that ideological and political characteristics make a difference. Poland in 1989, still reflecting the income distribution tendencies under former Communist rule, had a pattern more similar to its wealthier European neighbors than to the Latin American nations at comparable levels of GNP. It is also intriguing that the only Communist nation in our set of 12—China—had a similar income distribution to that of the advanced capitalist nations.

The association of industrialization and high productivity with more equal distribution of income has been true historically and tends to be true today. The first stages of industrialization and modernization may actually increase inequality in the distribution of income by creating a dual economy and society—a rural sector, with wide variation of landholding and status, and an urban industrial commercial sector, with its own differentials in income and consumption patterns. This pattern appears in the table, if we contrast inequality in India with even greater inequality in the somewhat richer countries of Mexico and Brazil. These inequalities, already present in most preindustrial societies, tend to increase at the same time as education and communication are spreading; this pattern helps explain the political instability of many developing countries. Income inequality is increasing at the same time that awareness of it is increasing. Inequality, then, is an issue all developing nations must face.

The fact that distributive equity improves somewhat in the later stages of economic growth should not be construed to mean that the issue of inequality disappears in the advanced nations. Interest groups such as trade unions and agricultural organizations are also strongly developed in these nations, and bargaining over the distribution of the economic and social product in the form of wages, or the imposition of the tax burden, often takes on highly conflictual, even violent, proportions. In the United States in the last decade, income inequality has increased substantially as a consequence of changes in economic structure, the rise of the single-parent family, and an increasingly regressive tax burden.

DILEMMAS: POPULATION GROWTH, ECONOMIC DEVELOPMENT, AND ENVIRONMENT

The issue of economic inequality has a very important international side. We have already shown in our discussion of rich and poor countries that the contrasts in productivity per capita are very large. We have also shown that internal inequality tends to increase as poor countries develop their economies. Mexico and Brazil are good examples. Students of these problems have proposed a variety of policy solutions which might mitigate the hardships and inequities that attend these processes. One of these studies sponsored by the World Bank, appearing in several editions in the 1970s and 1980s bore the title *Redistribution With Growth.*[4] The policies recommended in these studies were specifically intended to avoid the extreme cases of grossly "unequal development" such as in Brazil and Mexico. The economists involved in these studies pointed to two countries of East Asia, Taiwan and South Korea, which had combined rapid economic growth with a more equitable distributive pattern. In these countries early land reforms had equalized opportunity at the outset of the developmental process. Investment in education, in agricultural inputs and rural infrastructure (principally roads and water), and in labor-intensive industries, and an emphasis on export-oriented growth, had produced remarkable results. These results were based on a sound program of exploiting their *comparative advantage* in cheap and skilled labor which enabled them to compete effectively in international markets. Thus policies leading to growth of a more equitable kind (a solution to the dilemma of growth and inequality within nations) were well understood by the last decades, although putting them into practice can be very difficult, especially where substantial inequalities have already emerged. But these prospects were not reconciled with the prospects of population expansion, which was acquiring momentum in these same decades and which was particularly rapid in Third World countries.

We have already noted that although economic development brings many benefits, it also imposes serious costs on the environment. Another book appearing in the last years under the title *The Population Explosion*[5] drew sharp attention to the great burden on the environment which had resulted from the population growth and industrial development of the nineteenth and twentieth centuries. Even with recent extraordinary remedial measures, our arable soil, our forests, the quality of our air and water, the welfare of our plant and animal life, and the continuity of our climate had been seriously damaged by this combination of recent economic and demographic growth. It has become clear that we now must cope with a second dilemma along with the first one of combining economic growth with equity, that of counteracting the effect of the combined growth of the economy and the population on the environment.

Table 1.3 puts the second dilemma in sharp relief. The table divides world population into three strata—that of low-income economies (averaging $340 per annum), middle-income economies (averaging $2,490 per annum), and high-income economies (averaging $22,600 per annum). In 1992 the low-income economies had a population total of more than 3 billion, or 60 percent of the total world population; the middle-income group had roughly one-fourth of the total population, and the high-income population was 15 percent. Assuming that population would increase to 8 billion from its base of 5.5 billion in 1992, and assuming a more rapid growth of population in the poorer countries, a rapid rate of economic growth in the Third World, comparable to that of the East Asian "Little Tigers," would result in very great burdens on the environment indeed.

These prospects are frightening, and they have produced a mixed literature of both light and heat. Economist Amartya Sen warned us recently of a "danger that

Table 1.3   POPULATION BY ECONOMIC DEVELOPMENT LEVEL IN 1992 AND
PROJECTED TO 2025 (IN MILLIONS US$)

| Economic | In 1992 | | Projected to 2025 | |
Development Level	Number	Percent	Number	Percent
Low-Income Economies	3,191	59	5,062	62
Middle-Income Economies	1,416	26	2,139	27
High-Income Economies	828	15	922	11
Total	5,437	100	8,123	100

Source: World Bank, *World Development Report 1994* (New York: Oxford Univ. Press, 1994), Tables 1 and 25.

in the confrontation between apocalyptic pessimism on one hand, and a dismissive smugness, on the other, a genuine understanding of the nature of the population problem may be lost."[6] He points to the following tendencies: The first impact of "modernization" on population is to increase it rapidly through the introduction of sanitation measures and modern pharmaceuticals that reduce the death rate. As an economy develops, however, public policies and changing incentives tend to reduce fertility. With education (particularly of women) and improved health and welfare associated with development, the advantages of lower fertility become clear, and the rate of population growth declines. This happened in Europe and North America as they underwent industrialization, and this appears to be taking place in the developing world. Thus the general rate of yearly population growth in the world has declined in the last two decades from 2.2 percent to 1.7 percent. The rate of population growth in India, for example, rose to 2.2 percent in the 1970s, and has declined since then. Latin America peaked at a higher rate and then came down sharply. The great problem area is Sub-Saharan Africa with an average growth rate of more than 3 percent each year.[7]

But while the trend is in the desired direction, the rate of decline in population, and its geographic incidence leaves us with problems of a very serious order. One of our countries, China, has confronted this problem with a solution that Amartya Sen calls an "override" policy under which the state coerces the fertility decisions of its people through abortion and contraception. China has produced dramatic results at great costs. India and other countries have had some success in following what Sen calls a "collaborative" approach, involving governmental intervention in influencing family choices, as well as counting on such influences as the market and education on choices.[8] The case of Kerala in southern India is a dramatic example of what can be accomplished by the "collaborative" approach, where expanding education particularly among women, and otherwise improving conditions, has reduced fertility to a greater extent than in China, and even in Sweden, the United States, and Canada.

Amartya Sen tells us that humankind can resolve these dilemmas by drawing on our knowledge of, and experience with, these demographic-economic-environmental processes, without heavy coercion. The destructive costs and irreversible tendencies prophesied by the "Apocalyptic pessimists" are not necessary, but avoidable. To avoid them, however, requires sacrifices and foresight, difficult to mobilize in a world divided into almost 200 independent countries where powerful interests support the status quo.

ETHNIC AND RELIGIOUS DIFFERENCES

Countries are divided not only according to differences in income, wealth, and opportunity, but also by physical differences, language, culture, religion, and history. Even before the end of the Cold War and probably associated with the spread of education and of the mass media, ethnic autonomy movements in parts of old countries—such as the United Kingdom (the Scots and Welsh), Canada (the Quebecois), France (the Bretons), Spain (the Catalonians and the Basques)—sought to break free or achieve more independence. And since the end of the Cold War, many newly established or newly free states of the former Soviet bloc have been coming apart at their ethnic and religious seams. The successor countries of the Soviet Union—such as Georgia, Armenia, and Azerbaijan—are involved in conflicts with their neighbors over boundaries, as well as in internal conflicts over ethnic and religious separatism. In the former Yugoslavia, secession of a number of provinces triggered several wars. The most brutal of these has taken place in Bosnia-Herzegovina, where a newly proclaimed Muslim regime faced rebellion and a murderous "ethnic cleansing" campaign by the large Serbian minority, backed by their fellow Serbs who constitute the majority in the remaining Yugoslavian state. Intervention by the UN, NATO, and the United States to contain Serbian aggression and mediate a settlement has thus far met with frustration.

In the Third World the boundaries established by former colonial powers often cut across ethnic lines. In 1947 the British withdrew from their Indian empire, and divided the subcontinent into a northern Muslim area—Pakistan—and a southern Hindu area—India. The most immediate consequence was a terrible civil conflict and "ethno-religious" cleansing incidental to the exchange of populations. There still is a very large minority (almost 100 million) of Muslims in India. Twenty years ago the Ibo "tribe" of Nigeria fought an unsuccessful separatist war with the rest of Nigeria, led by the Islamic northern "tribes"—the Hausa-Fulani—resulting in the deaths of millions of people. As we write these words the Tutsi and Hutu peoples of the small African state of Rwanda have been engaged in a civil war of extermination, with hundreds of thousands of people slaughtered, and millions fleeing the country in fear of their lives.

Vestiges of imperial conquest (by Russia, Britain, France, Spain, Portugal, and the Netherlands) are one source of contemporary division. The migration of labor, forced or voluntary, across state boundaries, is another. Illustrative of the consequence of coercive labor migration, is the presence of descendants of Africans forcefully enslaved in the seventeenth to the nineteenth centuries, and transported to North and South America. Illustrative of its voluntary form, are the many Indians, Bangladeshi, Egyptians, and Palestinians seeking better lives in the oil sheikhdoms of the Persian Gulf and the Arabian peninsula; the Mexican and Caribbean migrant workers in the United States; and the Turkish, Algerian, southern

Italian, Spanish, Yugoslavian, and Greek migrants to the advanced economies of Central and Northern Europe. Some of the contemporary migration is politically motivated, triggered by civil war and repression. A recent book refers to the contemporary world as living through an "Age of Migration,"[9] comparable in scale to that of the late nineteenth and early twentieth centuries.

Political conflicts and divisions based on language, ethnicity, and religion once were thought to have been subordinated or even eliminated by "modern" differences between social classes, occupations, interests, and ideologies. In the post–Cold War world though, ideological differences have come to be overshadowed by ethnic and religious ones. In earlier editions of this book we had not given enough attention to ethnolinguistic and religious questions. The prominence, visibility, and even ferocity of contemporary conflicts over ethnic and religious issues requires that we provide some background information on these differences.

Such terms as *ethnic, ethnicity, ethnic conflict, ethnocentrism, and ethnic "cleansing"* have entered into the modern vocabulary. Max Weber, in his classic introduction to sociological theory *Economy and Society,* defined ethnic groups as "those human groups that entertain a subjective belief in their common descent because of similarities of physical type or of customs or both, or because of memories of colonization and migration. . . . [I]t does not matter whether or not an objective blood relationship exists."[10] This point that ethnicity is based on subjective belief rather than a necessary physical reality is stressed by leading contemporary authority Donald Horowitz,[11] who points out that the concept of ethnicity has to be elastic since groups physically quite similar, but differing by language, religion, customs, marriage patterns, and historical memories (for example, the Serbs, Croats, and Muslim Bosnians) may believe themselves to be descended from different ancestors and hence genetically and physically different as well. In the course of many centuries originally homogeneous populations may become substantially intermixed genetically with other populations, although the culture may continue, and intermarriage with other ethnic and religious groups may be strongly discouraged. This is true, for example, of the Jewish population of Israel, come together after more than two millenia of dispersion over the globe.

Examining the distribution of languages and of religions around the world may give some indication of how the world is divided along ethnic lines. Anthropologists and linguists tell us that there are approximately 5,000 different languages in use in the world today, classified into a much smaller number of language families. Some experts say there are as many as 200 language families, while others estimate the number to be much smaller, perhaps 20. Most of these languages are spoken by relatively small tribal groups in North and South America, Asia, Africa, and Oceania. Only 200 of these languages have a million or more speakers, and of these only 8 may be classified as world languages. English is the most truly international language, with a quarter of a billion speakers in North America, 60 million in Europe, and 20 million in Asia, as well as several million in Africa. While most of the 100 million French speakers are in Europe, they are substantially represented in North America, and in Africa as well. Spanish (300 million) and Portuguese (160 million) are spoken in Europe and Latin America; to a much lesser extent in Africa. Russian (165 million) is spoken in Europe and Asia; German (100 million) almost entirely in Europe. The language with the largest number of speakers, though in several dialects, is Chinese (1.1 billion), spoken almost entirely in Asia. The major languages with the greatest international spread are those of the former imperialist powers—Great Britain, France, Spain, and Portugal.[12]

Christianity is the largest and most widely spread religion, having twice the numbers of the Muslims, who are the next most numerous (see Table 1.4). The Christians are divided into three groups—Roman Catholics, Protestants, and Orthodox—with the Catholics dominant in Europe and Latin America, and a more equal distribution of Catholics and Protestants in Africa, Asia, and North America. The Protestants are divided into many denominations. The most significant recent developments have been the rise of left-inclined "Liberationist" Catholicism in parts of the Third World, and the spread of evangelical and pentacostal denominations such as the Baptists and the Assembly of God, which have been successful in missionary activities particularly in Latin America and Africa. The Muslims are almost entirely concentrated in the two continents of Asia and Africa. They have been particularly successful in missionary activities in Sub-Saharan Africa.

If we place on top of this complex template of languages spoken—a template produced by a many millenia-long differentiation of original speech patterns, and overlaid by the language imports of ancient migrations and more recent imperialist penetrations—if we place on top of this, the religious beliefs, customs, practices, and memories as they have generated and spread around the world, and the sense of ethnonational identity produced by centuries, even millenia-long historical struggles, then, we have a picture of the lines of potential ethnic cleavage in the political geography of the world. The lines in this complex picture become even darker and stronger if we also identify the many cases where ethnic differences coincide with economic inequalities due to historic and/or contemporary discrimination, linkages between custom, occupational choice, education patterns, and many other connections.

Where the cleavage lines crisscross within the boundaries of countries, where they are cumulative (combining language, race and ethnicity, religion, and history), and especially where they coincide with economic inequalities, they explain the violence and intractability of political struggles in various parts of the world—Bosnia, Ulster, Rwanda, South Africa, Palestine, Georgia, Armenia-Azerbaijan, the Indian Punjab and Kashmir, Sri Lanka, rural Mayan Chiapas in Mexico, the inner cities of the United States, the foreign worker housing projects and ghettoes in European and American cities unable or unwilling to digest Hispanics, Caribbean migrants, Turks, Algerians, Pakistanis, Indians, and the like. Many of these spots are intermittently in political flame, with right-wing ethnocentrists pitted against minorities demanding improvements in their condition, or regionally concentrated ethnic groups demanding autonomy or independence. The areas inhabited by large Russian minorities in the successor countries of the Soviet Union—Ukraine, Estonia, Latvia, Kazakhstan, and Kirgizia—are potential hot spots, as are such parts of the United States as Florida, Texas, and California where Caribbean and Mexican migrant workers are concentrated.

In Table 1.5 we provide examples of politically significant "ethnicity" in our selected 12 countries. The countries appear on the rows of the table, the ethnic

Table 1.4 ADHERENTS OF ALL RELIGIONS BY SEVEN CONTINENTAL AREAS (MID-1993, IN MILLIONS)*

	Africa	Asia	Europe	Latin America	North America	Oceania	Eurasia	Total Number	Total Percent
Christian	341.0	300	410.0	443.0	241.0	23.0	112.0	1,869	34.0
Muslims	285.0	668	14.0	1.4	3.0	0.1	43.0	1,004	18.0
Nonreligious and atheists	3.0	900	73.0	22.0	26.0	3.6	135.0	1,153	21.0
Hindus	1.6	746	0.7	0.9	1.3	0.4	—	751	14.0
Buddhists	—	332	0.3	0.6	0.6	—	0.4	334	6.0
Folk and Tribal	70.0	170	—	1.0	—	—	—	240	3.0
New and Other	—	138	1.7	2.0	0.7	—	—	124	2.0
Sikhs	—	19	0.2	—	0.3	—	—	20	0.2
Jews	0.4	6	1.5	0.1	7.0	0.1	2.0	18	0.3
Total	703.0	3,291	502.0	475.0	282.0	28.0	30.0	5,575	99.0

* Adherents as defined in *World Christian Encyclopedia* (1982).

Table 1.5   EXAMPLES OF ETHNICITY: ITS BASES AND THEIR SALIENCE*

	Physical Differences	Language	Intermarriage	Religion	Negative Historical Memories
Brazil: Blacks	XX	O	XX	X	X
China: Tibetans	X	XX	XX	XX	XX
Egypt: Copts	O	O	XX	XX	X
France: Algerians	X	X	XX	XX	XX
Germany: Turks	X	XX	XX	XX	O
India: Muslims	O	X	XX	XX	XX
Japan: Buraku-min	O	O	XX	O	XX
Mexico: Mayan	X	X	XX	X	XX
Nigeria: Ibo	O	X	XX	XX	XX
Russia: Chechens	X	XX	XX	XX	XX
United Kingdom: Scots	O	O	O	X	X
United States: Afro-Americans	XX	X	XX	O	XX

* Salience is estimated at the following levels: O = none or almost none; X = some; XX = much importance in affecting political differences.

"traits" on the columns. Five sets of traits are included, beginning with physical differences, then language, intermarriage, religion, and negative historical memories. The importance of these differences in our 12 cases is suggested by three ratings— 0, X, and XX. Table 1.5 tells us that the important bases of these exemplary ethnic groupings lie mainly on the right side of the table in the areas of intermarriage, religion, and historical memories. Language differences play a role of much importance in three cases, of some importance in five; and physical differences are of much importance in two, and of some importance in five of the twelve cases.

The political problems resulting from these examples of ethnicity range from demands for civil rights and equality of treatment as in the cases of the Afro-Americans and Afro-Brazilians, the Japanese Buraku-min and the Mexican Mayans; demands for autonomy-independence of the Chinese Tibetans, the Russian Chechens, the Nigerian Ibo; and right-wing ethnocentrism as among the Indian Hindus 9, and the German and French radical right. Keep in mind that these are examples of the ethnic phenomenon in the politics of our 12 selected countries.

Religious Fundamentalism

Another worldwide development agitating the politics of many countries is the rise of *religious fundamentalism*. The phenomenon got its name in the decades before World War I when Protestant clergymen on the eastern seaboard of the United States banded together to defend the "fundamentals" of religious belief against the secularizing inroads of science and "critical" biblical scholarship. Rejecting the accommodative response of their own denominational leaderships, the "funda-mentalists" adopted a militant posture, affirming the "inerrancy" of the Bible in all respects, forming closed ritually observant enclaves to defend themselves against these secularizing trends, and declaring their compromising leadership as hereti-cal. Orthodox Jews and pious Muslims encountering the same modernizing threat to their beliefs and practices formed similar movements in Europe, the Middle East, and the United States in the decades after World War II.[13]

Christianity, Judaism, and Islam are all "religions of the book," though not pre-cisely the same book. They share the Old Testament; but Christians add the New Tes-tament, and Muslims add the Koran. Each religious tradition adds other sacred inerrant documents—the Jews have the *Talmud* and the Shulchan Arukh; the Mus-lims have their collection of Koranic legal interpretations called the Shariya; Catholic-Christians have papal encyclicals, and the like. Hence, Christian, Jewish, and Muslim fundamentalists share this belief in the "inerrancy," the absolute truth, of the sacred books. They are also alike in forming enclaves in militant defense against their own "mainstream" clergy. Because these three religions acknowledge the ancestry of Abra-ham, they are called the Abrahamic religions, and the fundamentalist movements in these three Abrahamic religious traditions have much in common. Islamic funda-mentalism, however, is much more aggressive in its pursuit of political power than Christian fundamentalism because of the absence of a tradition of "separation of church and state" in Islamic history and culture. While political Catholicism in Europe has been slow to accept the separation of church and state, and only in recent decades may be said to have yielded to a limited role, Islamic fundamentalist move-ments as in Iran, Egypt, and Algeria acknowledge no limits to their striving for politi-cal power, and where they are present in large numbers, they strive to form theocrat-ic regimes as in the case of Iran. Jewish fundamentalist movements in Israel work with other orthodox groups in pressuring the major parties to embody the Jewish canon law in the public law as it relates to marriage and divorce, the enforcement of dietary regulations, and the respect for the sabbath. Christian fundamentalism in the United States operates mainly as a militant pressure group in relation to such issues as abor-tion, school prayer, and the like; as factions on school boards and local governments; and at the national level, as the "Christian Right" within the Republican party.

The rise of fundamentalist movements is a factor that has been affecting the politics of the entire world in the last decades. Where they have developed into large-scale political movements as in the Islamic countries of the Middle East and in the Hindu and Buddhist countries of South Asia, they form or seek to form theo-cratic and ethnotheocratic states, planning to reverse, or reversing, trends in fami-ly and social policy and imposing religious restrictions on education policy. There is, however, an inherent limit to the spread of fundamentalism. Islamic and Jewish fundamentalism are unlikely to ally with each other and pursue common goals. Indeed, Shia and Sunni Islamic groups are unlikely to form alliances. Hindu Indi-an and Buddhist Sri Lankan fundamentalism are strongly nationalist and also unlikely to form alliances. Hence fundamentalism is not an international move-ment comparable to communism and socialism. The political significance of the spread of fundamentalism lies in its polarizing and fragmenting effects on the internal politics of an increasing number of countries. The strength and militancy of fundamentalist movements inhibits efforts at population control, and slows or reverses the emancipation of women.

WORLD TRENDS AND POLITICAL PROBLEMS

Table 1.6 lists the trends and issues that now influence and divide the politics in most of the countries in the world. In the upper part of the left-hand column are the main economic and social changes. In the right-hand column we list the problems and issues that have arisen from these changes. At the bottom left we list the major political trends, and in the lower right we list the main "political pathologies." Note the major economic and social developments: the growth and spread of *technology and* the rise of the *service economy,* the *liberalization* of the market from governmental and traditional controls, and the growth of *international trade.* Along with these economic developments go two significant social developments: the growth of population as a consequence of improved sanitation, nutrition, and medical services, and "social mobilization" in the sense of the *urbanization* of the population; and the *secularization* of culture in the sense of the spread of *education and literacy,* and the increasing spread of modern *communication.* Some sociologists refer to these latter developments as the growth of *civil society.*

While these developments have obvious positive consequences for productivity and welfare, they also have negative or problematic consequences, raising new political issues, influencing political party systems, change of regimes, and the like. These are listed in the upper right column of Table 1.6. The growth of technology and the services, and the spread of the market economy results in inequality of wealth and income, a trend which has become quite marked in the advanced industrial societies in recent decades, and which tends to be a feature of economic growth in the developing economies. Increasing inequality of income and wealth sharpens class antagonisms and intense partisanship.

The opening up of international trade leads not only to comparative advantage, and hence greater productivity, but results in industrial relocation from region to region, and in labor migration from region to region. The political battles over *NAFTA (the North American Free Trade Agreement),* and *GATT (the General Agreement on Tariffs and Trade)* illustrate the impact of international trade on domestic economics and politics. Uneven economic growth produces massive immigration from the economically stagnant to economically dynamic areas and nations, setting in motion nationalist and ethnocentric reactions of a politically destabilizing sort.[14]

Economic growth in combination with population growth has a downside in environmental deterioration—overfishing, overgrazing, overcultivating, destruction of forest, pollution of air, land, and water, and the like—leading to the formation of environmental movements, or *environmentalism,* which cut across the earlier bases of party division in the countries affected.

The two social trends in the upper left-hand column of Table 1.6—population expansion, and social mobilization—result in a complex process of social and cul-

Table 1.6   WORLD TRENDS AND POLITICAL PROBLEMS

Economic and Social Developments	Political Problems and Issues
Growth of Technology and Service Economy	Growing Inequality of Wealth and Income
Liberalization and Marketization	Industrial Relocation and Labor Migration
Growth of International Trade	Environmental Deterioration
Population Expansion	Decay of Inner Cities
	Attrition of Family and Community
Social Mobilization: Urbanization, Education, Communication	Ethnic Mobilization
	Rise of Religious Fundamentalism

Political Trends	Political Pathologies
Democratization	
Decentralization	Political Fragmentation and Polarization
Regionalization	Declining Effectiveness of Policy-making Institutions
Globalization	

tural transformation. Social mobilization includes urbanization, the spread of education and literacy, and the growth of the communication media. In the modern urban setting people are exposed to an increased flow of information and ideas. Women enter into the labor force in increasing numbers, reducing the birth rate, weakening the family, and attenuating the rearing of children. Labor migration from less developed regions and countries into the labor markets of the cities contributes to "inner city" decay which has a mixed economic and ethnic basis. Migrant and minority groups caught in this "ghettoization" compete with indigenous labor and make welfare demands which feed into the ethnonationalism of the dominant population. Indigenous ethnic groups, exposed to education and the media, become more sharply aware of their ethnic identity and mobilize to support their interests. The secularizing state and civil society threaten religious groups which may respond by the formation of militant and reactive movements. Ethnic mobilization may lead to demands for autonomy, even for separate nationhood; and fundamentalist movements may lead to efforts to gain control of the state in order to stem and reverse the processes of secularization.

We list four distinct political trends in the world today—*democratization, decentralization, regionalization,* and *globalization.* Samuel Huntington, in his book *The Third Wave,*[15] tells us that democracy has appeared in world history in three waves (if we exclude the classic Greek and medieval Italian city-states). The first one, the century-long wave beginning with the emergence of general manhood suffrage in the United States in 1828, and continuing through the nineteenth century up to the late 1920s, brought democracy to some 30 countries of Europe and North America. Huntington defined democracy in this wave as requiring at least a

50 percent male suffrage and an executive responsible to a popular or a parliamentary vote. The second wave, which Huntington called the "short wave," lasted from 1943 until 1962. While quite a number of countries in Europe, East Asia, Africa, and Latin America became formally democratic in these years, most of them collapsed quickly and turned into authoritarian regimes of one kind or another. The "third wave," beginning in 1974 had involved some 30 countries in Southern Europe, East Asia, Latin America, and Eastern Europe. As of the time of publication of his book in 1991, the number has risen in recent years to include the successor states to the Soviet Union and a number of transitional cases in Africa. Not all of the newly democratizing countries are succeeding in consolidating their new institutions. In some, perhaps in many, democratic processes may fail to produce stable institutions and effective public policies and give way to one or another form of authoritarianism.

If the eighteenth and nineteenth were the centuries during which the concentration of power in the nation-state occurred, in the post–World War II decades power has been receding from the nation-state outward to the private economy, downward to local governments, and upward to regional organizations, and to the global level. The growth of governmental control over the economy and the ideals of socialism and social democracy, which dominated the economics and politics of the 1930s until the 1970s, has subsided and reversed in the last two decades. There has been a trend toward some *decentralization.* Regional, provincial, and local governmental units have been acquiring powers at the expense of the central governments, which are increasingly viewed as overbureaucratized and not effectively responsive to popular demands and needs.[16] The *European Community (EC)* and the North American Free Trade Association (NAFTA) are examples of *regionalization;* and the increasing powers and roles of the UN, and related institutions such as the World Bank and the International Monetary Fund, are examples of *globalization.*

The industrialized countries of Western Europe, after centuries of costly and destructive wars, have found that the peaceful and free exchange and movement of ideas, products, and persons across national boundaries greatly enhances productivity. Step by step in recent decades Western Europeans have created a common market economy, and they are currently poised at the threshold of even greater integration. Originally consisting of six countries—France, Germany, Italy, Belgium, the Netherlands, and Luxembourg—the European Community has expanded to include 12—adding Britain, Ireland, Spain, Portugal, Greece, and Denmark. Austria, Finland, and Sweden have been admitted in 1995, and a number of Eastern European countries have been invited to apply. In this process of integration the Europeans have been creating regional institutions with limited policymaking power and with resources that have been employed on such common projects as the provision of development aid to the poorer countries and regions. These institutions include a Commission consisting of 20 members, two each from the five larger countries—France, Germany, Italy, Spain, and the United Kingdom—and one each from the ten smaller ones. The Commission is responsible for administering the EC treaties and the policies enacted by the Council of Ministers, a body consisting of the Foreign Ministers of the 15 member governments. The European Parliament consists of more than 500 deputies elected directly by the voters of the constituent countries. It has budgetary powers, and is responsible for the admission of new members. A Court of Justice interprets treaties and legislation and seeks to resolve differences between European Community and national legislation. An Economic and Social Committee is representative of the various economic interests in the member countries and is consulted by the Commission and the Council of Ministers on the impact of European Community policies. The European Community might be called a "confederated" government (see Chapter 7) in which the governing institutions have policymaking authority, but they must rely on the member governments for enforcement, implementation, and revenue.[17]

The United Nations, formed at the end of World War II and limited in its scope and impact by the Cold War, has been acquiring new powers and responsibilities since the collapse of the Soviet Union. UN forces are deployed as peacekeepers as of early 1994 in 17 countries in Asia, Africa, Europe, and North America. Nine of these have been established since the end of the Cold War. These peacekeeping operations, involving more than 100,000 men and women peacekeepers, have the primary function of separating combatants in domestic and international conflicts, and facilitating the settlement of these disputes and the formation of effective governing institutions. The UN has acquired increased authority in the emerging world security structure, conferring international legitimacy on such regional security organizations as NATO (North Atlantic Treaty Organization), and both constraining, supporting, and replacing the unilateral actions of individual nation states.

The impingements of these economic, social, and political developments on the politics of individual countries varies from country to country, depending on the level of economic development and resources, ethnic and religious composition, geographic location, historical experience, and the like. The political problems listed at the bottom right of Table 1.6 are not only the consequences of the political developments listed in the bottom left-hand column, but have resulted from the economic and social changes listed in the upper part of the table. Environmental deterioration, growing economic inequality, economic dislocation and migration as well as ethnic mobilization and religious fundamentalism contribute to political fragmentation and polarization, making it more difficult to form stable governments. Growing economic affluence, coupled with the rise of a more restive, communication- and information-driven civil society impairs the effectiveness of aggregative and deliberative institutions—interest groups, political parties, parliaments, and political executives. It is more difficult to structure political alternatives when leaders of political parties and interest groups can no longer muster and discipline their followers as effectively as used to be the case, and when political leaders are losing much of their power to control the deliberative processes of parliamentary institutions to such new forces as the electronic media.

KEY TERMS

agricultural labor force	globalization
comparative advantage	GATT
civil society	government
centralization	gross national product GNP
decentralization	income inequality
democratization	liberalization
privatization	nation
regionalization	NAFTA
religious fundamentalism	NATO
service economy	population
ethnicity	purchasing power parity PPP
ethnocentrism	state
European Community	technology
environmentalism	United Nations
	wealth inequality

END NOTES

1. The Vatican and Switzerland are not members of the UN but maintain permanent observer missions at the UN headquarters. Taiwan was expelled from the UN in 1971.
2. See World Bank, *World Development Report, 1994*, New York, Oxford University Press, 1994, p. 245, for a discussion of the new Purchasing Power Parity (PPP) measure of Gross National Product.
3. *Ibid*, p. 230.
4. Hollis Chenery et al., *Redistribution With Growth* (New York: Oxford Univ. Press, 1981).
5. Paul and Anne Ehrlich, *The Population Explosion* (New York: Simon & Schuster, 1990).
6. Amartya Sen, "Population: Delusion and Reality," *New York Review of Books* 41, (Sept. 22, 1994), 62 ff.
7. World Bank, *World Development Report* (New York: Oxford Univ. Press, 1994), Table 25, pp. 210–11.
8. Amartya Sen, "Population," p. 64.
9. Stephen Castles and Mark J. Miller, *The Age of Migration: International Population Movements in The Modern World* (New York: Guilford, 1994).
10. Max Weber, *Economy and Society,* ed. Guenther Roth and Claus Wittich (Berkeley, CA: Univ. of California Press, 1978), p. 389.
11. Donald Horowitz, *Ethnic Groups in Conflict* (Berkeley, CA: Univ. of California Press, 1985), pp. 52–53. Also J. Milton Yinger, *Ethnicity* (Albany, NY: State Univ. Press, 1994).

12. Erik V. Gunnemark, *Countries, Peoples, and Their Languages: The Geolinguistic Handbook* (Gothenburg: Sweden: Lanstryckeriet, 1991).
13. See, among others, Martin Marty and Scott Appleby, *Fundamentalism Observed* (Chicago: Univ. of Chicago Press, 1991).
14. Stephen Castles and Mark J. Miller, *The Age of Migration; International Population Movements in The Modern World* (New York: Guilford, 1994).
15. Samuel Huntington, *The Third Wave: Democratization in the Late Twentieth Century* (Norman, OK: Univ. of Oklahoma Press, 1991).
16. Robert D. Putnam, *Making Democracy Work: Civic Traditions in Modern Italy* (Princeton, NJ: Princeton Univ. Press, 1993); a fascinating study of decentralization in Italy, and the differences in performance in Northern and other parts of Italy.
17. Stanley Hoffman and Robert Keohane, eds., *The New European Community* (Boulder, CO: Westview Press, 1991).

SUGGESTED READINGS

Chenery, Hollis, et al. *Redistribution With Growth.* New York: Oxford University Press, Fourth Printing, 1981.

Cornelius, Wayne, et al. [Eds] *Controlling Immigration: A Global Perspective.* Stanford, CA: Stanford University Press, 1995.

Ehrlich, Paul and Anne. *The Population Explosion.* New York: Simon and Schuster, 1990.

Hoffman, Stanley, and Robert Keohane, Eds. *The New European Community.* Boulder, Colorado: Westview Press, 1991.

Horowitz, Donald. *Ethnic Groups in Conflict.* Berkeley: University of California Press, 1985.

Huntington, Samuel. *The Third Wave: Democratization in the Late Twentieth Century.* Norman, Oklahoma: University of Oklahoma Press, 1991.

Marty, Martin, and Scott Appleby, *Fundamentalism Observed.* Chicago, Illinois: University of Chicago Press, 1991.

Putnam, Robert. *Making Democracy Work: Civic Traditions in Modern Italy.* Princeton, New Jersey: Princeton University Press, 1993.

Weiner, Myron. *The Global Migration Crisis: Challenge to States and to Human Rights.* New York: HarperCollins, 1995.

World Bank, *World Development Report.* New York: Oxford University Press, 1994.

Chapter
2

Concepts in Comparative Politics

WHY WE COMPARE

The great French interpreter of American democracy, Alexis de Tocqueville, recalling the way in which his ideas about French institutions and culture entered into the writing of *Democracy in America,* observed, "Although I very rarely spoke of France in my book, I did not write one page of it without having her, so to speak, before my eyes." And more generally about the comparative method he said, "Without comparisons to make, the mind does not know how to proceed."[1] Tocqueville was telling us that comparison is fundamental to all human thought. We add that it is the methodological core of the humanistic and scientific methods as well. From a humanist perspective, comparing the past and present of our nation and comparing our experience with that of other nations deepen our understanding of our own institutions. Examining politics in other societies permits us to see a wider range of political alternatives and illuminates the virtues and shortcomings in our own political life. By taking us out of the network of assumptions and familiar arrangements within which we usually operate, comparative analysis helps expand our awareness of the possibilities of politics.

Comparative political analysis helps us develop explanations and test theories of the ways in which political processes work and in which political change occurs. Here the logic and the intention of the comparative methods used by political scientists are similar to those used in more exact sciences. The political scientist cannot design experiments to control and manipulate political arrangements and observe the consequences. It is possible, however, to describe and explain the different combinations of events and institutions found in the politics of different societies. More than two thousand years ago, Aristotle in his *Politics* contrasted the economies and social structures of the many Greek city-states, in an effort to determine how the social and economic environment affected political institutions and policies. A modern political scientist, Robert Dahl, in his studies of democracy, compares the economic characteristics, cultures, and historical experiences of many contemporary nations in an effort to discover the combinations of conditions and characteristics that are associated with that form of government.[2] Other theorists, in their attempt to explain differences between the processes and performance of political systems, have compared constitutional regimes with tyrannies, two-party democracies with multiparty democracies, and stable governments with unstable regimes. The end of the Cold War has left a world engaged in vast experiments in alternative approaches to economic growth, alternative strategies for transitions to democracy, alternative forms of controlling and using the powers of government. All governments are grappling with new issues of preserving our environment, old issues of opportunity and economic security for citizens, and ancient issues of conflicts of ethnic identities and religious values. In a world made ever smaller by instantaneous communication and interdependent economies, these problems and achievements spill across national boundaries. Comparative analysis is a powerful and versatile tool. It enhances our ability to describe and understand political processes and political change in any country by offering concepts and reference points from a broader perspective. The comparative approach also stimulates us to form general theories of political relationships. It encourages and enables us to test our political theories by confronting them with the experience of many institutions and settings. The primary goal of this volume is to provide us with access to this powerful tool for thought and analysis.

HOW WE COMPARE

In its earlier five editions over the last 20 years, and in its current edition *Comparative Politics Today* follows a *structural-functional approach*. Some writers have argued that structural-functionalism is static and conservative in its methodology, that it is biased in favor of the status quo, since it describes a set of institutions at a particular time. We offer two answers to this criticism. First, we argue that this approach to the description and comparison of political institutions and processes is elementary common sense. There is no other way of comparing political systems, except by describing how different ones are organized and what their different parts do. To describe political institutions precisely and comprehensively at some particular cross section of time, is not to defend them, but to try to comprehend them. We would use a structural-functional approach to compare Nazi Germany, which we reject with horror, with a democratic, welfare state such as Sweden, which some of us may admire. Second, we recognize the need to supplement the structural-functional approach with a dynamic developmental approach, since we want to know not only *how* a political system functions, but *why* as well. A structural-functional approach does not tell us *why* Germany or France developed as they did in the 1930s and 1940s. It tells us *what* changes occurred in these regimes. The explanation of *why* they changed requires that we bring in the economic, social, cultural, and international context in an historical, dynamic way.

A FEW DEFINITIONS

It may be useful to define some of the common terms used in political science and comparative politics that are used frequently in the chapters of this book. We talk about *politics* and *public policy*, and about *states, governments, regimes,* and *nations,* and *political systems.* By *politics* we refer to the activities associated with the control of human behavior among a given people and in a given territory, where this control may be backed up by authoritative and coercive means. *Politics* refers to the processes and conflicts over questions as to how these authoritative and coercive means are to be employed—who or what agencies are to employ them and for what purposes *(public policies).* Authoritative and coercive control is typically exercised by *states* and *governments.* We use these two terms interchangeably, although some political scientists give an especial *oomph* to the concept of the *state.* For our purposes we use either of these terms to mean the legally empowered agencies having these authoritative and coercive powers. The term *regime* refers to a particular format of a state or a government, as the "prereform regime of England," "Wilhelmine Germany," "Third Republic France," "Tsarist Russia," and the like. The regime is the particular historical configuration of a given state or government. By *nation* we refer to a people residing in a given territory having a common language, history, and culture, who may or may not have their own state or independent government. Such countries as the Soviet Union, Yugoslavia, and Czechoslovakia were multinational states that have now separated and formed their own states and governments. The decline of the Cold War, lifting the pressure of the ideological confrontation, made this ethnic mobilization and separation possible.

Since the term *political system* is the main organizing concept of this book, we shall be elaborating its meaning in some detail below. Here it is only necessary to justify adding this term to the political science vocabulary. There is more to politics than authoritative and coercive activities. For example, there are political organizations such as political parties, or pressure groups which do not have authoritative and coercive powers, except insofar as they can control the agencies of the state or the government. There are the *media of communication*—press, radio, television, and the like—which effect elections, legislative deliberations, and enforcements of laws and regulations. Then there is a whole host of institutions beginning with the family and including communities, churches, schools, colleges, and universities, corporations, foundations and thinktanks, which influence how leaders and voters think and act about politics and public policy. We use the term *political system* to refer to this whole collection of related, interacting institutions and agencies.

COMPARATIVE SYSTEMS: STRUCTURE AND FUNCTION

We need to discuss in some detail three concepts which we use throughout this book—*system, structure, and function. System* suggests an object having moving parts, interacting with a setting or an environment. The political system is a set of institutions concerned with formulating and implementing the collective goals of a society or of groups within it. The decisions of the political system are normally backed up by legitimate coercion, and obedience may be compelled. We discuss *legitimacy* at greater length in Chapter 3, but we need to say a word about it here. By *legitimacy* we mean that those who are ruled believe in the "right" (whether by law or by custom) of the rulers to "rule" in the sense of implementing their decisions by force if necessary. The legitimacy of a political system may vary a good deal. The legitimacy of the American system was quite high in the decade after World War II; it declined substantially during and after the Vietnam War. Low legitimacy may be the reason for breakdowns in political organization and failures in public policy. Policy failures in turn can be the cause of declining legitimacy. The dissolution of the Soviet system in 1991 came after a failed and costly war in Afghanistan, a nuclear power disaster in Chernobyl, and an apparently irreversible decline in economic productivity.

Political systems do many things. They wage war or encourage peace; cultivate international trade or restrict it; open their borders to the exchange of ideas and artistic experiences or close them; tax their populations heavily or lightly, equitably or inequitably; regulate behavior more or less strictly; allocate resources for education, health, and welfare, or fail to do so; pay due regard to the interdependence of humanity and nature, or permit nature's capital to be depleted or misused. In order to carry on these many activities, political systems have institutions, agencies, or *structures,* such as political parties, parliaments, bureaucracies, and courts, which carry on specific activities, or perform *functions,* which in turn enable the political system to formulate and enforce its policies.

Figure 2.1 tells us that a political system exists in both a domestic and an international environment, molding these environments and being molded by them. The system receives *inputs* from these environments and attempts to shape them through its *outputs.* In the figure, we use the United States as the central actor, and we include some of the other countries as our environmental examples—Russia, China, Britain, Germany, Japan, Brazil, and Egypt. Figure 2.1 is quite schematic and oversimplified. Exchanges among countries may vary in many ways. For example, they may be dense or "sparse"; United States–Canadian relations exemplify the dense end of the continuum, while United States–Nepalese relations would be at the sparse end. The United States has substantial trade relations with some nations and relatively little trade with others. Some countries have an excess of imports over exports, whereas others have an excess of exports over imports. With such countries as the NATO nations, Japan, South Korea, Israel, and Saudi Arabia, military exchanges and support have been of great importance to the United States. The interdependence of nations—the volume and value of imports and exports, transfers of capital, the extent of foreign travel and international communication—has increased enormously in the last decades. We might represent this process as a thickening of the input and output arrows in Figure 2.1. Fluctuations in this flow of international transactions and traffic attributable to depression, inflation, protective tariffs, war, and the like may work havoc with the economies of the nations affected.

The interaction of the political system with its domestic environment may be illustrated by the emergence of the "postindustrial" society in the United States.

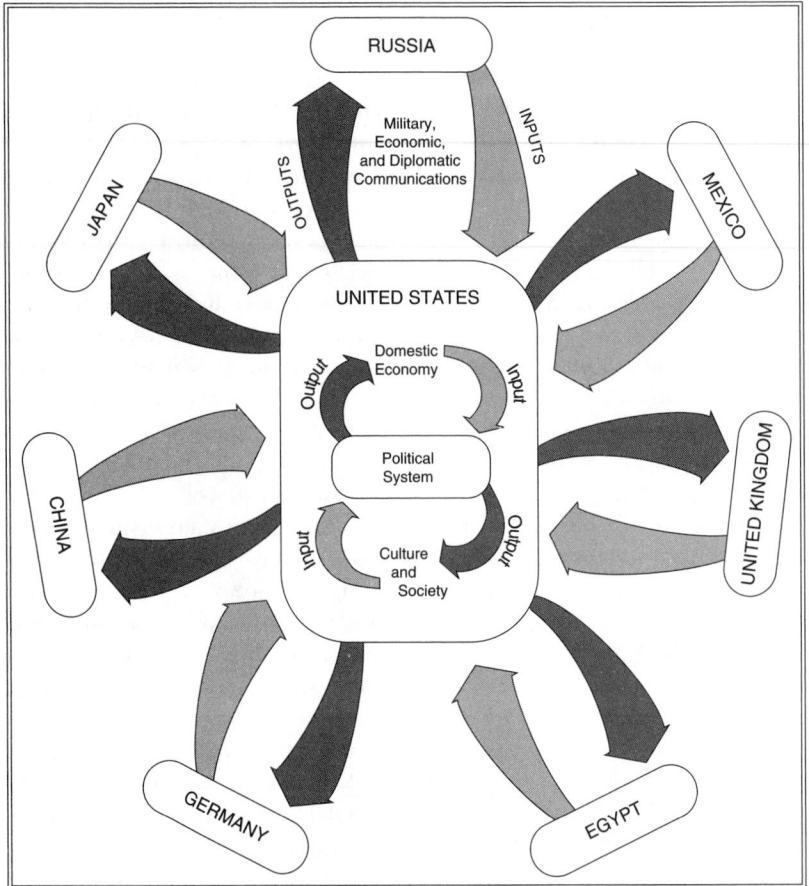

Figure 2.1 The political system and its environments.

The composition of the American labor force, and consequently its citizenry, has changed dramatically in the last century. Agricultural employment has declined to a relatively small percentage, employment in heavy extractive and manufacturing industries has decreased substantially, and the newer, high-technology occupations, the professions, and the service occupations have increased sharply as a proportion of the labor force. The last half-century has also witnessed significant improvements in the educational level of the American population, although the quality of education particularly at the primary and secondary levels has come in for very serious criticism in recent years. These and other changes in American social structure have transformed the social bases of the party system. There are now as many independents among American voters as loyal Democrats and Republicans. Workers of the older, primarily European, ethnic stocks have ceased being a solid support for the Democratic party, and they now tend to divide their votes almost equally between the two parties. On the whole, these changes in the labor force have been associated with a more conservative trend in economic policy and with efforts to cut back welfare and other expenditures. A more educated and culturally sophisticated society has become more concerned with the quality of life, the beauty and healthfulness of the environment, and similar issues. In input-output terms, socioeconomic changes have transformed the political demands of the electorate and the kinds of policies that it supports.

Thus, a new pattern of politics results in different policy outputs, different kinds and levels of taxation, changes in regulatory patterns, and changes in welfare expenditures. The advantage of the system-environment approach is that it directs our attention to the interdependence of what happens within and between nations and provides us with a vocabulary to describe, compare, and explain these interacting events. If we are to make sound judgments in politics, we need to be able to place political systems in their environments, recognizing how these environments both set limits on and provide opportunities for political choices. This approach keeps us from reaching quick and biased political judgments. If a country is poor in natural resources and lacks the skills necessary to exploit what it has, we cannot fault it for having a low industrial output or poor educational and social services. Similarly, a country dominated and exploited by another country with a conservative policy cannot be condemned for failing to introduce social reforms.

The policies that leaders and political activists can follow are limited by the system and its institutions. However, in this era of rapid change, if the goals of the leadership and the political activists change, one set of political institutions may quickly be replaced by another. One of the most dramatic illustrations of such an institutional transformation was the breakdown of control by the Communist parties in Eastern Europe, and their replacement by multiparty systems, once the leadership of the Soviet Union lost its confidence in the Soviet system and the future of socialism. Once the Soviet leadership decided to give up the Communist Party power monopoly in the Soviet Union and accept political pluralism and internal economic reform, it had no choice but to adopt a permissive and conciliatory policy toward its former satellites. The notion of interdependence goes even further than this relationship between policy and institutions. The various structural parts of a political system are also interdependent. If a government is based on popularly elected representatives in legislative bodies, then a system of election must be instituted. If many people enjoy the right to vote, then the politicians seeking office will have to mobilize the electorate and organize political parties to carry on election campaigns. As the policymaking agencies of the political system enact laws, they will need administrators and civil servants to implement these laws, and they will need judges to determine whether the laws have been violated and to decide what punishments to impose on the violators.

POLITICAL STRUCTURES OR INSTITUTIONS

Figure 2.2 locates within the political system the familiar political institutions and agencies—interest groups, political parties, legislatures, executives, bureaucracies, and courts. The difficulty with this sixfold classification is that it will not carry us very far in comparing political systems with each other. Britain and China have all

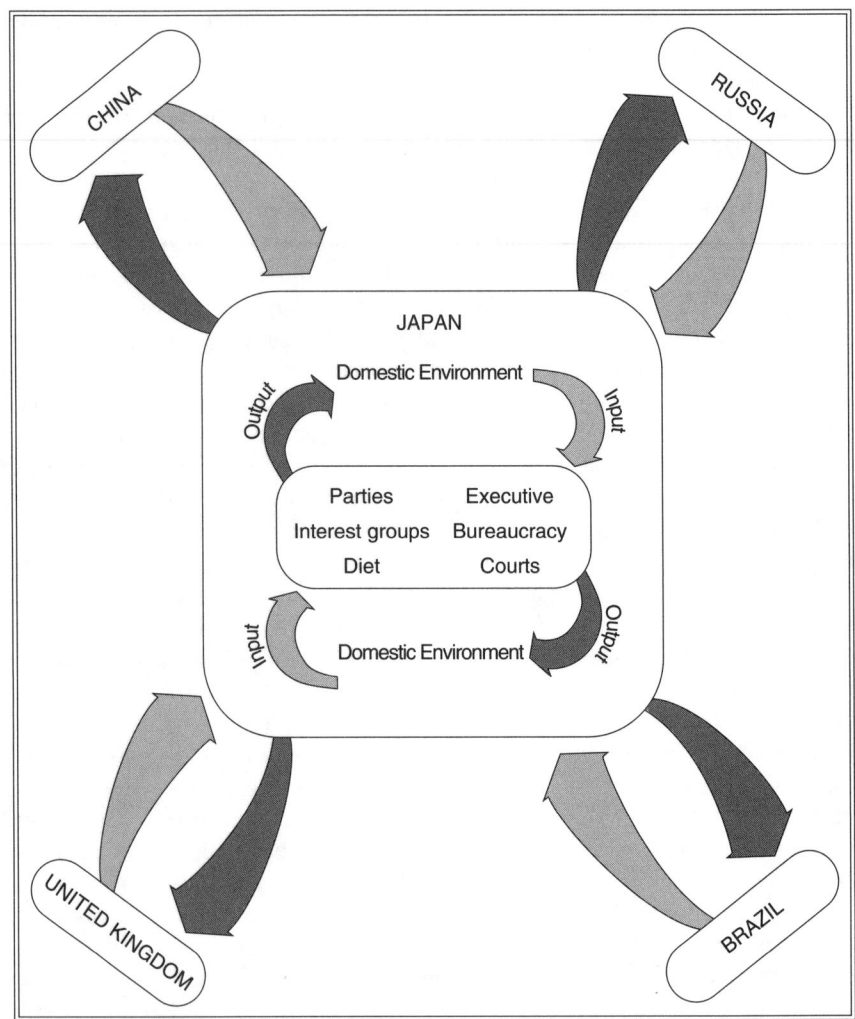

Figure 2.2 The political system and its structures.

six types of political institutions, at least in name; however, they are organized differently in the two countries, and they function in dramatically different ways. Britain has a monarch—a queen—who performs ceremonial functions, like opening Parliament and conferring knighthoods and other honors. China does not have a specialized ceremonial executive. There is a president, elected by the National People's Congress, who performs the ceremonial functions as well as some political functions. The political executive in Britain consists of the prime minister, the ministers assigned to the Cabinet, and the larger ministry which consists of all the heads of departments and agencies. All these officials are usually selected from Parliament. There is a similar structure in China, called the State Council, headed by a premier and consisting of the various ministers and ministerial commissions.

But while the British prime minister and Cabinet have substantial policymaking power, the State Council in China is closely supervised by the general secretary of the Communist Party, the Politburo, and the Central Committee of the party. Both Britain and China have legislative bodies—the House of Commons in Britain and the National People's Congress in China. But while the House of Commons is a very important institution in the policymaking process, the Chinese Congress meets for only brief periods, legitimating and ratifying decisions made mainly by the Communist Party authorities.

When we get to the level of political parties in the two countries, the differences become even larger. Britain has a competitive party system. The majority in the House of Commons and the Cabinet are constantly confronted by an opposition party or parties, competing for public support and looking forward to the next election when they may unseat the incumbent majority. In the Chinese case the Communist Party is the dynamic and controlling political force in the whole political process. There are no other political parties. The principal decisions are taken in the Politburo and to some extent in the Central Committee of the Communist Party. The governmental agencies implement the policies, which have to be initiated and/or approved by the top Communist Party leaders. British interest groups are autonomous organizations that play important roles in the polity and the economy. Chinese trade unions and other professional organizations have to be viewed as parts of the official apparatus, dominated by the Communist Party, that perform mobilizing, socializing, and facilitating functions. Thus, an institution-by-institution comparison of British and Chinese politics that did not spell out functions in detail would not bring us far toward understanding the important differences in the politics of these countries.

Figure 2.3 shows how we relate structure to function, and process to policy and performance. (The functions and processes shown in the figure are discussed in greater detail in Chapters 3 through 8.) In the center of Figure 2.3 under the heading "Process functions" are listed the distinctive activities necessary for policy to be made and implemented in any kind of political system. We call these *process functions* because they play a direct and necessary role in the process of making policy. Before policy can be decided, some individuals and groups in the government or the society must decide what they want and hope to get from politics. The political process begins as these interests are expressed or articulated. The many arrows on the left of the figure show these initial expressions.

To be effective, however, these demands must be combined into policy alternatives—such as higher or lower taxes or more or less social security benefits—for which substantial political support can be mobilized. Thus, the arrows on the left are consolidated as the process moves from *interest articulation* to *interest aggregation*. Alternative policies are then considered. A coalition that commands substantial political resources such as votes backs one of them, and authoritative *policymaking* takes place. The policy must be enforced and implemented, and if it is challenged or violated there must be some process of *adjudication*. Each policy may affect several different aspects of a society, as reflected in the many arrows for the *implementation* phase. These process functions that we have been describing are performed by such political structures as parties, legislatures, political executives, bureaucracies, and courts.

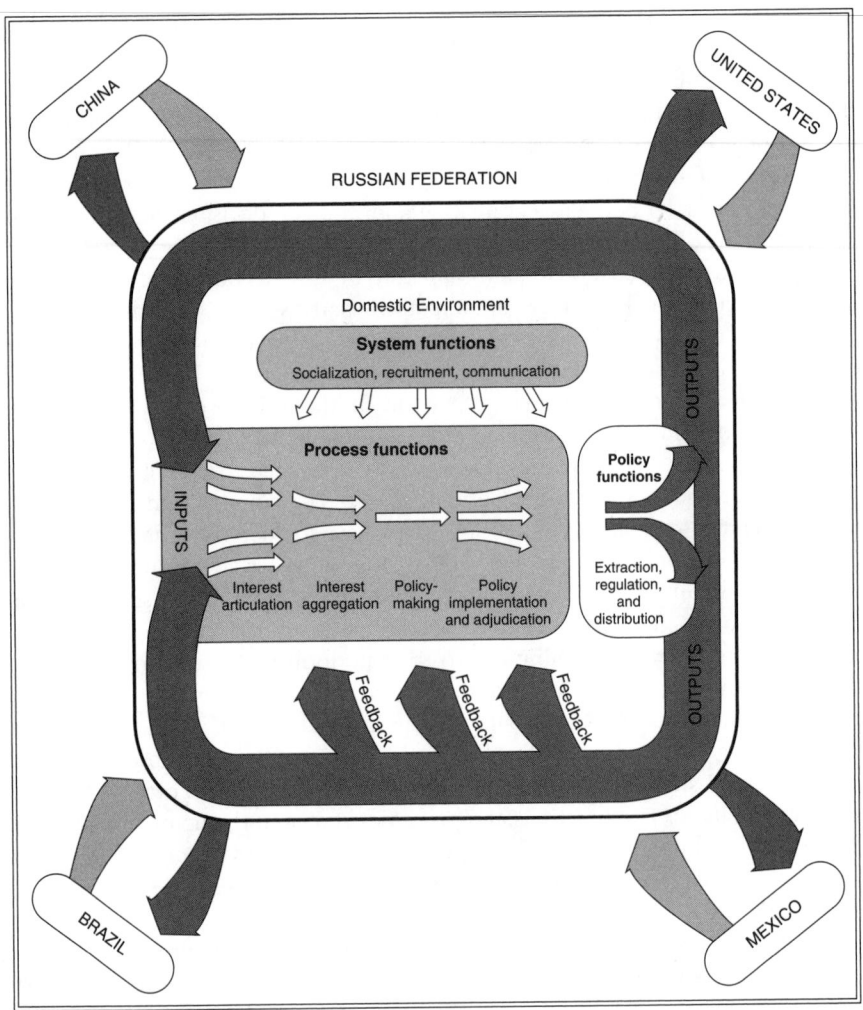

Figure 2.3 The political system and its functions.

The three functions listed at the top of the figure—socialization, recruitment, and communication—are not directly involved in making and implementing public policy but are of fundamental importance to the political system. The arrows leading from these three functions to all parts of the political process suggest their crucial role in underpinning and permeating the political process. *Political socialization* involves families, schools, communications media, churches, and all the various political structures that develop, reinforce, and transform attitudes of political significance in the society. *Political recruitment* refers to the selection of people for political activity and government offices. *Political communication* refers to the flow of information through the society and through the various structures that make up the political system. We refer to these three functions as *system functions,* because they determine whether or not the system will be maintained or changed, whether, for example, policymaking will continue to be dominated by a single authoritarian party or military council, or whether competitive parties and a legislature will replace them.

The third set of functions, listed at the right of the figure, treats the outputs— the implementations of the political process. We call these the *policy functions,* the substantive impacts on the society, the economy, and the culture. These functions include the various forms of regulation of behavior, extractions of resources in the form of taxes and the like, and distribution of benefits and services to various groups in the population. The *outcomes* of all these political activities, in a cyclical fashion, result in new inputs, in new demands for legislation or for administrative action, and in increases or decreases in the amount of support given to the political system and incumbent officeholders. These functional concepts describe the activities carried on in any society regardless of how its political system is organized, or what kinds of policies it produces. Using these functional categories, we can determine how institutions in different countries combine in the making and implementation of different kinds of public policy.

AN ILLUSTRATIVE COMPARISON: RUSSIA IN 1987 AND 1994

Figures 2.4 and 2.5 offer a simplified graphic comparison of structures and functions in Russia before and after the disintegration of the Soviet Union. The figures demonstrate the effects of two revolutionary changes—the end of the single-party political system dominated by the Communist Party of the Soviet Union, which held together the vast, multinational Soviet state, and the dissolution of the Soviet Union itself as a state into its 15 member republics. The demise of the Communist regime occurred over roughly a three-year period (1989–1991), while the formal collapse of the Union occurred with startling rapidity after the failure of the August 1991 coup d'état against Mikhail Gorbachev and his policies of reform. In December 1991, the Soviet Union was formally declared defunct.

As a result of these two remarkable events, Russia, the core republic of the old union, became an independent non-Communist state. Even before the August 1991 coup, Boris Yeltsin—long a bitter rival to the Soviet president, Mikhail Gorbachev—had been elected president of Russia in a popular election in June 1991. After the coup, Yeltsin decreed a ban on the political activity of the Communist Party, and he himself remained outside any organized political party. Besides the presidency, Russia was ruled by its legislature, called the Supreme Soviet, and the government (the heads of the ministries), which answered to the president. Organized parties competed for public favor but remained in their infancy as organizations linking the citizens to government. The mass media, free of the political and ideological constraints imposed under Communist rule, were rapidly seeking commercial acceptance by selling advertising and seeking new sponsors. New orga-

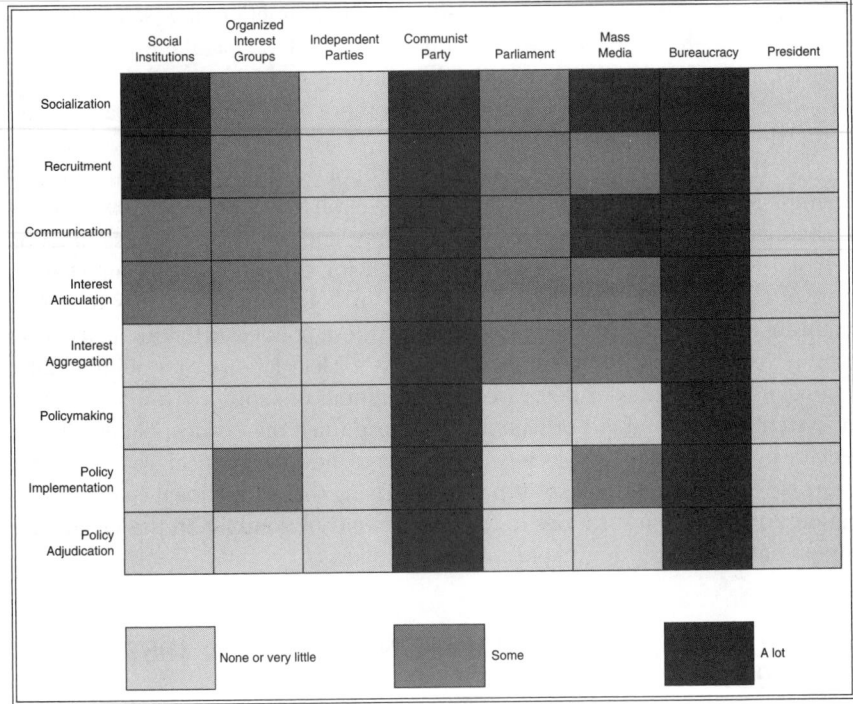

Figure 2.4 The Russian political system in 1987.

nized interest groups, such as business associations and labor unions, were rapidly becoming part of the political landscape. The two figures offer several sharp contrasts, therefore, reflecting the impact of these changes on Russia's political life.

In 1987 the Communist Party was still the dominant political structure, penetrating schools and media, the arts and public organizations, government and courts, with its influence. Through it, General Secretary Gorbachev was beginning to wage his campaign for *glasnost,* or freer discussion and disclosure, but *glasnost* was a centrally mandated campaign through which Gorbachev intended to build support for his policy of restructuring *(perestroika)* of Soviet society. For this reason, all the cells of the chart in the column marked "Communist Party" are shaded dark, as are the cells under the column marked "Bureaucracy." Although social institutions such as the family, occupations, arts, and hobby groups exercised some influence over such system-level functions as socialization, recruitment, and communication, it was the Communist Party and state bureaucracy that dominated process-level functions. Under their tutelage, the mass media played an important role in giving voice to society's aspirations, grievances, and values. The media in 1987 were becoming a particularly important player in the political system under the impact of *glasnost.*

By 1992 the political system had undergone a peaceful revolution. The Communist Party was outlawed and its property confiscated, although various minor splinter groups competed for the right to succeed to the Communist Party's ideo-

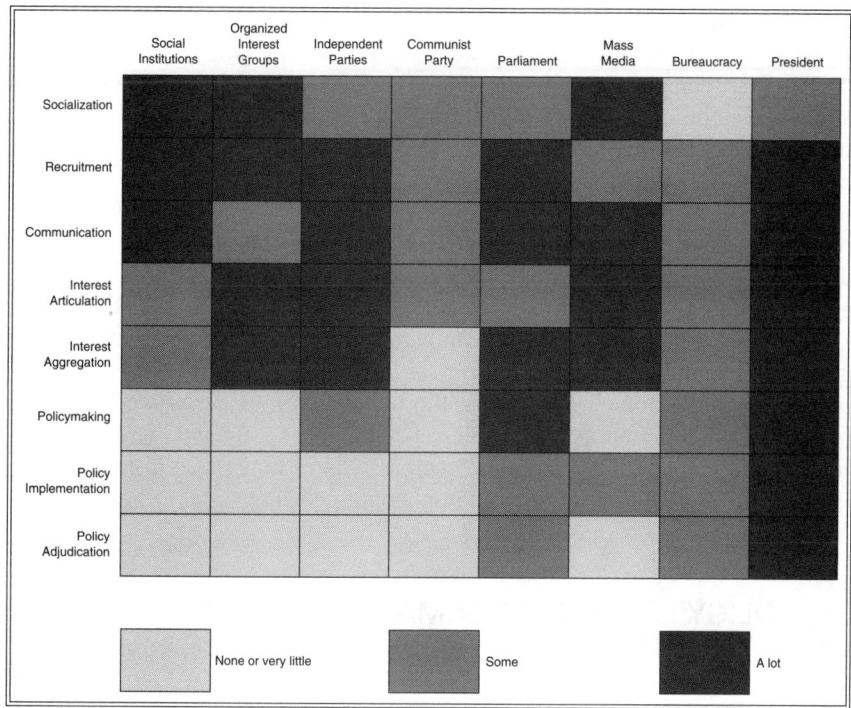

Figure 2.5 The Russian political system in 1994.

logical heritage. The bureaucracy, however, remained an important element in the political system, although adapting itself to the new trend of movement toward a market economy by adopting quasi-commercial forms. Political parties and interest groups were proliferating throughout Russia though few had significant clout or scope of operation. Parties as such were not represented in the government and had virtually no local organizations to speak of.

Two policymaking institutions had become very important in the system, the president and the Supreme Soviet. The presidency, occupied by Boris Yeltsin, was becoming the predominant institution: Many feared that Yeltsin was accumulating uncontrollable power. The Supreme Soviet, on the other hand, retained the constitutional power to pass laws and review the performance of the executive branch, although in both functions it was regularly frustrated by the inertia of the vast state bureaucracy, by its inability to compel compliance with its laws, by its weak links with the electorate, and by Yeltsin's tendency to rule by decree. Nonetheless, the freedom enjoyed by ordinary citizens to articulate their interests and to organize to advance them had expanded enormously. Moreover, before the Soviet Union broke up, Russia, though by far the largest of the republics, had lacked the means of self-government, since it was ruled by the Soviet Union directly. Now, as a result of the collapse of Communism, Russia had emerged as the principal successor of the economic and strategic assets of the Soviet Union. The great dilemma before Russia was whether the young structures of democracy could withstand the wrenching dislocations brought about by the breakdown of the old Soviet regime, and the emergence of a private economy.

The brief comparisons presented here are meant to illustrate the use of the structural-functional approach. This approach enables us to examine how similar functions are performed in different countries, or in the same country at two different points in time. Similarly, we may examine changes or contrasts in the functions performed by the same structures over time or across different political systems. In a country undergoing as rapid and dramatic transition as Russia in the 1990s, this framework helps us to analyze changes in the distribution of power among the major institutions making up the political system. Neither the analysis of structures nor that of functions is complete without the other. A structural analysis tells us the number of political parties, or the organization of the legislature, and how the executive branch, the courts, the bureaucracy, the mass media, interest groups, and other elements of the political system are set up and by what rules or standards they operate. A functional analysis tells us how these institutions and organizations interact to produce and implement policies.

THE POLICY LEVEL: PERFORMANCE, OUTCOME, AND EVALUATION

The important question is what these differences in structure and function do for the interests, needs, and aspirations of people. Figures 2.1 and 2.3 suggest the relationship between what happens in politics and in the society, and between what happens in the society and the international environment. The structural-functional differences determine the give-and-take between politics and environment, and the importance of that give-and-take for such goals and objectives as welfare, justice, freedom, equality, peace, and prosperity. At the left of Figure 2.3 are arrows signifying inputs of demands and supports from the society and the international system and inputs from the independent initiatives of political leaders and bureaucrats. At the right are arrows signifying outputs and outcomes, the end products of the political process, the things a government does for and to its people.

We have to distinguish between the efforts, the things a government does, and the actual outcome of these efforts. Governments may spend equal amounts on education and health, or defense, but with different consequences. Not only government efficiency or corruption, but the underlying cultural, economic, and technological level, as well as changes in its environment, play a role in the effectiveness of politics. Americans spend more per capita on education than any other people in the world, but their children perform less well in important school subjects than do children in some other countries that spend substantially less. The United States and the USSR spent enormous sums on defense in the last decades, and yet both countries were held at bay by small countries resolved to resist at all costs, and because of these failed efforts, they were weakened internally. The outcome of public policy is never wholly in the hands of the people and their leaders in the various nations of the world. Conditions in the internal environment, conditions and events in the larger external world, and simple chance may frustrate the most thoughtfully crafted programs and plans. We call the outputs of a political system—its extractions, distributions, regulations, and symbolic acts, its *performance.*

Finally, we must step even further back to consider the whole situation of political system, process, and policy, and the environment, to evaluate what political systems are doing. Evaluation is complex because people value different things and put different emphasis on what they value. We will refer to the different things people may value as political "goods." In Chapter 8 we discuss goods associated with the system level, such as the stability or adaptability of political institutions; goods associated with the process level, such as citizen participation in politics; and goods associated with the policy level, such as welfare, security, and liberty. To evaluate what a political system is doing, we must look at each of these areas and assess performance and outcomes. We must also be aware of how outcomes affect individuals and subgroups in the society, of specific changes that may often be overlooked in presenting averages, and of the continuing problem of building for the future as well as living today. This last problem affects both poor nations, which wish to survive and alleviate suffering today, but also improve their children's lot tomorrow, and rich nations, which must deal with the costs to their children of polluted and depleted natural resources as the result of the thoughtless environmental policies of the past.

KEY TERMS

adjudication	policymaking
function	political communication
implementation	political recruitment
inputs	political socialization
interest aggregation	political system
interest articulation	process functions
media of communication	regime
outcomes	structure
outputs	system
policy functions	system functions

END NOTES

1. Alexis de Tocqueville to Ernest de Chabrol, October 7, 1831, and Louis de Kergolay, October 18, 1847, *Alexis de Tocqueville: Selected Letters on Politics and Society,* ed.

Roger Boesche (Berkeley, CA: Univ. of California Press, 1985) pp. 59 and 191. See also, George Wilson Pierson, *Tocqueville and Beaumont in America* (New York: Oxford Yniv. Press, 1938).

2. Robert A. Dahl, *Polyarchy: Participation and Opposition* (New Haven, CT: Yale Univ. Press, 1971).

SUGGESTED READINGS

Almond, Gabriel A., and G. Bingham Powell Jr. *Comparative Politics: System, Process, Policy.* Boston, Little Brown, 1978.

Collier, David. "The Comparative Method", in *Political Science: The State of the Discipline II.* American Political Science Association, Washington, D. C.,1993.

Dogan, Mattei, and Dominique Pelassy. *How To Compare Nations: Strategies in Comparative Politics.* Chatham, N. J.: Chatham House Publishers, 1990.

Przeworski, Adam, and James Teune. *The Logic of Comparative Social Inquiry.* New York: Wiley, 1970.

King, Gary, Robert O. Keohane, Sidney Verba. *Scientific Inference in Qualitative Research.* New York: Cambridge University Press, 1993.

SYSTEM, PROCESS, AND POLICY

Gabriel A. Almond
G. Bingham Powell, Jr.

Chapter
3

Political Culture and Political Socialization

POLITICAL CULTURE

People's attitudes affect what they will do. The collective political attitudes, values, feelings, information and skills of the people in a society affect the way politics works in that society. Conditions that are tolerable to citizens in one country may be intensely frustrating and a source of rebellion in another. Constitutional arrangements that sustained liberty in England were turned into instruments of repression in South Africa and Northern Ireland. To understand the propensities for present and future behavior in a society, we must begin with its distribution of political attitudes--what we call its *political culture.*

Political culture does not explain everything about politics. Even people with similar values and skills will behave differently when they face different opportunities or challenges. Nor is political culture immutable. New experiences can change the attitudes of individuals; new generations can change the configuration of an entire political culture. But political culture is a critical element in comparing different countries at the same time or the same country at different times. If we do not take it into account, our understanding will be seriously distorted.

In approaching any specific political system it would be useful to develop a map of the important contours of its political culture, as well as the corresponding map of its structures and functions. In this chapter we begin by describing such a map. Then, we discuss *political socialization*, the function that explains how individuals form their political attitudes and thus, collectively, how citizens form their political culture. We conclude with observations about the political cultural trends in world politics today.

MAPPING THE THREE LEVELS OF POLITICAL CULTURE

One way of mapping a nation's political culture is to describe citizens' attitudes to the three levels of the political system: system, process, and policy. At the *system* level we are interested in the citizens' and leaders' views of the values and organizations that hold the political system together. How should policymakers be selected and when should citizens obey the laws? At the *process* level we are interested in individuals' propensities to become involved in the process: to make demands, obey the law, support some groups and oppose others. At the *policy* level we want to know what policies citizens and leaders expect from the government. What goals are to be established and how are they to be achieved?

System Propensities

Perhaps the most important single aspect of the political culture is the *legitimacy* of the government. Citizens perceive that a government is legitimate to the degree that they believe it has the rightful power to compel obedience. When citizens believe that they ought to obey the laws, then legitimacy is high. If they see no reason to obey, or if they comply only from fear, then legitimacy is low. Because it is much easier to get compliance when citizens believe in the legitimacy of the government, virtually all governments, even the most brutal and coercive, try to make citizens believe that their laws ought to be obeyed and that it is acceptable to use force against those who resist. A government with high legitimacy will be more effective in making and implementing policies and more likely to overcome hardships and reversals.

Citizens may accord legitimacy to a government for different reasons. In a traditional society, legitimacy may depend on the ruler's inheriting the throne and on the ruler's obedience to religious customs such as making sacrifices and performing rituals. In a modern democracy, the legitimacy of the authorities will depend on their selection by citizens in competitive elections and on their following constitutional procedures in lawmaking. In other political cultures, the leaders may base their claim to legitimacy on their special grace, wisdom, or ideology, which they claim will transform citizens' lives for the better, even though the government does not respond to specific demands or follow prescribed procedures.[1]

Whether legitimacy is based on tradition, ideology, citizen participation, or specific policies has important implications for the efficiency and stability of the political system. These bases of legitimacy set the rules for a kind of exchange between citizens and authorities. Citizens obey the laws and in return the government meets the obligations set by its basis of legitimacy. As long as the obligations are met, citizens are supposed to comply and provide support and appropriate participation. If customs are violated—the line of succession is broken, the constitution is subverted, or the ruling ideology is ignored—then the government must expect at least resistance and perhaps rebellion.

In systems in which legitimacy is low or the claimed bases for legitimacy are not accepted, citizens often resort to violence as a solution to political disagreement. Legitimacy may be undermined where: (1) citizens dispute the boundaries of the political system, as in Northern Ireland and the components of the former Yugoslavia; (2) citizens reject the current arrangements for recruiting leaders and making policies, as when they take to the streets to demand free elections in a dictatorship; or (3) citizens lose confidence that the leaders are fulfilling their part of the bargain of making the right kinds of laws or following the right procedures.

The Soviet Union disintegrated because all three kinds of legitimacy problems appeared. After Communist ideology failed as a unifying force, there was no basis for a national political community in the absence of common language or ethnicity. Similarly, general loss of confidence in the Communist Party as the dominating structure for choosing leaders, arranging for their symbolic ratification in one-party elections, and transforming the society to one of equity and prosperity, led many to call for new arrangements. Finally, shortages of food and consumer goods caused citizens to lose faith in the government's short-term economic and political policies. Gorbachev failed in his efforts to deal with all three problems at the same time.

Process Propensities

As shown in Figure 3.1, in a hypothetical modern industrial democracy a sizable proportion (60 percent) of adults may be involved as actual and potential participants in political processes. They are informed about politics and can and do make political demands, giving their political support to different political leaders. We call these people *participants.* Another 30 percent are simply *subjects;* they passively obey government officials and the law, but they do not vote or involve themselves in politics. A third group of people (10 percent) are hardly aware of government and politics. They may be illiterates, rural people living in remote areas, or older women unresponsive to female suffrage who are almost entirely involved in their families and communities. We call these people *parochials.*[2]

Such a distribution would not be unusual in modern democracies. It provides enough political activists to ensure competition between political parties and sizable voter turnout, as well as critical audiences for debate on public issues and pressure groups certain to propose new policies and protect their particular interests.

The second column in Figure 3.1 depicts a largely industrialized authoritarian society, such as the former Soviet Union. A rather small minority of citizens becomes involved in the huge one-party system, which penetrates and oversees the society, as well as deciding its policies. Most of the rest of the citizens are mobilized as subjects by the party, the bureaucracy, and the government-controlled mass media. Citizens are encouraged and even coerced to cast a symbolic vote of support in elections, and to pay taxes, obey regulations, accept assigned jobs, and so forth. Thanks to the effectiveness of modern societal organization and communications, and to the efforts of the authoritarian party, few citizens are unaware of the government and its influence on their lives. Hence, we see that most of the society is made up of subjects, rather than parochials or participants. If such a society suddenly attempts democratization of its politics, many citizens must learn to become participants as well as subjects.

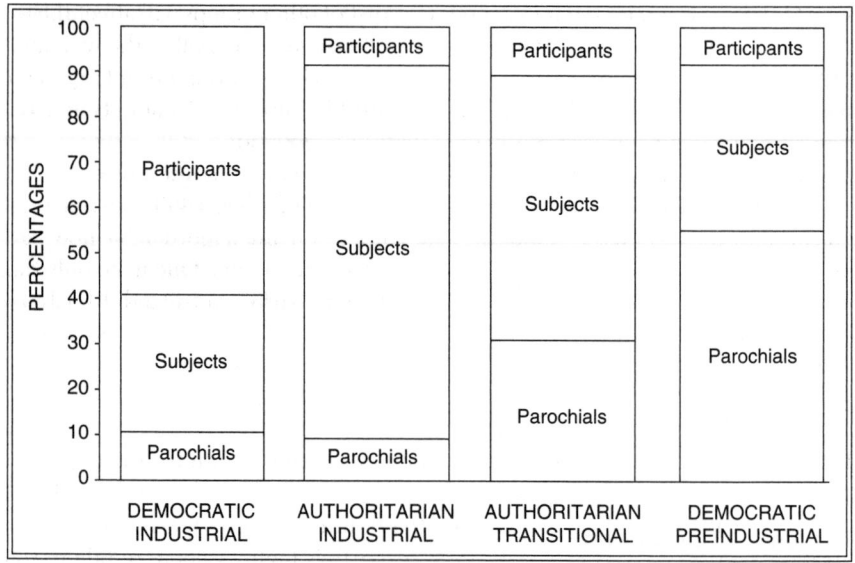

Figure 3.1 Models of political culture: Orientations toward involvement in the political process.

The third column shows an authoritarian system in a society that is partly industrial and partly modern, exemplified by such countries as Indonesia or Egypt. In spite of an authoritarian political organization, some participants—students and intellectuals, for example—would oppose the system and try to change it by persuasion or more aggressive acts of protest. Favored groups, like businessmen and landowners, would discuss public issues and engage in lobbying. But most people in such a system would be passive subjects, aware of government and complying with the law, but not otherwise involved in public affairs. The parochials—poor and illiterate slum dwellers and peasants or farm laborers working and living in large landed estates—would have little conscious contact with the political system.

Our fourth example is the democratic preindustrial system, perhaps one like India, which has a predominantly rural, illiterate population. In such a country there would be many fewer political participants, chiefly educated professionals, businessmen, and landowners. A much larger number of employees, workers, and perhaps independent farmers would be directly affected by government taxation and other official policies. But the largest group of citizens would be illiterate farm workers and peasants, whose knowledge of and involvement with the national public sector would be minimal. In such a society it is a great challenge to create a more aware citizenry that can participate meaningfully and shape public policies through democratic means.

A second critical feature of the process culture is people's beliefs about other groups and themselves as group members. Do individuals see the society as divided into social classes, regional groups, or ethnic communities? Do they identify themselves with particular factions or parties? How do they feel about groups of which they are not members? The political trust of other groups will affect the willingness of citizens to work with others for political goals, as well as the willingness of leaders to form coalitions with other groups.[3] The governing of a large nation requires forming large coalitions, and there must be substantial amounts of trust in other leaders to keep bargains and be honest in negotiations.

Beyond the question of trust, but related to it, is the question of hostility, an emotional component to intergroup and interpersonal relations. The tragic examples of ethnic, religious, and ideological conflict in many nations show how easily hostility can be converted into violence and aggressive action. One need only think of the terrible toll of civil war in Rwanda, Lebanon, Northern Ireland, El Salvador, or the former Yugoslavia.

Policy Propensities

If we are to understand the politics of a country, we must understand the issues people care about and their underlying images of the good society and how to achieve it. Citizens in different nations attach different importance to various policy outcomes. In some societies private property is highly valued; in others communal possessions are the rule. Some goods, such as material welfare, are valued by nearly everyone. But societies differ nevertheless: Some emphasize equality and minimum standards for all, while others emphasize the opportunity to move up the economic ladder. Some cultures put more weight on welfare and security, and others value liberty and procedural justice. (Different kinds of political goods are discussed further in Chapter 8.)

Moreover, the combination of learned values, strategies, and social conditions will lead to quite different perceptions about how to achieve desired social outcomes. One study showed that 73 percent of the Italian Parliament strongly agreed that a government wanting to help the poor would have to take from the rich in order to do it. Only 12 percent of the British Parliament took the same strong position, and half disagreed with the idea that redistribution was laden with conflict.[4] Similarly, citizens and leaders in preindustrial nations disagree about the mixture of government regulation and direct government investment in the economy that helps or hinders economic growth.

Consensual or Conflictual Political Cultures

Political cultures may be consensual or conflictual on issues of public policy and, more fundamentally, on their views of legitimate governmental and political arrangements. In a *consensual political culture,* citizens tend to agree on the appropriate means of making political decisions and tend to share views of what the major problems of the society are and how to solve them. In more *conflictual political cultures* the citizens are sharply divided, often on both the legitimacy of the regime and solutions to major problems.

In many countries citizens and elites use the language of "left" and "right" (in the United States, "liberal" and "conservative") to discuss the issues and actors involved in national debates about political issues. Although such language is always a simplification of the complexity of political choice, it is a useful simplification, helpful to communication among participants and observers alike. One useful aspect of the "left" and "right" language is that it enables us to visualize the distributions of citizens and parties along an ideological spectrum. (See Figure 3.2 below and Figure 6.1 in Chapter 6.)

In the United States, Britain, and Germany many citizens place themselves at the center of such an "ideological spectrum," with most of the rest at the moderate left or right. Very few place themselves at the extreme left or extreme right.[5] The more conflictual distributions in the political cultures of such countries as France, Italy, and Greece both encourage and reflect the more intense political debates in these countries. Such debates have been associated with disputes over a regime's legitimacy, as well as disagreements on political issues. In all three countries, however, the divisions seem to have gradually become less conflictual over the last 20 years.

While the elite debates about "left" and "right" in many modernized democracies have often focused on economic issues (such as the involvement of government in the economy), other issues—such as religion, defense, and the environment—also can play an important role. In younger democracies and, especially in nondemocracies, the language of "left" and "right" (or some other language, such as "progressive" and "conservative"), often focuses on democratization itself, or on the centralization of political power.[6] Whatever the substantive content, conflictual political cultures, with many citizens at the "extremes" and fewer in the "center," are a serious problem for any society.

When a country is deeply divided in political attitudes, and these deep differences are sustained over time, we speak of the distinctive groups as *political subcultures.* The citizens in these subcultures have sharply different points of view on at least some critical political issues, such as the boundaries of the nation, the nature of the regime, or the correct ideology. Typically, they affiliate with different political parties and interest groups, read different newspapers, and even have separate social clubs and sporting groups. Thus, they are exposed to quite distinctive patterns of learning about politics. Such organized differences once characterized the electorates in France and Italy, contrasting communist and Catholic subcultures, although these subcultural differences have declined substantially.

Where political subcultures coincide with ethnic, national, or religious differences, as in Northern Ireland, Bosnia, and Lebanon, the divisions can be very enduring and threatening. Earlier expectations in the United States that all the immigrant groups would assimilate into a common American culture have proven to be unfounded. Many individuals of English, Scotch, Irish, German, Scandinavian, Jewish, Italian, Greek, African, Chicano, or Asian origins, for example, continue to share common political and policy propensities with their fellow ethnics. These influences are mediated and sustained by family, community, school, peer group, interest groups, political parties, and media of communication. The fragmentation of the Soviet empire, the breakup of Yugoslavia, and the impulses toward autonomy and secession among the Scots, the Welsh, the Bretons, the Basques, and the like, reflect the lasting power of language, culture, and historical memory to create and sustain the sense of ethnic and national identity among parts of contemporary states. As we discussed in Chapter 1, Samuel Huntington has predicted that the places in the world where the great traditional cultures collide will be major sources of political conflict in the next century.[7]

Figure 3.2 reflects the sharpness of subcultural division as translated directly into political support in Northern Ireland. In the 1980s and early 1990s five parties contested the national elections in Northern Ireland. Two of these parties appealed mainly to Protestants and stood above all for regaining the Protestant domination over Northern Ireland politics that had prevailed from 1922 until direct British intervention in the early 1970s. The Democratic Unionist party, in particular, stood for direct resistance to any compromises. Two of the parties appealed mainly to Catholics. Sinn Fein called for both armed and electoral struggle leading to union with the Republic of Ireland, while the Social Democratic and Labour party (SDLP) called for negotiated compromises involving Ireland, Britain, and the two communities in Northern Ireland. One party, the Alliance, tried to rally moderate forces in both Protestant and Catholic communities against continuing conflict.[8]

The parties are shown across the bottom of the figure, with the cross-community moderate party in the center and the most extreme parties at the respective far left (Sinn Fein) and far right (Democratic Unionist). The choices of Protestant voters are shown with an unbroken line, while the Catholic voters' choices are shown with a dotted line. The clarity of division between the Catholic and Protestant subcultures is dramatized by the huge gap in the center—neither community supported the only party appealing for support across religious lines. Protestants voted overwhelmingly (91 percent) for the two Protestant parties, and Catholics voted almost as overwhelmingly (87 percent) for the two Catholic parties. The citizenry is not quite perfectly polarized, for the more moderate of the two community parties won more support within each community. But a third or more of each com-

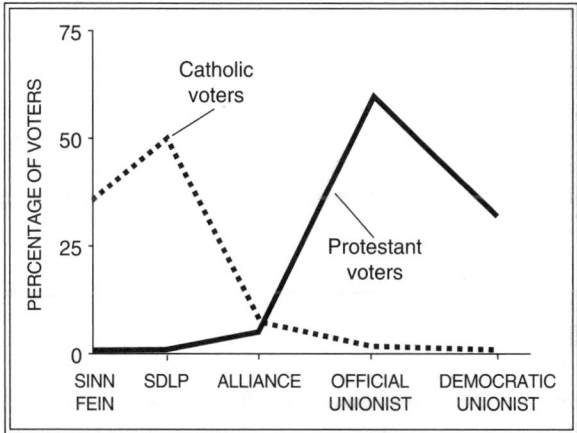

Figure 3.2 Voting polarization in Northern Ireland in the 1983 general election. (*Source:* Calculated from data in Ian McAllister and Richard Rose, based on a 1983 election survey. The parties received very similar rates in 1983 and 1987. Data from Ian McAllister and Richard Rose, *Voters Begin to Choose* London: Sage, 1986.)

munity did support the most extreme party available to it. Conflictual subcultures of this kind pose very difficult problems for any political system. In Northern Ireland the conflicts between subcultures have destroyed local democratic politics, driven thousands from their homes, and cost about 3,000 lives in the last 25 years. In 1994 a cease-fire was finally achieved between the hostile factions, but it remains to be seen if it can lead to peaceful accommodation. While these costs pale in comparison to the ghastly toll of civil wars in Lebanon, Bosnia, and Rwanda, they testify to the enduring problems of conflictual subcultures even in modernized and economically developed societies.

POLITICAL SOCIALIZATION

Political cultures are sustained or changed as the citizens acquire their attitudes and values. We use the term *socialization* to refer to the way children are introduced to the values of their society. *Political socialization* is the part of this process that shapes political attitudes. Most children acquire elementary but distinctive political attitudes and behavior patterns at a relatively early age.[9] While some of these attitudes will be elaborated and revised as the child develops, others may remain parts of the political self throughout life.

At any specific time an individual's *political self* will be a combination of several feelings and attitudes in varying proportions. At the deepest level there are general identifications and beliefs such as nationalism, ethnic or class self-images, religious and ideological commitments, and a fundamental sense of one's rights and duties in the society. Subcultural divisions often have such power to generate commitment and fear because they are constructed from these deep self-images. Individuals also acquire less emotional knowledge about political and governmental institutions. Finally, there are fleeting views of current events, policies, issues, and personalities. All these attitudes change, but those in the first group usually were acquired earliest, have been most frequently reinforced through messages and behavior, and tend to be the most durable.

Political socialization never really ceases; therefore, the political self is always changing. Many of life's most common experiences—becoming involved in new social groups and roles, moving from one part of the country to another, shifting up or down the social and economic ladder, becoming a parent, finding or losing a job—modify our political perspective. More dramatic experiences, such as immigration to a new country or suffering through an economic depression or a war, can sharply alter even quite basic political attitudes.

Three general points about political socialization need to be emphasized. The first is that political socialization can take the form of either *direct* or *indirect* transmission and learning. Socialization is direct when it involves the explicit communication of information, values, or feelings toward politics. Civics courses in public schools are direct political socialization, as are the efforts of Islamic fundamentalist movements to indoctrinate children in such countries as Iran and Pakistan.

Political socialization is indirect when political views are inadvertently molded by our experiences. Such indirect political socialization may have particular force in a child's early years. For example, the child's development of either an accommodating or an aggressive stance toward parents, teachers, and friends is likely to affect the adult's posture toward political leaders and fellow citizens in later life. Or, growing up in a time of deprivation and hardship may leave the future adult with a more materialistic set of value priorities.[10]

The second major point is that socialization continues throughout an individual's life. Attitudes established during childhood are always being adapted or reinforced as the individual passes through a variety of social experiences. Early family influences can create a favorable image of a political party, but subsequent education, job experience, and the influence of friends may dramatically alter that early image. Furthermore, certain events and experiences—a war or an economic depression—may leave their mark on the whole society. Such events seem to have their greatest impact on young people just becoming involved in political life, such as first-time voters, but most people are affected to some degree. When experiences bring about drastic changes in the attitudes of older members of the society, we speak of *political resocialization*.

Political socialization transmits and transforms a nation's political culture. It is the way one generation passes on political ideas and beliefs to succeeding generations, a process called cultural transmission. It transforms the political culture when it leads the citizens, or some of them, to view and experience politics in a different way. In times of rapid change or extraordinary events, such as the formation of a new nation, political socialization may even create a political culture where none existed before.

The third point is that patterns of socialization in a society can either be unifying or divisive. As we have already suggested, subcultures in a society can have their own distinctive patterns of socialization. As they provide their members with their own newspapers, their own neighborhood groups, perhaps their own schools, the young acquire distinctive subcultural attitudes, their elders are reinforced in them. These divisive patterns of socialization can have momentous impact on the society.

AGENTS OF POLITICAL SOCIALIZATION

Political socialization is accomplished through a variety of institutions and agents. Some, like civics courses in schools, are deliberately designed for this purpose. Others, like play and work groups, are likely to affect political socialization indirectly.

The Family

The direct and indirect influences of the family—the first socialization structure that an individual encounters—are powerful and lasting. The most distinctive of these influences is the shaping of attitudes toward authority. The family makes collective decisions, and for the child these decisions may be authoritative—failure to obey may lead to punishment. An early experience with participation in family decision making can increase the child's sense of political competence, providing skills for political interaction, and encouraging active participation in the political system as an adult. By the same token, patterns of obedience to parental decisions can help to predispose the child's future performance as a political subject. The family also shapes future political attitudes by locating the individual in a vast social world; establishing ethnic, linguistic, and religious ties and perception of social class; affirming cultural and educational values and achievements; and directing occupational and economic aspirations.[11]

A revolution in women's resources and expectations in recent decades has profoundly affected the politics of advanced industrial nations. The trend toward gender equality in education, occupation, and profession has transformed the structure of the family. The attenuation of sharp differences between the sexes in self-images, in parental roles, and in the relations of men and women to the economy and the political system, is significantly affecting patterns of political recruitment, political participation, and public policy. A more open family, equality of parenting, and the early exposure of children to child care and preschool group experiences have modified the impact of the family in the socialization process in ways we still do not fully understand.

The School

Educated persons are more aware of the impact of government on their lives and pay more attention to politics. They have been given mental skills and background that change their ability to interpret and act on new information. They have more information about political processes and undertake a wider range of activities in their political behavior. These effects of education have appeared in studies of political attitudes in many nations.[12]

Schools provide adolescents with knowledge about the political world and their role in it. They provide children with more concrete perceptions of political institutions and relationships. Schools also transmit the values and attitudes of the society. They can play an important role in shaping attitudes about the unwritten rules of the political game, as the traditional British public schools tried to instill the values of public duty, informal political relations, and political integrity. Schools can reinforce affection for the political system and provide common symbols, such as the flag and pledge of allegiance, for an expressive response to the system. When a new nation comes into being, or a revolutionary regime comes to power in an old nation, it usually turns immediately to the schools as a means to supplant "outdated" values and symbols with new ones more congruent with the new rulers' ideology.

In some nations the agents of socialization do not provide unifying political socialization, but send starkly different messages to different groups. The educational system in South Africa had until recently as one of its main goals the development and perpetuation of differences between the races. The apartheid culture was supported both by inculcating attitudes of separateness and by providing different skills and knowledge. There was no mixing of white and black children. White children learned early that their parents and other siblings treated blacks as inferior people. As they grew older they learned that whites were different and superior to blacks. White children in South Africa were required by law to attend primary and secondary school, where the environment has been exclusive as it was at home. The school experience usually confirmed and strengthened the attitudes acquired by white children at home.

Education for the black majority was terribly different. After forcing most of the private mission schools to close, the government dealt with black education through a separate government department that provided segregated elementary education for most African children and secondary education for a few. In 1979, after several years of improvement, the government still spent more than ten times as much per student on white education as on black African education.[13] Black dissatisfaction with the quality of education, as well as with the unsuccessful government efforts to force the use of Afrikaans (the native language of most white South Africans) as the medium of instruction in the 1970s and 1980s, was one of the major sources of the unrest that fueled the challenge to white-dominated politics in the 1990s. The new South African government is committed to a huge challenge: to alter profoundly (with a limited budget) the role of the school system from a perpetuator of difference to a provider of unifying symbols and equal skills to children of all races.

Religious Institutions

The religions of the world are carriers of cultural and moral values, which inevitably have political implications, affecting politics and public policy. The great religious leaders have seen themselves as teachers, and their followers have usually attempted to shape the socialization of children through schooling and to socialize converts of all ages through preaching and religious services. While the frequency of church attendance varies greatly in different societies and religions, the presence of religious identity and organizations is felt in most political systems. Where the churches systematically teach values that are at least in part at odds with the controlling political system, as in the years of tensions between the Communist regime and the Catholic Church in Poland, or in the conflict between Islamic fundamentalists and secular governments in Algeria and Egypt, or in the efforts of American fundamentalists to introduce prayer in the schools, the struggle over socialization can be of the greatest significance in the society.

The emergence of aggressive religious fundamentalism in recent decades has had a major impact on the society and politics of countries as diverse as the United States, India, Israel, Lebanon, Iran, Pakistan, Algeria, and Nigeria. Such fundamentalism is a defensive reaction against the diffusion of rational and scientific views of nature and human behavior, and the spread of secular and libertarian values and attitudes. It usually defines for its believers a world that is uncompromisingly divided into forces of spiritual goodness and forces of darkness and evil. Believers must identify themselves by distinctive and separate behaviors and fight in the great struggle between these forces.[14] While the influence of fundamentalism has been most visible in the Middle East and among Muslim countries, it is important in Christian countries as well. There are both Protestant and Catholic versions of fundamentalism in the United States and in European and Latin American countries. Versions of fundamentalism are also to be found, combined with ethnic and nationalist tendencies, among the Confucian, Buddhist, and Hindu countries of East, Southeast, and South Asia.

Broadly speaking, the rise of fundamentalism has shifted the center of political gravity to the right, and has often raised conservative social, moral, and religious issues to the top of the contemporary policy agenda. Religious institutions of many kinds offer, of course, moral and ethical guidance that may be grievously needed by individuals making choices in complex secular societies. However, its uncompromising themes and the sharp boundaries of identity and behavior required of its members often makes fundamentalism a deliberately conflictual and uncomfortable presence in national politics.

Peer Groups

Although school, family, and religious movements are the agents most obviously engaged in socialization, several other social units also shape political attitudes. One is peer groups, including childhood play groups, friendship cliques, school and college fraternities, and small work groups, in which members share relatively equal status and close ties. Individuals adopt the views of their peers because they like or respect them or because they want to be like them. It may be awkward or painful to be "different."

A peer group socializes its members by motivating or pressuring them to conform to the attitudes or behavior accepted by the group. An individual may become interested in politics or begin to follow political events because close friends do so. High school seniors may choose to go on to college because other students with whom they identify have chosen to do the same. In such cases, the individual modifies his or her interests and behavior to reflect those of the group in an effort to be accepted by its members.[15] The international youth culture symbolized by rock music, T-shirts, and blue jeans may have played a major role in the failure of Communist officials to mold Soviet and Eastern European youth to the "socialist personality" that was the Marxist-Leninist ideal. Likewise, groupings such as the "skinheads" that have sprouted up among lower-class youth in many Western countries have adopted political views that have no other source than peer interactions.

Occupation, Class, and Status

Historically, and still in parts of the world such as some Latin American countries, societies have been divided into landowning aristocracies and peasants and other lower-class groups. Even as recently as the Victorian Age in Britain, Prime Minister Disraeli could speak of England as consisting of "two nations"—the upper and lower classes, differing in height, health, dress, speech, lifestyle, attitudes, and values. Industrialization produced a new social structure in advanced countries such as Britain and Germany, where working classes emerged, concentrated in particular neighborhoods, developing their own forms of speech, dress, recreation and entertainment, and their own organizations, including powerful trade unions and political parties. One could speak of the emergence of a proletarian political culture in these areas. The rise of "postindustrial" society has meant the breakup of these large social formations. White-collar workers and professionals in Europe, North America, Japan, and other parts of East Asia now outnumber blue-collar workers, with the result that the political processes in these countries have become more complex, more fluid.

Mass Media

Modern societies cannot exist without widespread and rapid communication. Information about events occurring anywhere in the world becomes general knowledge in a few hours. Much of the world has become a single audience, moved by the same events and motivated by similar tastes. There is no part of the world so remote that its inhabitants lack the means to be informed almost simultaneously about events elsewhere: mass-produced and inexpensive transistor radios are omnipresent, even in Third World villages far removed from political power centers, and the mass media—newspapers, radio, television, magazines—play an important part in internationalizing attitudes and values around the globe.

Television, enlisting the senses of both sight and sound, may have a powerful emotional impact on large public audiences. American disillusionment with the war in Vietnam in the late 1960s and early 1970s was in considerable part the result of the bringing of the battlefield into the living room, made possible by television coverage of military action. More recently, an increasing cynicism about politics and politicians in the United States seems to be encouraged by a tendency by the news media to emphasize strategies and competition over substantive policy questions and generally to portray candidates more negatively.[16] Greater use of "attack" advertising in political campaigns in the 1990s also seems to contribute to viewers' loss of confidence in the electoral process and the responsiveness of public officials.[17]

In 1989 the movements for democracy throughout Eastern Europe fed on the knowledge of each others' tactics and successes, given extra impact by newspapers, television, and radio newly free to report these exciting events in and beyond their own nation. In addition to providing specific and immediate information about political events, the mass media also convey, directly or indirectly, the major values on which a society agrees. Certain symbols are conveyed in an emotional context, and the events described alongside them take on a specific emotional color. Mass media controlled by an authoritarian government can be a powerful force in shaping political beliefs, although citizens will soon ignore reports that are inconsistent with their personal experiences, and word-of-mouth transmission of inconsistent attitudes is often a powerful antidote to the effectiveness of direct mass-media socialization.

Interest Groups

Interest groups, associations, and organizations of one kind or another also play important roles in the shaping of popular attitudes. These include economic groups, such as trade unions, manufacturer and trade associations, chambers of commerce, and agricultural groups. Among these economic groups, trade unions may have had the most important consequences for politics. In most advanced industrial countries, the rise of trade unions has transformed political culture and politics, creating new political parties and ushering in the "welfare state." Other occupational and professional associations, such as peasant and farmer groups, manufacturers, wholesalers and retailers, medical societies, and associations of lawyers, are important agencies influencing political attitudes in modern and modernizing societies. They enlist large numbers of trained professionals, and ensure their loyalty by defending their members' economic and professional interests. Because these associations relate to occupational strata, they promote and intensify occupational and class-related political values.

Also important in political socialization are ethnic societies, such as organizations of Americans of Polish, Italian, Greek, Chinese, or Jewish origin; civic associations, such as parent-teacher associations and leagues of women voters; and policy groups, such as taxpayers' associations, and "pro-life" and "pro-choice" organizations. Groups such as these—relying on the use of the media and the mails—disseminate large quantities of information and exhortation on political, social, and economic issues to mass and elite audiences.

Political Parties

As specialized political structures, parties play a deliberate and important role in political socialization. Political parties attempt to mold issue preferences, arouse the apathetic, and find new issues as they mobilize support for candidates. Political parties such as the Republicans and Democrats in the United States or Labour and Conservatives in Britain typically draw heavily on traditional symbols of the nation or a class and reinforce them. A competitive party system may focus criticism on the government's *incumbents* (officeholders), but it often reinforces support for the basic structures and processes. Parties also keep citizens in contact with the political structures. Most individuals are concerned with politics only in a limited way, but a steady flow of party activities, culminating in an election every few years, keeps citizens involved in their citizenship, their participant roles.

In competitive party systems, party socialization activities can also be divisive. In their efforts to gain support, leaders may appeal to class, language, religion, and other ethnic divisions and make citizens more aware of these differences. In the 1960s in Belgium, the small Flemish and French separatist parties emphasized language differences and split the traditional Belgian party system, which had been stable for 50 years, aroused massive political conflict, and brought about major policy changes, including constitutional revisions. Leaders of preindustrial nations often oppose competitive parties because they fear such divisiveness in their new nations. Although this is sometimes a sincere concern, it is also self-serving to incumbent leaders, and is becoming increasingly difficult to justify against widespread contemporary demands for multiparty systems.

In the ex-Communist nations until recently and in many preindustrial nations, governments have used a single party to attempt to inculcate common attitudes of national unity, support for the government, and ideological agreement. The combination of a single party and controlled mass media is potent: The media present a single point of view, and the party activities reinforce that perspective by involving the citizen more directly and personally. Yet, as demonstrated recently in Eastern Europe and the USSR, years of directed socialization by media and party cannot compete with citizens' personal experiences in shaping underlying attitudes.

Direct Contact with Governmental Structures

In modern societies, the wide scope of governmental activities brings citizens into frequent contact with various bureaucratic agencies. One study found that 72 percent of adult Americans had interacted with at least one government agency in the preceding year; about a third had interacted with more. The most frequent contacts were with tax authorities, school officials, and the police.[18] The scope of government intervention in daily life, and hence the necessity for contacts with government, is greater in many Western European nations than in the United States, and it is greater yet in the still surviving Communist countries.

These personal experiences are powerful agents of socialization, strengthening or undercutting the images presented by other agents. No matter how positive the view of the political system that has been taught in school, a citizen who is harassed by the police, ignored by welfare agencies, or unfairly taxed is unlikely to feel much warmth toward the authorities.

In their study of citizen attitudes in five nations, Almond and Verba found marked differences across countries in the expectations that citizens had of their treatment by police and bureaucrats.[19] Italians, and particularly Mexicans, had quite dismal expectations as to equality and responsiveness of treatment. American blacks also reported quite negative expectations in these 1960 interviews. It is quite likely that these expectations were in large measure a response to actual patterns of treatment by government.

TRENDS IN CONTEMPORARY POLITICAL CULTURES

Each community's political culture exists uniquely in its own time and place. The attitudes and beliefs of its citizens are shaped by their personal experiences and by the *agents of political socialization* in the society. Yet, in any historical period trends may also emerge that affect many communities. Such trends reflect two kinds of factors: similar environmental conditions and exposure to the same historic events. We can understand the value trends of our time—modernity and secularism; reactions to modernity such as postmaterial values, fundamentalism and ethnic awareness; democratization; marketization—as reflecting both general societal developments and specific historic events.

Industrialization, modern technology, and the rise of the modern media of communication have affected similar changes in political culture across national boundaries. Alex Inkeles and David Smith's study of the development of modern attitudes in six nations emphasizes how factory experience can create an awareness of the possibilities of organization, change, and control over nature. They report how one Nigerian worker replied to a question about how his new work made him feel. "Sometimes like 9 feet tall with arms a yard wide. Here in the factory I alone with my machine can twist any way I want a piece of steel all the men in my home village together could not begin to bend at all."[20]

For almost two centuries now, the *secularizing* influences of science and control over nature have shaped political cultures, first in the West and increasingly throughout the world. This trend toward cultural *modernization* continues to have powerful effects as it penetrates societies (or parts of societies) that have been shielded from it. Exposure to modernity through work, education and the media shapes individual's personal experiences and sends messages about modernity and performance in other societies. It encourages citizen participation, a sense of individual equality, the desire for improved living standards and increased life expectancy, and government legitimacy based on policy performance. It also frequently disrupts familiar ways of life, traditional bases of legitimacy, and political arrangements that depend on citizens remaining predominately parochials or subjects.

Of course, the legitimacy of any government rests on a complicated mixture of procedure and policy. In traditional societies the time frame is a long one. If crops fail, enemies invade, and floods destroy, then, eventually, as in Imperial China, the emperor may lose the mandate of heaven, or the chiefs their authority, or the feudal lords their claim to the loyalty of their serfs. But in modern secular societies, there is a more direct and explicit connection between acceptable policy outcomes and the granting of legitimacy to the government. The belief that human beings can shape the environment puts pressure on political leaders to perform well. If they do not, they will lose legitimacy, and their ability to govern will be undermined; perhaps the regime will even be threatened if the incumbents are not replaced. The ease with which Communist governments were swept away in Eastern Europe in 1989 shows how deeply their legitimacy had been undermined by their own performance, despite the efforts at direct socialization from above.

A related response to modernization and the societal conditions that accompany it seems to be the resurgence of *ethnicity,* or ethnic identities, in many parts of the world.[21] Increased citizen skills and self-confidence often encourage suppressed groups and peoples to express their identities and demand equal treatment. Development of education and communication skills may encourage a flourishing of literature in a local language whose previous tradition has been informal and oral. This development can further intensify awareness of common symbols and history. While resurgence of distinctive local cultures enriches the global society, clashes between cultures and subcultures can also be particularly deadly bases of political conflict. Moreover, the migration of peoples into new areas, made possible by easier transportation and communication, and encouraged by wars, political conflicts, and the desire for economic betterment, can seem to threaten the way of life of the invaded society. The exposure to values from other cultures may sharpen defensive assertion of one's own, at least in the short run. Although such exposure may eventually lead to greater tolerance, there are no guarantees of this outcome.

Modernization and the focus on material prosperity have also generated reactions against them. We have already discussed the current movements towards religious fundamentalism, expressing resistance to science and secularism, reasserting "fundamental" values of the religious faiths. These movements are only the most recent of a long series of efforts to reassert deeper human meaning and deeper certainty about humanity's purpose against modernity's corrosion of traditional values. These antisecular reactions, like ethnic resurgence, can lead to intense conflict, especially in disputes over education policy, but extending to many areas of social life.

Yet another cultural response to modern conditions appears in studies of political culture in the United States and Western Europe, reporting shifting value priorities for the political agenda in these "postmodern" societies. New generations that have grown up under conditions of international peace and economic prosperity are less concerned with material well-being and personal security than their parents.[22] Groups that came of age in the 1960s and 1970s tend to be less oriented to the work ethic than the earlier generations and relatively more concerned about social and cultural issues than about economic policy. These studies suggest that even the retreat from political activism in the 1980s did not lead to a renewed focus on material questions, but rather toward more private, nonpolitical forms of expression. The trend towards postmaterialist values seems to have been slowed by the more recent economic recessions, but it continues to alter the value priorities of the political agenda. Issues of the environment and equal opportunity for self-expression for all individuals have become more central, although traditional economic issues remain salient. Politicians in all pluralist democracies are struggling to identify the most important beliefs in contemporary culture, which seems no longer to fit a simple left-to-right spectrum of ideologies.

The trend to *democratization* (discussed further in the next chapter), reflects both long-run responses to modernity and immediate reactions to current events. In the long run, the weakening of traditional sources of legitimacy devalues many alternatives to democracy, while the development of skills of individual citizens makes their claim to equal participation in policymaking (at least indirectly) more plausible.

In the short term, democracy was given a huge boost by the collapse of the Soviet Union and, more broadly, the apparent failure of Communist authoritarianism to compete successfully with liberal democracy in modern societies. At the moment, the dominant international powers are democracies, giving prestige to the democratic idea and, often, material support to would-be democrats. As Huntington's historical review suggests, earlier "waves" of democratization followed the victories of democracies over authoritarian challengers in World War I and World War II.[23] Huntington's analysis also reminds us that these previous waves experienced reversals, in which some new democracies proved unable to sustain themselves. These reversals became associated with new antidemocratic ideologies and new challenges. Despite the generally favorable long-term value trends, we do not discount the possibility of new reversals and challenges; indeed, failures of democratization seem inevitable, as deep divisions and limitations make any stable government difficult in some societies.

The failure of the Soviet-dominated command control economies in the Soviet Union and Eastern Europe to keep up with their free(er) market counterparts in the West has given great prestige to the movement towards *marketization*. That is, to a movement to rely on free markets and private profit incentives, rather than political control of decisions about investment and wages, to create efficient economic production and growth—within a framework of government-secured property rights. This movement had already appeared in the United States and many Western Europe nations in the 1980s. Increased government involvement in the economies of the industrialized nations had begun to run into serious problems of inefficiency and economic stagnation; the political victories of Reagan in the United States and Thatcher in Britain gave further prestige to efforts to roll back government involvement.

Moreover, the difficulties of Third World nations attempting to modernize their economies with government-controlled economic development plans also left freer markets as a more plausible alternative. The successes of the Asian "tigers" of South Korea, Taiwan, and Singapore in achieving rapid economic growth in a structure of government encouragement of marketization encouraged this movement, which even affected policy directions in officially Communist China. It is difficult to disentangle the fundamental political economy issues here from the effects of contemporary events. The trend to marketization reflects itself a counter to a long period of increasing government intervention in economies. At the moment there seems to be no particular mixture of free market and government intervention that is without flaws and without need to adapt to local economic conditions. Modern technology seems to offer advantages for both marketization and a role for government. We expect much further experimentation and that the current trend to marketization may also encounter reversals or countertrends in the future.

These trends in contemporary political culture make clear it is not a static phenomenon. Our understanding of political culture must be dynamic. It must encompass how the agents of political socialization communicate and interpret historic events and traditional values. It must juxtapose these with the exposure of citizens and leaders to new experiences and new ideas. It must understand also that the gradual change of generations means continuing modification of the political culture as new groups of citizens have different experiences on which to draw.

KEY TERMS

agents of political socialization	modernization
conflictual political culture	parochials
consensual political culture	participants
democratization	political culture
direct and indirect socialization	political resocialization
ethnicity	political self
fundamentalism	political socialization
incumbents	political subcultures
legitimacy	secularization
marketization	subjects

END NOTES

1. This concept of legitimacy and its bases in different societies draws upon the work of Max Weber. See, for example, Max Weber *Basic Concepts in Sociology,* trans. H. P. Secher (New York: Citadel Press, 1964), Chs. 5–7.

2. These terms were developed in Gabriel A. Almond and Sidney Verba, *The Civic Culture: Political Attitudes and Democracy in Five Nations* (Princeton, NJ: Princeton Univ. Press, 1963).

3. On the importance of trust, see Almond and Verba, *The Civic Culture,* Ch. 10; Ronald Inglehart, *Culture Shift in Advanced Industrial Society* (Princeton, NJ: Princeton Univ. Press, 1990), Ch. 1; and Robert D. Putnam, *Making Democracy Work: Civic Traditions in Modern Italy* (Princeton, NJ: Princeton Univ. Press, 1993), esp. Chs. 4 and 6.

4. Robert Putnam, *The Beliefs of Politicians* (New Haven, CT: Yale Univ. Press, 1973), p. 108; and see Putnam, *Making Democracy Work.*

5. See, for example, the data reported in *Zentralarchiv fur empirische Sozialforschung, Political Action: An Eight Nation Study 1973–1976* (Cologne, Germany: Univ. of Cologne, 1979), pp. 35–36; and in Jacques-Rene Rabier, Helene Riffault, and Ronald Inglehart, *Euro-Barometer 28: Relations with Third World Countries and Energy Problems,* November 1987 (Ann Arbor, MI: Inter-University Consortium for Political and Social Research, 1989), pp. 325–26.

6. John Huber and Ronald Inglehart, "Expert Interpretations of Party Space and Party-Placement in 42 societies," *Party Politics* 1:1 1995, pp. 73–111.

7. Samuel P. Huntington, "The Clash of Civilizations," *Foreign Affairs* 72 (Summer 1993) pp. 22–49.

8. More detailed discussion of the positions offered by the parties, and of the fears and hopes of each community and its leaders, can be found in Padraig O'Malley, *The Uncivil Wars: Ireland Today* (Boston: Houghton Mifflin, 1983).

9. See Almond and Verba, *The Civic Culture,* Ch. 12; M. Kent Jennings, Klaus R. Allerbeck, and Leopold Rosenmayr, "Generations and Families," in Samuel H. Barnes, Max Kaase, et al., *Political Action: Mass Participation in Five Western Democracies* (Beverly Hills, CA: Sage, 1979), Chs. 15 and 16.

10. Ronald Inglehart, *The Silent Revolution* (Princeton, NJ: Princeton Univ. Press, 1977); Barnes and Kaase, *Political Action;* Inglehart, *Culture Shift.*

11. Richard E. Dawson, Kenneth Prewitt, and Karen Dawson, *Political Socialization,* 2nd ed. (Boston: Little, Brown, 1977), Ch. 7.

12. For example, see Sidney Verba, Norman H. Nie, and Jae-on Kim, *Participation and Political Equality: A Seven-Nation Study* (New York: Cambridge Univ. Press, 1978); Almond and Verba, *The Civic Culture;* Barnes and Kaase, *Political Action,* Ch. 4.

13. Leonard Thompson and Andrew Prior, *South African Politics* (New Haven, CT: Yale Univ. Press, 1982), p. 119.

14. See, among others, Martin Marty and Scott Appleby, *Fundamentalism Observed* (Chicago: Univ. of Chicago Press, 1991).

15. Dawson, Prewitt, and Dawson, *Political Socialization,* Ch. 9.

16. Thomas E. Patterson, *Out of Order* (New York: Knopf, 1993).

17. Stephen Ansolabehere, Shanto Iyengar, Adam Simon, and Nicholas Valentino, "Does Attack Advertising Demobilize the Electorate?" *American Political Science Review,* 88 (Dec. 1994), pp. 829–838.

18. Robert G. Lehnen, *American Institutions: Political Opinion and Public Policy* (Hinsdale, IL: Holt, Rinehart & Winston, 1976), p. 183.

19. Almond and Verba, *Civic Culture*, pp. 108---109. And see Dwaine Marvick, "The Political Socialization of the American Negro," *Annals of the American Academy,* 361 (Sept. 1965), pp. 112–27.

20. Alex Inkeles and David H. Smith, *Becoming Modern* (Cambridge, MA: Harvard Univ. Press, 1974), p. 158.

21. Donald Horowitz, *Ethnic Groups in Conflict* (Berkeley: Univ. of California Press, 1985).

22. Inglehart, *Silent Revolution;* Inglehart, *Culture Shift.*

23. Samuel P. Huntington, *The Third Wave: Democratization in the Late 20th Century* (Norman: Univ. of Oklahoma Press, 1991).

SUGGESTED READINGS

Aberbach, Joel D., Robert D. Putnam, and Bert A. Rockman. *Bureaucrats and Politicians in Western Democracies.* Cambridge, Mass.: Harvard University Press, 1981.

Almond, Gabriel A., and Sidney Verba. *The Civic Culture.* Princeton, N.J.: Princeton University Press, 1963.

—, eds. *The Civic Culture Revisited.* Boston: Little Brown, 1980.

Baker, Kendall, Russell Dalton, and Kai Hildebrandt. *Germany Transformed: Political Culture and the New Politics.* Cambridge, Mass.: Harvard University Press, 1981.

Brown, Archie, and Jack Gray. *Political Culture and Political Change in Communist States.* New York: Holmes and Meier, 1977.

Eckstein, Harry. "A Culturalist Theory of Political Change." *American Political Science Review.* 82 (Sept. 1988), pp. 789–804.

Horowitz, Donald. *Ethnic Groups in Conflict.* Berkeley: University of California Press, 1985.

Inglehart, R. *Culture Shift in Advanced Industrial Society.* Princeton, N.J.: Princeton University Press, 1990.

Inkeles, Alex, and David H. Smith. *Becoming Modern.* Cambridge, Mass.: Harvard University Press, 1974.

Jennings, M. Kent, and Richard Niemi. *The Political Character of Adolescence.* Princeton, N.J.: Princeton University Press, 1974.

Patterson, Thomas E. *Out of Order.* New York: Alfred A. Knopf, 1993.

Putnam, Robert. *The Beliefs of Politicians.* New Haven, Conn.: Yale University Press, 1973.

—, *Making Democracy Work: Civic Traditions in Modern Italy.* Princeton, N.J.: Princeton University Press, 1993.

Pye, Lucian W., and Sidney Verba, eds. *Political Culture and Political Development.* Princeton, N.J.: Princeton University Press, 1965.

Sears, David O. "Political Socialization," in F. I. Greenstein and N. W. Polsby, *Handbook of Political Science,* Vol. 2, Ch. 2. Reading, Mass.: Addison-Wesley, 1975.

Wylie, Laurence. *Village in the Vaucluse.* Cambridge, Mass.: Harvard University Press, 1957.

Chapter *4*

Political Structure and Political Recruitment

*P*olitical structures are the organized ways that people carry out political activities. The most obvious structures are familiar political institutions, such as parties, elections, legislatures, executives, and bureaucracies. The function of political recruitment determines which people are selected to become active members of these structures and how long they remain there.

ELECTIONS: AN EXAMPLE

The election is one of the most common political structures in the modern world. Nations that hold no elections, such as Saudi Arabia, are unusual. The election's most obvious component, the act of voting by the individual citizen, is one of the simplest and most frequently performed political actions. The citizen enters a voting booth and indicates support for a political candidate, party, or policy proposal by making an "x", or pressing a stylus next to the candidate's name, or by pulling a lever. The number of voters can easily be counted and the votes determined.

Most elections are apparently about the *recruitment* of political leaders. Yet, in fact, elections vary greatly in the functions they perform in the political system. Few structures illustrate so clearly the need for a structural-functional approach to describing political systems. A brief discussion of contemporary elections can usefully introduce our treatment of political recruitment and political structures.

Figure 4.1 shows levels of voter participation in national elections from the late 1970s to the present in several countries. In Britain, Germany, and the United States, as in most of the world's democracies, most citizens are eligible to *participate* and they may choose between competing political parties and candidates. In the Western European democracies at least three-quarters of the citizens usually

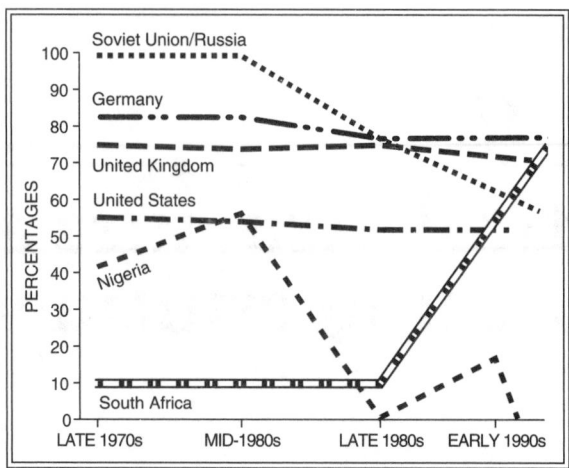

Figure 4.1 Electoral turnout in recent national elections in selected nations—percentage of population 18 years and older. (*Sources:* Turnout estimates calculated by the authors, using voter participation data from Thomas Mackie and Richard Rose, *The International Almanac of Electoral History,* 2nd ed. New York: Free Press, 1982, *The European Journal of Political Research,* and *Keesing's Contemporary Archives;* and population of voting age calculated from United Nations Demographic Yearbooks. Estimates for Germany are for West Germany only in 1976 and 1983; combined Germany in 1990).

voted; in the United States about half the electorate went to the polls in presidential elections.

In modern democracies such as these, citizens' choices affect the recruitment of leaders to the top offices of government. Shifts in citizen support bring to power new coalitions committed to new policies. The desire for office, to attain or retain political power, encourages leaders to modify policies to meet citizen expectations. Despite its simplicity, the implications of the vote can be profound. Citizens can influence interest aggregation and policymaking through this role in recruitment.

In other countries in the table, however, the elections have played a somewhat different role. In South Africa competitive elections have long given white voters the opportunity to shape recruitment and policies. But the large black majority has been excluded from the electoral process. The total voter turnout of about 10 percent reported in Figure 4.1 for the 1970s and 1980s combines average participation by whites (around 70 percent), with no participation at all by blacks. The dramatic increase in citizen voting participation in the legislative elections of April 1994 reflects the enfranchisement of the black majority and the large colored and Asian minority. Over 80 percent of the citizens participated in the dramatic election that brought South Africa its first black prime minister and a coalition government in which two black parties held a majority of cabinet posts.

In Nigeria in the late 1970s and early 1980s all citizens had the opportunity to shape recruitment and policy through competitive elections. By 1983 participation included around half the citizens. But elections did not remain a significant recruitment structure for long. The new president elected in 1983 was in office only a few months before being deposed by a military coup. Seven years later, coincident with a surge in democratization in Africa, Nigeria began gradually moving back toward an elected civilian government with local balloting in 1990, state-level elections in 1991, and federal legislative elections in 1992. However, the military government mandated a restricted process under which politicians from former civilian regimes were disqualified (as tainted by corruption) and which offered voters a choice of only two parties, both created by the government. Turnout was adversely affected by a spreading cynicism about the meaningfulness of the vote. Citizens' doubts were confirmed when the military annulled the presidential election of June 12, 1993, even before the votes were announced, and appointed an Interim National Government to organize new elections. In November 1993 a new military coup by Defense Minister General Sanni Abachi overturned the Interim National Government, banned all political activity, dissolved the legislature, dismissed the 30 elected state governors and thus ended even a limited role of elections in recruitment.

In the former Soviet Union until 1990 the people were able to vote for only one candidate, who was always a nominee of the Communist Party. The very high levels of voter participation reflected government-pressured expressions of symbolic support for the regime. Elections and voting in that system, as in Eastern Europe before 1989 and in China today, played a role in socialization, shaping citizens' attitudes. They had little to do with recruitment or policymaking.

In 1991 Russians participated for the first time ever in the choice of a national-level chief executive: Boris Yeltsin was elected president of Russia on the basis of a 60 percent majority in an election in which 70 percent of the registered voters participated—a normal level of voter turnout in European elections.[1] In the legislative elections of December 1993 about 55 percent of the eligible voters participated in the election of representatives from a wide array of parties.

In most countries, the average levels of voter participation are fairly stable over time. The dramatic changes noted above—those in Nigeria, the Soviet Union/Russia, and South Africa—are important but in different ways. In Nigeria the decline or absence of voter participation signifies the elimination and constraint of elections by military fiat. The decline in voter participation in the USSR/Russia since 1990, on the other hand, was actually a positive sign vis-à-vis the meaningfulness of Soviet elections in recruitment. It signified the withdrawal of coercion to show symbolic support for the one Communist Party candidate, and it went hand in hand with genuine opportunities for choosing between candidates. The tremendous increase in participation in South Africa reflected new eligibility of the black majority to play a role in competitive elections.

This brief consideration of electoral structures and voting participation underlines three points. First, we must take a structural-functional perspective and look at what elections actually do. The role of elections depends on who is allowed (or compelled) to participate and what sort of *competition* is permitted for what offices. We can understand relative and changing levels of citizen participation in elections only with such a perspective. Second, the political system is a system, and the implications and workings of election structures depend on other structures and functions as well. Is there freedom to communicate new information and to organize new parties? How are public policies actually made—are the elections for positions that are important in policymaking? Third, *recruitment* is a system function that in many ways affects the working of the political process and the resulting public policies. Where elections are meaningful in recruitment, they offer citizens influence in the policymaking process. They can directly bring to office policymakers committed to different policies. Competitive elections can also affect policy indirectly as elites work in their day-to-day policymaking to build election support or avoid election losses.

DEMOCRATIC AND AUTHORITARIAN POLITICAL STRUCTURES

Democracy means "government by the people." In small political systems, such as local communities, it may be possible for "the people" to share directly in debating, deciding and implementing public policy. In large political systems, such as contemporary states, democracy must be achieved largely through indirect participation in policymaking. Elections, competitive political parties, free mass media, and representative assemblies are political structures that make some degree of democracy, some degree of "government by the people," possible at the level of the nation-state. This indirect democracy is not complete or ideal. But the more citizens are involved and the more influential their choices, the more democratic the system.

In Chapters 5 through 7 we discuss in more detail different structures that perform the important policymaking functions in different societies. As our election example has already suggested, however, the most important general structural-functional distinction in classifying political systems is between democratic systems and authoritarian systems. In the *democratic systems* competitive elections give citizens the chance to shape the entire policymaking process through their selection and rejection of key policymakers. In the *authoritarian systems* the policymakers are chosen by military councils, hereditary families, dominating political parties, and the like. Citizens are either ignored or pressed into symbolic assent to the government's choices. In large societies the competitive election with eligibility for all is a necessary condition for meaningful "government by the people."

As political systems become more complex and more capable of penetrating and shaping the society, the probability of some form of citizen involvement increases, but the question of the freedom of participation also becomes more serious. In a modern society it is possible for the government to control and shape the flow of information and communication, the formation of attitudes and culture, and choices—if any—offered to citizens. On the other hand, it is also possible for independent social and political subsystems to exert autonomous influence on politics. High levels of education and information can build a participant political culture. Specialized social, economic, and political groups of all kinds can be springboards for the average citizen to make political demands and mobilize other people into political activity, even to build new political parties and support new alternatives in leadership. Thus, more developed political systems, especially in industrial societies, have greater potential for authoritarian control of citizens on a mass scale, as well as for democratic control by citizens on a mass scale.

Figure 4.2 illustrates the democratic-authoritarian distinction in national political structures. The placement of the nations shows how that distinction becomes more dramatic and clear-cut as a national political system develops more specialized and inclusive organizations for controlling the society. At the top right and top left of the figure are Britain and the former Soviet Union; both systems had many specialized structures for shaping their societies, including schools, mass media, party systems, and vast bureaucracies, and both are able to draw on literate and skilled populations. But in Britain and the other modern democracies these many structures and the involved population give citizens substantial ability to control their leaders. In the former Soviet Union and East Germany the policies made by the top leaders controlled citizens, whose sources of information, freedom to form groups, and patterns of involvement with the government were carefully directed from above. As suggested by the arrows for both authoritarian countries, the late 1980s and early 1990s saw important shifts toward democracy. East Germany has been incorporated into a democratic united Germany. The USSR was broken up into its constituent republics, most of which have introduced much more local autonomy, more freedom of information and activity, and electoral competition.

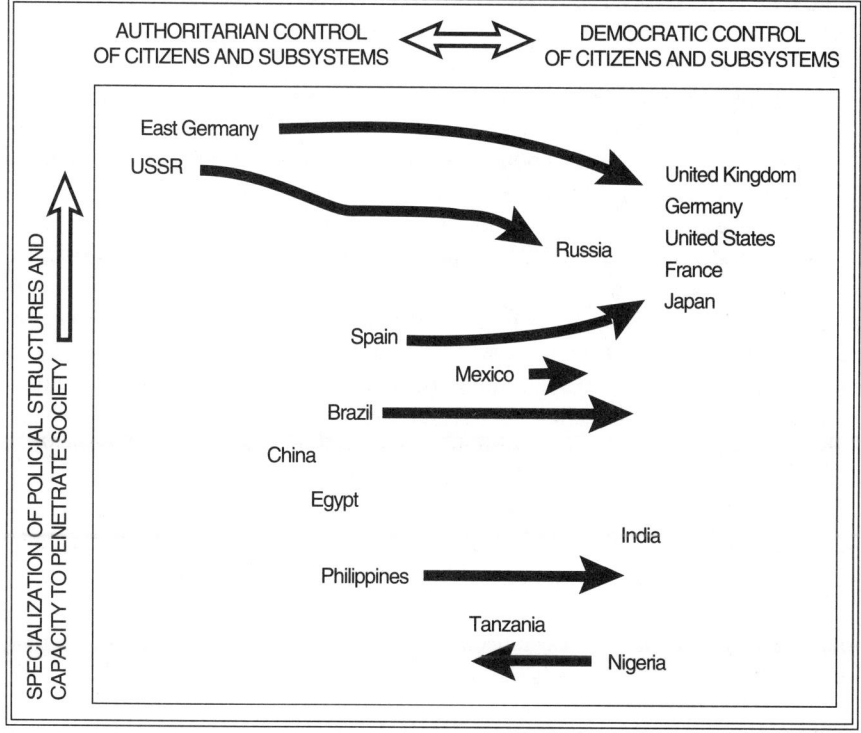

Figure 4.2 Democracy and authoritarianism in selected contemporary political systems: regimes and transitions.

In such systems as India, China, Egypt, the Philippines, Tanzania, and Nigeria, the development of specialized and integrated structures is much less complete. They show significant democratic or authoritarian leanings, but both the citizens' capacity for input and the leaders' capacity for manipulation and control are less. The democratic opportunities or authoritarian constraints in such systems are often very meaningful to educated elites or to those living in areas near the bureaucratic centers, but less relevant to the average citizen in the countryside.

Transitions toward democracy have been a major feature of world politics in the last 20 years, beginning with the collapse of authoritarian regimes in Southern Europe, extending to regimes in Latin America and Asia, and more recently in Eastern Europe and the Soviet Union. The generally democratic direction of the arrows of transition in Figure 4.2 reflects those trends with some specific examples (Spain, Brazil, the Philippines, East Germany, and the USSR/Russia). Many of those transitions have been relatively peaceful and reflect a negotiated response of authoritarian rulers to citizen pressures. Military forces have frequently stood aside or even supported the citizens against the dictators. The legitimacy of authoritarian regimes has been undermined everywhere, especially since the collapse of the model (and support) of the Soviet Union. Yet the table also shows us the case of Nigeria, where a democratic-leaning regime installed in 1979 was overthrown by a military coup shortly after its second competitive national election in 1983 and a partial movement towards redemocratization was again aborted by the military in 1993. Nigeria is not unique; Peru provides another recent case of (at least temporary) democratic breakdown. The arrows of transition can move in either direction.

It can be difficult to consolidate stable regimes, especially in the less economically developed societies. As Samuel Huntington has reminded us, the movement towards democracy in many nations from 1975 through 1990 might be considered a "Third Wave" of worldwide democratization.[2] The first of these waves began in the nineteenth century and culminated with the establishment of many new democracies after the victory of the Allies in World War I. But this wave reversed itself in the next 20 years and a number of democracies collapsed or were conquered by authoritarian states. After World War II a second democratic wave saw many newly independent ex-colonial states, as well as the defeated authoritarian powers, set up the formal institutions of democracy. Many of these would-be democracies failed in their first decade; another "reverse wave" in the 1960s and early 1970s swept away some older democracies (Chile, Greece, and Uruguay, for example) as well. While today's Third Wave of democratization is supported in part by the more favorable environments of more modernized societies, it seems likely that it will also experience reversals of the sort we see in Nigeria. It remains to be seen how much of the democratic gains will remain in the long run.

THE RECRUITMENT OF CITIZENS

Citizens become involved in the political process in two ways. *Participant activities* are those in which the average citizen makes some attempt to influence policy-making. She may write a member of Congress to urge passage of fair-housing legislation, or she may work to help a candidate favoring industrial development rather than environmentalism. *Subject activities* are those in which the average citizen is involved in policy implementation. Laws have been made, and the citizen responds to them, whether as taxpayer, welfare recipient, or simple law abider. Table 4.1 shows the major types of citizen involvement in politics and some examples of each type.

Citizens as Participants

In the next three chapters we will discuss the input functions of interest articulation, interest aggregation, and policymaking. As we can see in Table 4.1, citizens can become involved in each of these functions. In *interest articulation,* citizens make requests, demands, and pleas for policies. Some interest articulation involves only a citizen and his family, as when a veteran writes to his congressman for help in getting his benefits approved, or when a homeowner asks the local party precinct leader to see if she can have her driveway snowplowed regularly. These are *personal interest contacts,* and they are universal in all kinds of political systems including the authoritarian ones. Citizens may also become involved in politics as members of interest groups (discussed in detail in Chapter 5). They may include formal groups organized for interest articulation, such as professional groups like the American Medical Association, informal local groups like the signers of a petition submitted to a city council, or even the spontaneous gathering of outraged ghetto dwellers, whose smoldering resentment of poverty and injustice erupts in a sudden riot over an accusation of police brutality. Such interest group activity is also found in authoritarian systems, although it may be limited to methods of expression that are not openly confrontational with authorities.

Table 4.1   TYPES OF CITIZEN INVOLVEMENT IN POLITICS

Participant activities	Subject activities
Interest articulation	Resource provider
Personal interest contacting	Taxpayer
Informal group activity	Military draftee
Formal group activity	Juror
Protest activity	Resource receiver
Interest aggregation	Social security recipient
Voting in competitive elections	Welfare recipient
Party work in competitive elections	Veterans' benefit recipient
Policymaking	Behavior regulatee
Voting in referendum	Obeyer of laws
Member of town meeting, workers' council	Parent sending child to school
	Manufacturer obeying safety regulations
	Symbol receiver, provider
	Giver of pledge, loyalty oath
	Listener to political speeches
	Voter in noncompetitive election

Interest aggregation activities are those in which the citizen provides active political support—commits political resources—to a political leader or faction. The two major categories of citizen interest aggregation activities are voting and campaign activity in competitive elections. The great and ingenious invention of representative democracy makes these activities possible for the average citizen. By allowing freedom to organize and communicate and to form political parties and by making the recruitment of top policymakers dependent on winning elections, the structures of democracy allow citizens to affect policies. Citizens affect policies not merely by making requests or appealing to the conscience of leaders, but by being counted in the choice of leaders. Where citizens can take part in choosing leaders, other input activities, such as demands made by interest groups, will also receive more attention. A citizens' action group, labor union, or business lobby that can offer the votes of many members, or that can contribute money or stuff envelopes before election day, will receive serious attention when it raises policy issues.

Even in democratically oriented nations, of course, it is difficult for citizens to be very involved in direct policymaking. In the exceptional case, citizens may be directly involved when a referendum (a vote on substantive issues) is held. This is unusual in most nations, although in the state of California it has become quite common and rivals the state legislature in legislative impact. In general, however, because the average citizen does not make a living in politics, there is but limited time available to attend to political matters. But at the local level citizen involvement is somewhat more feasible, because citizens are better informed about issues and events. On one hand, there are some special forms of local self-government in which very broad participation does take place, such as the New England town meeting or apartment and house councils, workers' councils, and neighborhood associations. On the other hand, there are local policymaking roles that are part-time elite roles. American city council members, like other local officials in many societies, are not full-time in their public duties. They just cross the borderline between citizen and elite activity.

Who Participates?

Participation by citizens varies greatly by type of activity and types of political systems. Table 4.2 shows some types of citizen participation in five countries: the United States, Britain, Germany, France, and the former Soviet Union. At the top of the table we see the most ordinary and the most dramatic forms of citizen involvement in interest articulation: contacting officials and participating in lawful protest demonstrations. As already suggested, contacting local officials for help is found in all types of countries. In both the United States and the former USSR nearly a third of the electorate had contacted local officials at least sometimes. In the German and British democracies the degree of local activity is slightly less, but higher proportions of the electorate contact regional or national officials.

Participation in political protests, on the other hand, varies greatly within and across countries, depending on the types of issues, the skills of the organizers, and the acceptability of this type of action to citizens and governments. Peaceful protests have become an increasingly acceptable form of action to many citizens in the Western democracies over the past 30 years, although older citizens are still more inclined to view them suspiciously. By now 10 to 15 percent of the citizens in the United States, Britain, and Germany have at some time participated in such demonstrations. Although these protests have become increasingly a conventional form of participation, they are still more attractive to the young, the better educated, and the politically dissatisfied.[3] As shown in Table 4.2, France has had far more protest involvement than the other three democracies, with over a quarter of the population reporting having participated at some points. These numbers reflect both French traditions of popular protest and the difficulties citizens have often found in getting the attention of majoritarian governments of both right and left under the Fifth Republic. The final column shows that only 4 percent of Soviet citizens reported having participated in protests, reflecting the strong government repression of such activities until very recently. Given their current circumstances of serious discontent, substantial education, the absence of regularized party competition, and much looser government controls, we may expect to see dramatic increases in protest actions in Russia and other successor states to the old Soviet Union, such as Ukraine and Belarus.

Citizens' membership and participation in formal and informal groups and associations may be a form of indirect interest articulation, when the groups of

Table 4.2   CITIZEN PARTICIPATION IN FIVE NATIONS (PERCENTAGE)

Type of Participation	Nation				
	(West) Germany	United Kingdom	France	United States	USSR
Interest articulation					
Ever contact local officials	13%	21%	NA	34%	27%
Ever participate in peaceful protest demonstration	14%	10%	26%	12%	4%
Interest aggregation					
Average national voter turnout in competitive elections	85%	75%	78%	54%	76%
Ever persuaded others how to vote	45%	17%	NA	40%	31%
Ever worked for party or candidate	21%	8%	NA	30%	9%

Sources: All USSR data were generously provided by Raymond M. Duch and James L. Gibson based on their survey in conjunction with the Institute of Sociology, USSR Academy of Sciences, in European USSR in May 1990. Local contacting estimates in other countries are based on data reported in Norman H. Nie, Sidney Verba, Henry E. Brady, Kay L. Schlozman, and Jane Junn, "Participation in America: Continuity and Change," paper presented at the Annual Meeting of the Midwest Political Science Association, Chicago, 1988; George Moser, Geraint Parry, and Neil Day, "Political Participation in Britain," paper presented at the Annual Meeting of the American Political Science Association, Washington, D.C., 1986; M. Kent Jennings, Jan W. van Deth, et al., *Continuities in Political Action*, p. 55. Protest estimates from Russell J. Dalton, *Citizen Politics in Western Democracies*, p. 65. Voter turnout from G. Bingham Powell, Jr., "American Voter Turnout in Comparative Perspective," p. 38. Estimates for persuasion and party work from Barnes and Kaase, et al., *Political Action*, pp. 541–42.

which they are members undertake to speak for their members on issues of public policy. Thus, an American might join the Sierra Club primarily because of a love of nature and outdoor activity, but will also be counted among supporters of environmental measures when that association articulates its policy concerns. It is difficult to provide comparative cross-national measures of such involvement, but most studies suggest that Americans are particularly likely to be active members of formal and informal groups.[4] These activities are discussed at greater length in Chapter 5.

Table 4.2 also shows direct citizen involvement in several forms of interest aggregation. Democracies are remarkable in that competitive elections offer important political resources to all citizens. First, we see the average turnout of citizens in competitive national elections, which was also shown for some specific elections in Figure 4.1. Among the democracies, the United States stands out for its rather low levels of national voting participation: Only around half of the potential electorate, rather than three-fourths or more as in the average democracy, votes. The last two lines of the table show, however, that this comparatively poor American performance in voting does not simply reflect relative apathy. Americans are much more likely to try to persuade others how to vote than are their British counterparts, and they are much more likely to work for a party or candidate than either British or German citizens.

Russians participated in their first semicompetitive national election in the Soviet elections of 1990, and even here competition was allowed between candidates but not in a multiparty context. Their first experience with multiparty elections was in 1991. So the Russians have little experience with the broad opportunities for citizen involvement in interest aggregation. Nonetheless, turnout was a healthy 76 percent in the Soviet Union election of 1990, and 70 percent in the Russian election of 1991; in 1990, nearly a third of the Soviet electorate reported trying to persuade others how to vote, and 9 percent reported helping to prepare or distribute materials for candidates.

The paradox of American political participation, which contrasts low turnout in elections with relatively heavy involvement in other forms of political activity, results from the interaction of the two major factors that shape individual political involvement: the institutional setting and the resources of individuals. Voting participation is sharply affected by eligibility requirements and registration laws, by the organizational pervasiveness and mobilizing activities of political parties, and by the sharp contrast in party and candidate choices. In all these ways the American voting environment is less conducive to citizen turnout. Registration requirements mean that citizens who change addresses must make a new effort to reestablish their eligibility, while registration is automatic in many European nations. (Changes in American voter registration rules, such as a "motor voter" law, which would enable a person to register to vote when applying for or updating a driver's license, are trying to make this easier.) Party organizations are more centralized in Europe and are more extensive in many nations than in the United States. Traditionally, ideological contrasts between parties have been more dramatic in Europe, and parties often have strong, specialized links to economic or religious groups. For voting, such institutional factors outweigh the levels of citizen education and general interest, which seem to be higher in the United States than in much of Western Europe.[5]

For other forms of activity, the citizen resources of education and interest, as well as the extensive networks of organizations, tend to pull Americans into politics at a higher rate than citizens in most democracies.[6] In the case of campaign activity, the looser American electoral organizations, which are now centered on candidates more than parties, create both opportunities and needs for involvement by the general public. The rather low levels of campaign activity in Britain (8 percent in Table 4.2, as compared to 30 percent for the United States) reflect short campaigns dominated by nationally linked party organizations, as well as lower levels of education and general political interest.

Citizen participation reflects, then, the way citizens with various participant attitudes utilize opportunities offered by institutions and issues. Citizens who are well informed, confident of their ability to influence others, or attentive to political affairs, or who think it their duty to get involved, will make use of opportunities for participation. Skill and confidence are especially important in complicated activities like organizing new groups or rising to be a leader in an organization.

Much cross-national research has shown that better educated, wealthier, and occupationally skilled citizens are more likely, on average, to develop the attitudes that encourage participation.[7] The personal resources and skills that such people develop in their private lives can be easily converted into political involvement when duty calls or need arises. Consequently, these studies have shown that the better-off citizens in a society tend to be more active in politics than the less well-off. This tendency is least pronounced in the easiest activities, such as voting participation and personal contacting, and most pronounced in forming groups. The tendency for the better-off to dominate in the arenas of participation is also more pronounced in societies, such as the United States, with weak party organizations, weak working-class groups (such as labor unions), and without parties appealing distinctively to the interests of the lower classes. In nations with stronger working-class parties and labor unions, organizational networks may develop which to some extent counterbalance the greater information and awareness of the more affluent citizens.

Citizens as Subjects

One of the most pervasive of all citizen roles is that of taxpayer (see Table 4.1). This role has probably generated more citizen resistance to the efforts of authorities to promote compliance than any other. Tax revolts are a recurrent feature of political history in many nations and cultures. The demand of taxpayers to have a greater voice in policymaking in return for their assent to increased taxes is a prominent theme in the history of democracy. The American and French revolutions were in part precipitated by their governments' efforts to raise taxes. Antitax movements, antitax campaign promises, and even antitax parties were a regular feature of politics in many democracies in the 1970s and 1980s.

Resources must be extracted from the society for a wide range of government activities. Modern nonsocialist societies extract from a quarter to half of the national income in taxes and levies of various kinds. Communist political systems in the former Soviet Union and Eastern Europe extracted from half to three-quarters of the national income through taxation and profits on nationalized industries, and this is still true of China, North Korea, Vietnam, and Cuba (see Chapter 8). Many devices are used to compel citizens to become obedient providers of the necessary resources. The United States relies heavily on direct income taxes. The government withholds the income of individual earners, as well as corporations, who must file annual statements to request refunds when they have overpaid or must make additional payments when they have underpaid. An agency of the government, the Internal Revenue Service, monitors citizen taxation. Many state and local governments also tax incomes or use a host of indirect taxes, such as sales taxes. Although the primary sanction for compliance is coercion, with severe penalties provided for tax evasion, a normative emphasis on obedience to the law and good citizenship supplements coercion. In fact, some European nations have much higher levels of tax evasion than the United States. In France, tax evasion is virtually a time-honored custom, and government budget forecasters always anticipate a substantial shortfall.[8]

Citizen roles as receivers of governmental benefits are assumed much more readily, although here too government agencies must typically engage in substantial public education campaigns to inform citizens of the availability of benefits and how to receive them. Aid to the handicapped, to war veterans, to the aged, to the poor, and to various special groups takes a great variety of forms. Patterns of bureaucratic implementation typically require citizens to register or to make special applications for the benefits in question, whether these are welfare benefits, medical care, or loans to small business or for disaster relief. The agency must then monitor the system to see that only eligible citizens receive the benefits.

Modern societies are also covered by networks of regulations. Parents are commonly required to send children of certain ages to school for specific periods of the year. Compliance is achieved by a combination of incentive and coercion. On one hand, education is emphasized as a positive benefit to children and families. On the other hand, penalties are provided for failure to comply, unless educational requirements are met otherwise. It is, indeed, difficult to think of occupational and other major social and economic roles in modern societies that are not somehow linked to a form of government regulation. From traffic regulation to antitrust laws, the citizen in a complex society faces regulatory action. Yet, here too there is variation. In authoritarian political systems the regulation is usually more pervasive and often more arbitrary, and it extends to the control of internal travel, public gatherings, and public speech.

A final form of citizen subject role is the symbolic involvement role. Most political systems attempt to involve citizens with symbols of the community, regime, and authorities. In some countries, schoolchildren must learn and recite a pledge of allegiance; such activities can be controversial, as in the United States where complex legal battles have been fought over the efforts of citizens to resist this requirement for religious or ethical reasons. The mass media are filled with efforts by political leaders to invoke and reinforce symbols of national history and unity. Contemporary authoritarian systems, particularly the one-party states, press the symbolic involvement of citizens much further. In major efforts to socialize citizen attitudes through symbolic role-playing, these systems typically mobilize every citizen to cast a vote for the single party's candidate on election day and to participate in parades, work groups, and the like. For the same purpose, many have instituted vast recreational programs, particularly to further the involvement of the young. The penetrative party and bureaucratic organizations in these regimes usually are highly effective in mobilizing citizens to perform these symbolic roles, although the effect on attitudes would seem to fall short of the expectations of the rulers.[9] The rapid collapse of the Soviet Union and Eastern European regimes suggest that decades of symbolic participation did not build a strong belief in their legitimacy.

HOW MUCH PARTICIPATION?

A central phenomenon of the cultural rebellions of the 1960s and 1970s was the "participation explosion." There was widespread belief, particularly among the "baby boomers" (the unusually large cohorts born in the 1950s and 1960s) in participant democracy. Although these age cohorts have matured, recent research shows that this "participationism" persists. This is also true of those age groups born more recently.[10] The main thrust of this belief is that even in democratic countries political decisions are made by the establishment—the economically privileged and the politically powerful. The solution to this problem, claim the proponents of participant democracy, is to bring decision making down to the level of the community and small groups, back to the people. As a result, citizens would be able to grasp the issues and act politically in their own interest.

Other political theorists maintain that even in democracies there must be a division of political labor and influence, and that a country in which most people would be politically active much of the time would be impossible to govern.[11] The fundamental question is whether a direct, *participant democracy* is possible in modern nations confronted with contemporary conditions and problems.

Robert Dahl has faced this question and presented an analysis that merits some attention.[12] His argument starts with the idea that the preferences, values, and interests of all members of political communities should be taken into account in the decisions of democratic political systems. If all or most members of the community have the same interests and preferences, then there is no problem. However, since this unanimity never occurs, some kind of rule of decision is essential. The majority principle would seem to be an ethically acceptable solution, but in some cases majority rule may be impossible, because the interests of some minority may be so important that its members would not tolerate rule by majority. Language, religion, and property rights are examples of issues over which the application of majority rule may result in civil war, national fragmentation, and the destruction of democracy. In democracies, majority rule is normally limited in some areas, either through the acceptance of mutual guarantees protecting the interests of minorities (permitting free practice of religion, the right to speak and be educated in minority languages, and so forth) or through a reserved area of autonomous decisions in which government is prohibited from interfering (freedom of speech, press, assembly, petition, and so forth).

But these limits on majority rule are only the beginning of sound democratic logic.[13] Dahl argues that the ideal of participant democracy must confront the sheer numbers of people involved, the differences in interests and preferences, and the need for competence. It must also confront the economic aspects of participation—that is, what people must forgo in the way of time, energy, and money if they are active in politics. He concludes that its cost to the individual limits the role that direct participation can play in democratic government. Delegation of power to representatives (held accountable, to be sure, through elections) and to nonelected professionals and specialists is a necessary and desirable alternative.

Dahl concludes his discussion of the limits of participant democracy with the metaphor of Chinese boxes, the ancient toy consisting of a large box that contains smaller and smaller boxes. Just as there is a range of box sizes, political problems occur in all dimensions and at all levels. Problem-solving organizations must exist at each level if the problems are going to be solved at all. The big box is analogous to the international level, where, it becomes increasingly evident, problem-solving apparatus and capacity will have to develop if the human race is to survive. The tiny box is analogous to the local community, where direct participation of individuals in local political decisions like sewage disposal, education, and road maintenance is both possible and feasible, because many individuals not only want to solve these problems but are competent to judge the effectiveness of alternative solutions and are motivated to pay the costs of participating. As one moves from the tiniest box to the largest one, specialized competence becomes more important and the costs of participation become greater, necessitating reliance on elected representatives and appointed professionals.

None of this, however, argues that the ideal of participation has been fully realized in the contemporary nations characterized (properly) as democracies. Recent experiments in local community participation and in participation by workers and their representatives in the decision making of economic enterprises suggest that there are still opportunities for democratic creativity. And the recent mobilization and politicization of members of underprivileged minority groups, women, and young people in industrial democracies show that there are still bastions of privilege and inequality to conquer.

THE RECRUITMENT OF ELITES

Becoming Eligible: Bias Toward the Better-off

Every political system has procedures for the recruitment, or selection, of political and administrative officeholders. In democracies such as the United States, Britain, and France, political and administrative positions are formally open to any candidate with appropriate qualifications, such as age, residence, education, and the like. But political recruits, like political participants, tend to be people of middle- or upper-class background or those coming from the lower classes who have been able to gain access to education.[14] Of course, this somewhat overstates the case. The trade unions or leftist political parties in some countries may serve as channels of political advancement for people lacking in economic advantage or educational opportunity. Thus, the Labour party delegation in the British House of Commons and the Communist party delegation in the French National Assembly include a substantial number of workers. The workers have usually acquired political skills and experience, however, by holding offices in trade unions or other groups.

There is a reason for this bias in political recruitment. Political and governmental leadership, particularly in modern, technologically sophisticated societies, requires knowledge and skills hard to acquire in any way other than through education and training. Natural intelligence and experience in a trade union or cooperative society may, to a limited degree, take the place of substantial formal education. Even in leftist parties, however, the higher offices tend to be held by educated professional people rather than by members of the working class.

Communist countries, despite their ideologies of working-class revolution, were not able to avoid this bias. To advance into industrialism, or seek to do so, they inevitably had to depend on trained technicians. Even the running of an effective revolutionary party calls for technical competence and substantial knowledge. In the later decades of its existence, the Central Committee of the Communist Party of the Soviet Union was increasingly composed of persons with higher education who were recruited from the upper levels of the regional party organizations, the army, and the bureaucracy. The emergence in Communist countries of an educated, technically competent, and privileged ruling class violated their revolutionary populist ideology and friction resulted. Thus, we observe a cycle of recruitment of the technically competent followed by ideological and populistic attacks on bureaucracy and privilege. Nowhere was this more marked than in China, where the Great Proletarian Cultural Revolution of the late 1960s sought to destroy the powers and privileges of the party leadership and the governmental bureaucracy and bring power back to the people. Yet if countries are to make and implement developmental programs, they cannot escape this dependence on education and competence. In recent years China has returned to an emphasis on education and technological development and even experimented with encouraging greater individual initiative, then turned sharply back toward repression when that initiative took on a political cast. When students or journalists protest against the system, party officials sometimes punish them by sending them off to live in some poor, remote village—a reminder of their need for solidarity with the peasants!

Selection of Elite Policymakers

From among those who have been recruited to lower levels of the political elite, a much smaller number must be selected for the top roles. Historically, the problem of selecting the individuals to fill the top policymaking roles has been critical for maintaining the internal order and stability of government. Monarchs, presidents, generals, and party chairs exercise great power over policy directions. A major accomplishment of stable democracies has been to regulate the potential conflict involved in leadership succession and confine it to the mobilization of votes instead of weapons. When we refer generally to "recruitment structures," we are thinking of how nations choose their top policymakers and executives.

Table 4.3 shows these recruitment structures in a number of contemporary nations. The most familiar structures in the table are the presidential and parliamentary forms of competitive party systems. In the *presidential* form, as in the United States and France, parties select candidates for nomination, and the electorate chooses between these. Russia, like France, also provides for an important role for the prime minister, who can be removed by the elected legislature. The new Russian party system is in a very rudimentary stage of development, however.

The Mexican system appears similar, but the Partido Revolucionario Institucional (PRI) has such control over the electoral process that for half a century the electorate has merely ratified the party's presidential nominee. That nomination itself has been announced by the outgoing president after complex bargaining between party factions and other powerful groups. In 1994 Mexico seems to be moving to give the voters an honest role in choosing between alternative candidates, but many voters remain skeptical that a non-PRI president could really come to office.

In the *parliamentary* form, the chief executive is not selected directly by popular election. Rather, the parties select leaders, and the electorate votes to determine the strength of the party in the assembly. If a party or coalition of parties wins a majority, its leader becomes prime minister. Such elected assembly majorities usually support stable and effective governments, as in Britain and West Germany, and thus recruitment is tied directly to interest aggregation and policy creation. But in these systems party defections or a changing coalition can force a change in government if the assembly majority becomes too dissatisfied.

If no party or coalition wins a majority in the election, bargaining takes place among the factions in the legislative assembly to enable some prime minister to

Table 4.3 RECRUITMENT OF CHIEF EXECUTIVE IN SELECTED CONTEMPORARY NATIONS, 1995

Country	Chief executive structure[a]	Recruitment structures[b]	How often has type of government survived succession?[c]
United States	President	Party and electorate	Very often
Germany	Prime minister	Party and assembly	Often
Japan	Prime minister	Party and assembly	Often
France	President	Party and electorate	Often
United Kingdom	Prime minister	Party and assembly	Very often
Russia	President	Electorate	Never
Mexico	President	Elites, party, electorate?	Often (electorate new)
Nigeria	President	Military	Never
China	Party secretary	Party and military	Twice
India	Prime minister	Party and assembly	Often (one interruption)

[a] "Party secretary" refers to that position or a similar one as head of party in communist regime.

[b] "Party and assembly" refers to the typical parliamentary system.

[c] "Often" means that at least three successions have taken place; that is, a new individual has assumed the chief executive role three times under that type of government.

emerge who can command a majority of assembly seats—or who can at least receive passive support for the moment. Where the legislature does not include strong extremist or antidemocratic representation, such negotiated coalitions can also be quite stable.[15] Deeply conflictual party divisions can, however, lead to frequent changes in government in multiparty systems. In Italy, for example, the average prime minister has been able to govern for less than a year before being replaced.

In both the competitive presidential and parliamentary systems the tenure of the chief executive is periodically renewed. In the presidential system this is through fixed terms of office for the chief executive. In the parliamentary system there is a maximum term for the parliament. New elections must be held before the end of this term and a prime minister selected by the majority party or coalition of parties.

Table 4.3 also illustrates the role of noncompetitive parties. In Mexico, as we have seen, selection has taken place through a rather open process of oligarchic bargaining within and around the PRI and the incumbent president, who cannot succeed himself. Despite the somewhat closed recruitment process, the rule of no reelection forces periodic change in personnel, and often in policy, and the party and the semicompetitive elections do bring about some popular involvement.

In the former USSR, and in the other Communist regimes, the Communist Party long selected the first secretary or its equivalent, who was in effect the controlling force in the executive. Individual succession was not a simple matter. These systems provided no limited term for incumbents and no clear means of regularly assessing political support. The incumbents were difficult to oust once they had consolidated their supporters into key party positions, but they always had to be aware of the possibility of a party coup of the type that ousted Nikita Khrushchev from the Soviet leadership in 1964. As systems, however, the hierarchical party–selection structures seemed quite successful in maintaining themselves until the dramatic coup attempt against Gorbachev in August 1991. Although he was briefly restored to power, the events surrounding the coup stripped the Soviet presidency of any power, and legitimacy based on electoral success passed to the presidencies and legislative bodies of the constituent republics, most importantly to President Boris Yeltsin of Russia and the Russian Congress of People's Deputies. It remains to be seen how soon any of the republics, Russia included, will have in place stable systems of leadership succession.

The poorer nations, moving down the column of Table 4.3, show substantially less stability, and the regimes have usually had less experience at surviving succession crises. The regime in Nigeria is typical of governments in many nations not shown in the table. It experienced military rule from the civil war in the 1960s until 1979, then introduced a competitive presidential system, which was overthrown by a military coup shortly after its second free election in 1983. The military-based government moved toward a system of civilian rule in 1992–93, with state elections and then a presidential election between candidates of government-created parties. But the government announced that the presidential election was annulled before the results were announced. After another coup in November 1993, the military rulers abandoned, at least temporarily, the pretense that citizens could play a role in recruitment.

Many African nations are under military governments; some of them have experienced repeated coups against incumbent leaders. Military governments, stable or unstable, have also been common in Latin America and the Middle East. In China the Communist Party has remained in power but has suffered several periods of internal strife, and the army has been involved in recruitment at all levels. India's democracy, having persisted through assassinations and other crises, has been an exception to the rule among poorer nations. It has provided a number of executive successions with a single interruption by authoritarian emergency rule that postponed elections for several years in the 1970s.

It is indicative of the great need to mobilize broadly based political support behind the selection of chief executives in contemporary political systems that political parties are important selection structures in so many cases. The frequent appearance of parties also reflects, no doubt, the nature of legitimacy in secular cultures: the promise that the rulers' actions will be in the interest of the ruled.

CONTROL OF ELITES

Performance of the system functions is crucial for the stability of a political system. Elite recruitment is one of the most essential system functions. Traditional empires and dictatorships, in which self-perpetuation was a major goal of the rulers, seem to have focused on recruitment as the system function to be most carefully regulated. Lesser elites were controlled through the careful selection of loyalists to fill the supervisory roles in the military and civilian bureaucracies and through the provision of powerful inducements for continuing loyal performance. The conquering general or authoritarian dictator mixes rewards to favorites with severe penalties for failure or disloyalty.

Modern authoritarian systems have discovered that more efficient and effective control is achieved by simultaneous manipulation of political socialization, political recruitment, and political communication. Socialization efforts are made to instill loyalty, to recruit loyal activists, and to limit and regulate the flow of information. But if recruitment is made a part of a larger pattern of control, it is hardly neglected. Selection in the USSR was accomplished through a device called *nomenklatura*. Under this procedure important positions were kept under the direct supervision of a specific party agency whose officials had the final word on the advancement of anyone to such an office. Moreover, a complicated set of inducements was offered to make sure that chosen officials performed as they were supposed to. These inducements made it difficult for any but the topmost officials to have much freedom of action. Maximum control was ensured with normative incentives, such as appeal to party, ideology, and national idealism; financial incentives, such as better salaries, access to finer food and clothing, better housing, and freedom to travel; and coercive control, such as reporting by police, party, and bureaucrats. Demotion or imprisonment, even execution, were penalties for disapproved actions. To avoid that bane of authoritarian systems, the coup by police or military forces, the varied layers of command and inducement structures were interwoven, so that no layer could act independently.

Democratic systems, too, use selection and regulation to attempt to control the performance of government officials. In many parliamentary systems the prime minister and cabinet can be replaced without a national election if they lose the confidence of a majority of members of a parliament. In Germany, Social

Democratic Chancellor Helmut Schmidt was ousted by Helmut Kohl of the Christian Democratic party in October 1982. In Britain Conservative Margaret Thatcher's own party replaced her with John Major as prime minister in 1990. In the American system the Supreme Court has the authority to declare congressional or presidential actions unconstitutional, and impeachment procedures can be used against the incumbents in top roles, even the president (as seen in the events forcing President Nixon from office) or a Supreme Court justice, if their activities stray too far beyond legal bounds. Military officers and civil servants are also subject to removal from office or demotion for violating their oaths of office or for failing to perform their duties. These structures and procedures to ensure that the powerful perform their duties as expected are an essential part of political recruitment.

Above all, as we have emphasized, periodic renewal of the tenure of elected officials in competitive elections is a fundamental device for encouraging their responsiveness to citizens. It is deeply imperfect. It may be difficult to tell when elected officials are incompetent, deceitful, or just unlucky. The complexities of policymaking may baffle the attempt of even trained observers to assign responsibility for success and failure. The multiplicity of political issues may leave citizens torn between their candidate choices. Or, none of the choices may seem very palatable. Yet, deeply imperfect as it is, this remarkable recruitment structure, operating as part of a system of information, group activity and party competition, gives every citizen some influence on the policymaking process. For this reason we consider it the most significant democratic structure.

KEY TERMS

authoritarian system	participant democracy
competitive elections	personal interest contacts
democratic system	political recruitment
interest aggregation	parliamentary system
interest articulation	presidential system
nomenklatura	subject activities
participant activities	transitions toward democracy

END NOTES

1. *New York Times,* June 14, 1991.
2. Samuel P. Huntington, *The Third Wave: Democratization in the Late Twentieth Century* (Norman: Univ. of Oklahoma Press, 1991).
3. Samuel H. Barnes and Max Kaase, et al., *Political Action: Mass Participation in Five Western Democracies* (Beverly Hills, CA: Sage, 1979); Russell Dalton, Citizen Politics in Western Democracies (Chatham, NJ: Chatham House, 1988), Ch. 4; M. Kent Jennings and Jan W. van Deth, et al., *Continuities in Political Action* (New York: Walter de Gruyter, 1990).

4. Gabriel A. Almond and Sidney Verba, *The Civic Culture* (Princeton, NJ: Princeton Univ. Press, 1963); Sidney Verba, Norman N. Nie, and Jae-on Kim, *Participation and Political Equality* (Cambridge: Cambridge Univ. Press, 1978); Barnes and Kaase, et al., *Political Action.*

5. See G. Bingham Powell, Jr., "American Voter Turnout in Comparative Perspective," *American Political Science Review,* 80 (March 1986), pp. 17–44; and Robert Jackman, "Political Institutions and Voter Turnout in Industrial Democracies," *American Political Science Review,* 81 (June 1987), pp. 405–24. Also see Austin Ranney's discussion in Chapter 17 of other factors shaping American voter turnout and a cross-national comparison that examines only registered voters.

6. See Verba, Nie, and Kim, *Participation and Political Equality;* and Barnes and Kaase, et al., *Political Action.*

7. In addition to the references in the previous notes in this chapter, see Robert Lane, *Political Life* (Glencoe, IL: Free Press, 1959); and Alex Inkeles and David H. Smith, *Becoming Modern* (Cambridge, MA: Harvard Univ. Press, 1974).

8. See High Heclo, Arnold Heidenheimer, and Carolyn Teich Adams, *Comparative Public Policy,* 3rd. ed. (New York: St. Martin's Press, 1990), p. 191.

9. Archie Brown and Jack Gray, *Political Culture and Political Change in Communist States* (New York: Holmes & Meier, 1977), passim.

10. Ronald Inglehart, *Culture Shift in Advanced Industrial Society* (Princeton, NJ: Princeton Univ. Press, 1990).

11. See, for example, Seymour Martin Lipset, *Political Man* (Baltimore, MD: Johns Hopkins Univ. Press, 1981); Harry Eckstein, *A Theory of Stable Democracy* (Princeton, NJ: Center of International Studies, Princeton Univ. Press, 1961); Almond and Verba, *Civic Culture.*

12. Robert A. Dahl, *After the Revolution,* 2nd ed. (New Haven, CT: Yale Univ. Press, 1990). Also see his *Democracy and Its Critics* (New Haven, CT: Yale Univ. Press, 1989).

13. For a description of the majoritarian and nonmajoritarian practices, see Arendt Lijphart, *Democracies* (New Haven, CT: Yale Univ. Press, 1984). For some evidence of the advantages of nonmajoritarian constitutions and party systems in inhibiting violence and channeling participation through legitimate political channels in democracies, see G. Bingham Powell, Jr., *Contemporary Democracies* (Cambridge, MA: Harvard Univ. Press, 1982), Chs. 4, 6, 10.

14. See the general review of many studies by Robert Putnam, *The Comparative Study of Political Elites* (Englewood Cliffs, NJ: Prentice-Hall, 1976).

15. See Powell, *Contemporary Democracies,* Ch. 7; and Lawrence C. Dodd, *Coalitions in Parliamentary Governments* (Princeton, NJ: Princeton Univ. Press, 1976); Gary King, James E. Alt, Nancy E. Burns, and Michael Laver, "A Unified Model of Cabinet Dissolution in Parliamentary Democracies," *American Journal of Political Science,* 35 (1990), pp. 846–71; Paul Warwick, "Economic Trends and Government Survival in Western European Parliamentary Democracies, *American Political Science Review,* 86:4 (1992), pp. 875–87.

SUGGESTED READINGS

Barnes, Samuel H., and Max Kaase. *Political Action: Mass Participation in Five Western Democracies.* Beverly Hills, Calif.: Sage Publications, 1979.

Butler, David, Howard R. Penniman, and Austin Ranney, eds. *Democracy at the Polls.* Washington, D.C.: American Enterprise Institute, 1981.

Dahl, Robert A. *Polyarchy: Participation and Opposition.* New Haven, Conn.: Yale University Press, 1971.

—. *After the Revolution.* New Haven, Conn.: Yale University Press, 1971.

—. *Democracy and Its Critics.* New Haven, Conn.: Yale University Press, 1989.

Dalton, Russell J. *Citizen Politics in Western Democracies.* Chatham, N.J.: Chatham House, 1988.

Diamond, Larry, Juan J. Linz, Seymour Martin Lipset. *Politics in Developing Countries: Comparing Experiences with Democracy.* Boulder, Co.: Lynne Rienner, 1990.

Franklin, Mark N., Thomas T. Mackie, Henry Valen, et al. *Electoral Change: Responses to Evolving Social and Attitudinal Structures in Western Countries.* N.Y.: Cambridge University Press, 1992.

Gurr, Ted Robert. *Why Men Rebel.* Princeton, N.J.: Princeton University Press, 1970.

Hirschman, Albert. *Exit, Voice, and Loyalty.* Cambridge, Mass.: Harvard University Press, 1970.

Huntington, Samuel. *Political Order in Changing Societies.* New Haven, Conn.: Yale University Press, 1968.

—. *The Third Wave: Democratization in the Late Twentieth Century.* Norman: University of Oklahoma Press, 1991.

Lijphart, Arend. *Democracies: Patterns of Majorities and Consensus Governments in Twenty-One Countries.* New Haven, Conn.: Yale University Press, 1984.

Linz, Juan. "Totalitarian and Authoritarian Regimes, in F. I. Greenstein and N. W. Polsby, *Handbook of Political Science.* Reading, Mass.: Addison-Wesley, 1975.

Lipset, Seymour M. *Political Man.* London: Mercury 1963.

Marshall, T. H. *Class, Citizenship and Social Development.* New York: Doubleday, 1964.

O'Donnell, Guillermo, Philippe C. Schmitter, and Laurence Whitehead. *Transitions from Authoritarian Rule.* Baltimore: Johns Hopkins University Press, 1986.

Pateman, Carole. *Participation and Democratic Theory.* New York: Cambridge University Press, 1970.

Perlmutter, Amos. *Modern Authoritarianism: A Comparative Institutional Analysis.* New Haven, Conn.: Yale University Press, 1981.

Powell, G. Bingham, Jr. *Contemporary Democracies: Participation, Stability and Violence.* Cambridge, Mass.: Harvard University Press, 1982.

Rueschemeyer, Dietrich, Evelyne Huber Stephens, and John Stephens. *Capitalist Development and Democracy.* Chicago: University of Chicago Press, 1992.

Vanhanen, Tatu. *The Process of Democratization.* N.Y.: Crane Russak. 1990.

Verba, Sidney, Norman H. Nie and Jae-on Kim. *Participation and Political Equality.* Cambridge: Cambridge University Press, 1978.

Chapter
5

Interest Groups and Interest Articulation

Every political system has some way of formulating and responding to demands. As we saw in Chapter 4, the simplest form of *interest articulation* is the individual making a plea or request to a city council member or tax officer, or, in a more traditional system, village head or tribal chieftain. In larger political systems, individuals working together as an interest group are more likely to be effective in promoting their interests.

During the last hundred years or so, as societies have become internally more complex and more interdependent and the scope of government activity has widened, the quantity and variety of interest groups have grown proportionately. Interest group headquarters, sometimes numbering in the thousands, are to be found in capitals like London, Washington, Paris, Bonn, and Rome. Some of these headquarters are in buildings as imposing as those housing major governmental agencies. In countries with powerful local governments, interest groups will be active at the provincial or local level as well.

Interest groups have been organized on the basis of tribal membership, race, national origin, religion, and policy issues. Usually the most powerful, largest, and financially strongest groups are those based on occupation or profession, because the livelihoods and careers of men and women are affected most immediately by governmental policy and action. Most countries that permit their formation have labor unions, manufacturers' associations, farm groups, and associations of doctors, lawyers, engineers, and teachers.

TYPES OF INTEREST GROUPS

Interest groups vary in structure, style, financing, and support base, among other things, and these differences may greatly influence a nation's politics, its economics and its social life.

Individual Contactors

Individuals may act alone in contacting political officials, and under some conditions these activities may be quite important. We have seen in Table 4.2 that contacting officials about narrow personal or family matters remains common in the modern world. Indeed, it has probably increased in societies with large government bureaucracies. So, too, there may be an increase in individuals' efforts to articulate their opinions on broader issues, as when they write to their senator on foreign policy or approach their local zoning board about neighborhood improvement.

Individual efforts may become important when many people send similar messages or when an individual contactor is too influential to be ignored, as when a wealthy campaign contributor brings a personal problem to the attention of a politician or when a dictator's ranking subordinate asks a favor for his child. Individual efforts to articulate interests on broader issues, however, become closely intertwined, typically, with group awareness and intermittent group activities, which we will discuss in the following sections. (See also the discussion of patron-client networks and other groups in Chapter 6.)

Anomic Groups

Anomic interest groups are the more or less spontaneous groups that form suddenly when many individuals respond similarly to frustration, disappointment, or other strong emotions. They are flash affairs, rising and subsiding suddenly. Without previous organization or planning, individuals long frustrated may suddenly take to the streets to vent their anger as a rumor of new injustice sweeps the community or news of a government action touches deep emotions. Their actions may lead to violence, but not necessarily. Particularly where organized groups are absent or where they have failed to obtain adequate representation in the political system, smoldering discontent may be sparked by an incident or by the emergence of a leader. It may then suddenly explode in relatively unpredictable and uncontrollable ways.

Some political systems, including those of the United States, France, Italy, India, and some Arab nations, report a rather high frequency of violent and spontaneous anomic behavior.[1] Other countries are notable for the infrequency of such disturbances. Traditions and models of anomic behavior help turn frustration into action. In France protestors draw on two centuries of street barricade experience since the great Revolution of 1789.

From 1988 to 1990 pro-democracy rallies, protests, and riots spread rapidly across Eastern Europe. The long-suppressed discontent burst forth in many places as citizens realized that the Soviet Union would no longer support repressive local regimes and that many of these had lost the will and military support to crush dissent. News of other protests stimulated efforts and provided a model for similar action; each new success provided further encouragement.

In the United States, rioting and protests gathered momentum in the 1960s, and a decade of rioting and protests offered models for spontaneous political action that occurred in many African American neighborhoods after the assassination of Martin Luther King, Jr., in 1968. Los Angeles, which suffered severe damage from anomic violence in the 1960s, saw history repeated in April–May 1992, when riots and looting broke out over a large area of the city following the acquittal of four police officers accused of excessive violence in the beating of an African American suspect. The decayed centers of several British cities experienced similar upheavals in the mid-1980s. Wildcat strikes (spontaneous strike actions by local workers, not organized action by national unions) long a feature of the British trade union scene, also occur frequently in such continental European countries as France, Italy, and Sweden.

We must be cautious, however, about characterizing as anomic political behavior what is really the result of detailed planning by organized groups. The farmers' demonstrations in France and Britain and at the European Community headquarters in Brussels have owed much to indignation, but little to spontaneity.

Nonassociational Groups

Like anomic groups, nonassociational groups rarely are well organized, and their activity is episodic. They differ from anomic groups because they are based on common interests of ethnicity, region, religion, occupation, or perhaps kinship. Because of these continuing economic or cultural ties, nonassociational groups have more continuity than anomic groups. Subgroups within a large nonassociational group (such as blacks or workers) may, however, act as an anomic group, as in the spontaneous 1992 Los Angeles riots. Similarly, in 1986 riots broke out in Kazakhstan in the USSR when the provincial Muslim party leader was replaced by an ethnic Russian. Throughout the world, ethnicity, like occupation, has proved to have a powerful identity that can be a basis for collective activity.

There are two especially interesting kinds of nonassociational groups. One is the very large group that has not become formally organized, although its members perceive, perhaps dimly, their common interests. One example is a consumer interest group, such as users of lakes and rivers, but many ethnic, regional, and occupational groups also fit into this category. It can be very difficult to organize such groups. If many members share a rather small problem, none of them may find it sufficiently rewarding to commit the effort and time needed to organize the others. Moreover, if large collective benefits, such as cleaning up water pollution or ending discriminatory legislation, are achieved, they will be shared even by those who did not work to achieve them, so-called "free riders." Thus, many may prefer to wait for the rewards without sharing the cost or risk of action. The study of such *problems of "collective action"* is of great importance in understanding why some groups (including governments and revolutionary challengers) become organized and others do not, and why and under what circumstances the obstacles to collective action can be overcome.[2]

A second type of nonassociational group is the small village, economic, or ethnic subgroup, whose members know each other personally. Thus, in the Italian labor disorders of the 1960s and 1970s southern Italian migrants in northern Italian factories were often deployed as pickets in groups based on the villages of their origin.[3] The small, face-to-face group has some important advantages and may be highly effective in some political situations. If its members are well connected or its goals unpopular or illegal, the group may prefer to remain informal, even inconspicuous. Examples of the action of such groups include work stoppages and petitions demanding better wages and hospital conditions by doctors in Mexico City in the 1960s,[4] requests made by large landowners asking a bureaucrat to continue a grain tariff, and the appeal of relatives of a government tax collector for favored treatment for the family business. As the last two examples suggest, personal interest articulation may often have more legitimacy and be put on a more permanent basis by invoking group ties and interests.

Institutional Groups

Political parties, business corporations, legislatures, armies, bureaucracies, and churches often support institutional groups or have members with special responsibility for lobbying. *Institutional groups* are formal and have other political or social functions in addition to interest articulation. But either as corporate bodies or as smaller groups within these bodies (legislative blocs, officer cliques, groups in the clergy, departments, skill groups, and ideological cliques in bureaucracies), such groups express their own interests or represent the interest of other groups in the society. Where institutional interest groups are powerful, it is usually because of the strength provided by their organizational base. Such a group based in a governmental organization has direct access to policymakers.

In Italy, the Roman Catholic Church has been an institutional interest group with great influence in Italian politics. A major form of intervention has taken the form of religious education. In 1948 the Pope and bishops repeatedly admonished Catholics, under penalty of sin, to use their votes to defeat Socialists and Communists. In 1978 the Permanent Council of the Italian Bishops' Conference denounced "Marxists and Communists" in a warning against allowing the Communist Party to become a member of the governing coalition. Less overtly, the Church seeks influence by having members of the clergy call on officeholders to express opinions on matters of concern to the Church. In Islamic countries fundamentalist clergy actively lobby and make demands of governmental officials.

In authoritarian regimes, which prohibit or at least control other types of groups, institutional groups play a very large role. Educational officials, party officials and factions, jurists, factory managers, officers in the military services, and groups composed of many other institutionally based members have had significant roles in interest articulation in Communist regimes.[5] In preindustrial societies, which usually have fewer associational groups and where such groups usually fail to mobilize much support, the prominent part played by military groups, corporations, party factions, and bureaucrats is well known. We pointed out the frequency of military coups in such societies (see Chapter 4), but even where the military does not seize power directly, the possibility of such action forces close government attention to military requests.

In industrial democracies, too, bureaucratic and corporate interests use their great resources and special information to affect policy. In the United States the military-industrial complex consists of the combination of personnel in the Defense Department and defense industries who join in support of military expenditures. In most societies, civil and military bureaucracies do not simply react to pressures from the outside; in the absence of political directives they often act as independent forces of interest representation.

Associational Groups

Associational groups include trade unions, chambers of commerce and manufacturers' associations, ethnic associations, religious associations, and civic groups. These organizations are formed explicitly to represent the interests of a particular group. They have orderly procedures for formulating interests and demands, and they usually employ a full-time professional staff. In recent debates about health care in the United States there has been an enormous mobilization of pressure groups and lobbyists, representatives of doctors, health insurance organizations, consumer groups and the like in efforts to influence legislation.

Associational interest groups—where they are allowed to flourish—affect the development of other types of groups. Their organizational base gives them an advantage over nonassociational groups, and their tactics and goals are often recognized as legitimate in society. By representing a broad range of groups and interests, they may limit the influence of anomic, nonassociational, and institutional groups.

Some democratic theorists have been suspicious of associational "pressure" groups, stressing that the special demands and advantages of such groups may be contrary to the public interest or the interests of the less well-organized citizens. Students of American politics have sometimes emphasized the "business or upper-class bias of the pressure group system" in the United States.[6] Surveys of citizen behavior support this argument of a bias in American group activity, but they also show that associational groups in the United States and in other countries can be an important route into politics for citizens with fewer individual resources.[7] Moreover, associational group activity can help citizens to develop and clarify their own preferences, provide important information about political events, and articulate the interests of citizens more clearly and precisely than parties and elections.[8]

Even if initially organized for other purposes, the presence of associational groups can solve many of the problems of organization and mobilization faced by discontented, but scattered, individuals.[9] Once formed, even limited associational groups can provide an organizational base to help overcome the "collective action" problems faced by nonassociational groups (like peasants, workers, ethnic groups, consumers) as mentioned above.

In short, associational interest groups have an important role to play in democratic societies. One of the problems to be faced by the newly democratized nations of Eastern Europe is how to build a rich associational group life in societies in which organized groups have long been suppressed or controlled. These societies were dominated for over 40 years by institutional interest groups operating within the Communist Party and the bureaucracies. With the collapse of the Communist Party institutions, the bureaucratic groups could dominate interest articulation, with only sporadic input from anomic and nonassociational groups and within loose constraint from the new parties and legislatures. The process of building new, independent associational groups to articulate the specialized interests of different citizens is already underway and will be important to the democratic process. Similarly, many less economically developed nations face an urgent need to develop a "civil society" of associational groups to involve citizens in the political process and represent their interests if democratization is to have a chance for success.

Interest Group Systems

Research in comparative politics has drawn attention to systematic connections between interest groups and between the group and the government policymaking institutions. The differences in types of connections allow us to talk of different interest group systems in modern societies. All modern societies have large numbers of interest groups, but the patterns of relationship differ. It is useful to distinguish among pluralist, democratic corporatist, and controlled interest group systems.[10]

Pluralist interest group systems are characterized by many kinds of autonomous associational groups. Not only are there different associational groups for different interests, such as labor unions, business associations, and professional groups, but also articulation is fragmented within each type of interest. Many different labor unions, many different employer and business associations, many different ethnic, professional, and local groups—all simultaneously press demands on policymakers and on the implementing bureaucracies. Typically, some sectors and segments of society are more densely organized and more coordinated than others, but extensive coordination between groups is fairly rare. The United States is the best-known example of a strongly pluralist interest group system; Canada and New Zealand are also typically cited as examples. Despite its greater labor union membership and somewhat greater coordination of economic associations, Britain tends to fall on the pluralist side in most analyses, as do France and Japan.

Democratic corporatist interest group systems are characterized by much closer coordination between organizations making demands for groups in a particular sector of society. Moreover, these densely and centrally organized groups are systematically involved in making and implementing policy. They regularly and legitimately work with the government agencies and, usually, with political party organizations as partners in negotiating solutions to policy problems. The best-studied democratic corporatist arrangements have been in the area of economic problems. Countries with large and unified "peak" associations of business and labor that negotiated with each other and the government had better records than more pluralist countries in sustaining employment while restraining inflation in the 1970s and early 1980s.[11] The most thoroughly corporatist interest group systems are in Austria, the Netherlands, and the Scandinavian nations of Norway and Sweden. Substantial democratic corporatist tendencies are also found in Germany and Denmark.

Because different sectors of a society may vary in their organized interest groups and in their government relations, we must be cautious about generalizing too much about interest group systems. However, Table 5.1 shows the striking differences in organization of the labor movements in some industrialized societies. The countries are ranked by the average percentage of the total labor force that are members of unions. That percentage is shown in the middle column. We see that in Sweden about 90 percent of the nonagricultural work force is organized into unions. These unions have close ties with the Social Democratic party. Moreover, as shown in the last column, the labor movement in Sweden is relatively unified, scoring 8 on a 10-point scale. (In such countries as Norway, Denmark, and Austria, also shown in Table 5.1, more than half of the labor force is organized into highly coordinated unions.)

In Britain about half the labor force is unionized, but these unions are not as highly coordinated as those of the corporatist countries. The member unions in the British Trades Unions Congress have strong traditions of individual autonomy and are themselves relatively decentralized. Partially for that reason corporatist-type agreements to control wages and prices negotiated in the mid-1970s in Britain were not long sustained. The central negotiators could not get the local union organizations to honor the agreements, especially as real incomes fell. Soon thereafter, the Thatcher government moved away from direct negotiation with labor, and thus away from corporatism. West Germany had a somewhat lower level of union membership, but the German unions are relatively well coordinated and have been able to negotiate national wage policies with representatives of business and government.

Table 5.1 shows that union membership in Japan, France, and the United States is relatively low, with only about one worker in four or fewer belonging to a union.

Table 5.1   INTEREST GROUP SYSTEMS OF LABOR UNIONS

Type of System	Country	Nonagricultural Work Force Unionized, Early 1990s (percent)	Organizational Unity of Labor (10-point scale)
Democratic Corporatist	Sweden	95	8
	Austria	61	10
Mixed	Germany	44	8
	Britain	50	4
Pluralist	Japan	27	2
	France	26	2
	United States	18	4

Source: The Economist, August 18, 1990, p. 57. Unity of labor adapted from David R. Cameron, in John Goldthorpe, ed., *Order and Conflict in Contemporary Capitalism* (Oxford Univ. Press, 1984), p. 165, describing 1965–80.

Moreover, the union movements themselves are relatively fragmented and decentralized. In these countries there are few traditions of "social partnership" between government, unions, and employer associations. In the area of labor policy, at least, these are highly pluralist, not corporatist, interest group systems. However, corporatist-type arrangements among individual corporations, trade associations, and governmental bureaucracies (without organized labor involvement) are to be found in Japan.

In some democratic systems, for example France and Italy, associational interest groups such as trade unions and peasant associations have been controlled by the Communist Party or the Roman Catholic Church. Usually, these groups tended to mobilize support for the political parties or social institutions that dominated them. This lack of autonomy had serious consequences for politics. Denial of independent expression to interest groups may lead to outbreaks of violence. Subordination of interest groups by parties may limit the adaptability of the political process. However, these structures of subordination seem to be breaking down, particularly with the reorganization and weakening of the formerly Communist parties.

Finally, in thoroughly *controlled interest group systems,* the organized groups are penetrated and dominated by other institutions, such as parties and bureaucracies. The best examples are the traditional Communist systems in which the dominating party organizations penetrate all levels of society and exercise close control over all such associational groups as are permitted to exist. Unions and youth associations, for example, are completely subordinated to the Communist Party, and only rarely are they permitted to articulate autonomous interests of their members. This control was exercised in the Soviet Union and Eastern Europe; it continues in China, North Korea, Vietnam and Cuba. The authoritarian corporatist systems found in non-Communist nations like predemocratic Spain, Brazil, and Mexico also encouraged highly controlled interest groups. Interest articulation was limited to the official group leaders, who could use their positions in political institutions as a base from which to express their demands. As we have already noted, numerous institutional interest groups do emerge in these societies, especially from parts of the party and bureaucracy, such as the military, as do informal nonassociational groups.

ACCESS TO THE INFLUENTIAL

To be effective, interest groups must be able to reach key policymakers. Groups may express the interests of their members and yet fail to penetrate and influence policymakers. Political systems vary in the ways they organize and distribute political resources. Interest groups vary in the tactics used to gain access to the resource holders. Their tactics are shaped in part by the opportunities offered by the structure of policymaking, as well as by their own values and preferences.

It is useful to distinguish between legitimate or constitutional *channels of political access* (such as the mass media, parties, and legislatures) and illegitimate, *coercive access channels*. These channels correspond to the two major types of political resources that can be used in trying to get elites to respond. The first type is established by the legitimate structures of the government, which designate the resources to be used in policymaking. In a democratic political system, the appropriate resources may be votes in the national assembly. Various groups may attempt to gain control of these legislative votes by influencing the parties that win elections, or the voters who choose them, or through bargaining, persuasion, or promises of support to incumbents. However, direct violence remains as a second type of resource, a coercive channel of access for individuals and groups who feel that they are otherwise powerless.

If only one major legitimate channel of political access is available, as in a political system dominated by a single party, it becomes difficult for all groups to achieve access. Demands transmitted through that channel may be distorted as they work their way to key decision makers. The leadership thus may be prevented from getting information about the needs and demands of important groups. Over the long run, such misperceptions can easily lead to miscalculations by the leadership and to unrest among the dissatisfied groups, who may turn to violence.

Legitimate Access Channels

One important means of access to political elites in all societies is through personal connections—the use of family, school, local, or other social ties. An excellent example was the information network among the British elite based on old school ties originating at Eton, Harrow, or other "public" schools, or in the colleges at Oxford and Cambridge universities. The rise of the middle class professionals in control of the British Conservative party has reduced the value of these old school ties. Similarly, in Japan many alumni of the University of Tokyo Law School hold top positions among the political and bureaucratic elites and are able to act in concert because of these personal ties.

Although personal connections are commonly used by nonassociational groups representing family or regional interests, they serve other groups as well. Face-to-face contact is one of the most effective means of shaping attitudes and conveying messages. Demands communicated by a friend or neighbor carry much more weight than a formal letter from a stranger. In modern nations, personal connections are usually cultivated with special care. In Washington, D.C., the business of advising interest groups and individuals on access problems, for substantial fees, has become a profession (and, increasingly, a target of government regulation), carried on often by former officeholders prepared to use their personal governmental contacts for their lobbyist clients.

The *mass media*—television, radio, newspapers, and magazines—constitute an important access channel in democratic societies. Many interest groups spend a great deal of effort hiring skillful public relations specialists and purchasing direct advertising, trying to see that their interests receive favorable attention in the media. Interest groups such as the organizations of senior citizens encourage background reports on their needs, as well as coverage of their views on specific policies. When a cause receives national media attention, the message to policymakers has added weight because they know that millions of voters have been sensitized to the issue. Moreover, groups believe that in an open society, "objective" news coverage will have more credibility than sponsored messages. However, the confusion created by the number of messages and by their lack of specific direction can limit the effectiveness of the mass media for many less important groups.

The mass media can play an important part in mobilizing support for interest group efforts, leading to donations of time and money, as well as spontaneous expressions of similar demands from sympathizers. The loosening of government control from the media in the Communist regimes of Eastern Europe and the Soviet Union gave a huge boost to democracy movements. Reports of policy failures in economic policy, the environment, and social services helped undermine the legitimacy of the incumbent regimes. Reports of successful protests and demonstrations in other parts of the country, or in other countries, enhanced the confidence of demonstrators everywhere. The multitude of spontaneous, as well as coordinated, actions encouraged by mass media reports helped convince the ruling groups that their support had vanished.

Political parties can be important legitimate channels of access, but a number of factors limit their usefulness. Highly ideological parties with a hierarchical structure, such as most Communist parties, are more likely to control affiliated interest groups than to communicate the interest groups' demands. Decentralized party organizations, like those in the United States, whether inside or outside the legislative organization, may be less helpful than individual legislators or blocs would be. In a nation like Britain, on the other hand, the various components of the party organization, particularly parliamentary committees, are important channels for transmitting demands to the cabinet and the party in power. In nations like Mexico, where one relatively loosely structured party dominates the political system, the party provides a vital channel for the articulation of many interests.

Legislatures are a common target of interest group activities. Standard lobbying tactics include appearances and testimony before legislative committees, providing information to individual legislators and similar activities. In the United States political action committees raise campaign contributions for individual members of Congress and can usually be sure of some political attention in exchange. In Britain and France the strong party discipline in the legislature and in its committees lessen the importance of members of Parliament (MPs) and parliamentary committees as access channels for interest groups. In Germany and many other European democracies, the presence of strong committees and/or power divided among multiple parties encourage interest groups to use them as access channels. The combination of loose party discipline and decentralized committees as a source of much legislation makes the U.S. Congress a major target of group efforts.

Government bureaucracies are major access channels in most political systems. Contacts with the bureaucratic agencies may be particularly important where the bureaucracy has been delegated policymaking authority, or where interests are narrow and directly involve few citizens. A bureaucrat sympathetic to a group may try to respond to its demands without leaving bureaucratic channels, by exercising administrative discretion; he or she may also be very helpful in speeding consideration through the most appropriate channels of communication, or may help frame an issue in a manner most likely to receive a sympathetic hearing in the political arena. This is only possible, however, when focused opposition is insufficient to force open public discussion. Thus, a study of access channels used by groups in Birmingham, England, showed that on broad issues involving class, ethnic, or consumer groups, the associations tended to work through the political parties. On the many narrower issues, involving few other groups and less political conflict, the associations tended to turn to the appropriate administrative department.[12]

Protest demonstrations, strikes, and other forms of nonviolent but dramatic and direct pressure on government may be regarded by authorities as legitimate or illegitimate tactics, depending on the political systems involved. Such demonstrations may be either spontaneous actions of anomic groups or, more frequently, an organized resort to less conventional channels by organized groups. In democratic societies, protest demonstrations may be efforts to mobilize popular support— eventually electoral support—for the group's cause. The civil rights and anti-Vietnam War demonstrations in the United States were examples of such activity, as have been more recent pro-life and pro-choice rallies on the Mall in Washington. In nondemocratic societies, such demonstrations are more hazardous and represent perhaps more extreme dissatisfaction with alternative channels.

Protest demonstrations have been aptly described as a tactic of society's powerless, those who do not have access or resources to influence policymakers through conventional channels of party, legislature, and bureaucracy.[13] As a tactic of the powerless, protest activity is especially attractive to young people and minority groups, who are not among the elite. Protests have also been a favored tactic of groups whose ideological commitments focus on challenging the established social and political order.[14] Yet, since the 1970s protest demonstrations have increasingly been accepted as legitimate and used as a conventional channel for interest articulation by those who feel that disciplined parties and bureaucratic agencies are deaf to their complaints. Protests can supplement other channels, especially in gaining the attention of the mass media in an age when television comes to every household. Thus, we find doctors in Paris, civil servants in Sweden, and "gray panthers" (the elderly) in America using a tactic once limited to students and minorities.

Coercive Channels and Tactics

Most scholars who have written on the subject see acts of collective violence as closely associated with the character of a society and the circumstances that prevail there. In his studies of civil strife, Ted Robert Gurr has developed the concept of *relative deprivation* to explain the frustration or discontent that motivates people to act aggressively. Gurr defines relative deprivation as a "discrepancy between people's expectations about the goods and conditions of life to which they are entitled, on the one hand, and, on the other, their value capabilities—the degree to which they think they can attain these goods and conditions."[15] The sense of relative deprivation leads to frustration and anger; aggressive violence releases those feelings.

Feelings of relative deprivation are only a source of frustration, discontent, and anger. The more such discontent and anger persist, the greater the chance of collective violence. But other conditions are important also. People will tend to turn to violence if they believe it is justified and if they believe it will lead to success. If they believe that their government is illegitimate and the cause of their discontent, they will readily turn to political violence if there are no other means of bringing about change. To this end, it is the responsibility of the government and its institutions to provide peaceful alternatives to violence as a means of change.

This general analysis of violence should not blind us to the differences between types of violent political activity. A *riot*, for example, involves the spontaneous expression of collective anger and dissatisfaction by a group of citizens. Though riots have long been dismissed as aberrant and irrational action by social riffraff, modern studies have shown that rioters vary greatly in their motivation, behavior, and social background.[16] Most riots in fact seem to follow some fairly clear-cut patterns, such as confining destruction or violence to particular areas or targets. Relative deprivation seems to be a major cause of riots, but the release of the frustrations is not as aimless as is often supposed.

In the 1992 riots in Los Angeles and elsewhere, although the destruction began within hours of the acquittal of Rodney King's assailants, there was consensus among those involved that the trial outcome was only a proximate cause, a "spark" that ignited already volatile ingredients. The direction of violence against the property of Korean shopowners reflected widely felt ethnic hostility unrelated to Rodney King. There were at least a few who justified looting through comparison with the massive thefts from savings and loans and insider trading in the previous few years. Many more simply felt that society had moved on and left them in poverty and decay; clear examples of relative deprivation abounded. The immediate results were to make matters worse: over 50 people dead, mostly African Americans; thousands of businesses destroyed, with a loss of 14,000 jobs; and thousands of people left without access to necessary retail outlets. Although much of the mayhem seems poorly related to effective political action, it was a poignant cry for attention; and the slogan that emerged—"no peace without justice"—was a clear political message.

While deprivation may help fuel the discontent, *strikes* and obstructions, such as the recent efforts in the United States to block or prevent the blocking of entry into abortion clinics are typically carried out by well-organized associational or institutional groups. Many violent demonstrations are called "riots," but should not be. According to Ann Wilner, for example, violent protests in Indonesia during the rule of Sukarno were largely stage managed, "instigated, provoked, and planned by one or several members of a political elite," in order to test their strength, gain support from the undecided, frighten others from joining the opposition, and challenge higher authorities.[17] James Payne suggests that in Peru, violent demonstrations and riots under the civilian regimes of the early 1960s were "fully a part of the Peruvian pattern, not merely distasteful, peripheral incidents." The labor unions, in particular, found such tactics crucial to their survival.[18]

The influence of strikes and obstructions has varied, depending on the legitimacy of the government and coercive pressure from other groups. General strikes in Belgium were instrumental in bringing about expanded suffrage early in the twentieth century. But general strikes were disastrous failures for the sponsoring organizations in Italy in 1922 and Britain in 1927. Like the massive truckers' strike that helped bring down the government in Chile in 1972–73, these unsuccessful actions left deep bitterness in the societies. French peasant farmers' tactics of seizing public buildings, blocking roads, and the like, won major concessions from their government in the early 1960s, in part because the government was threatened by terrorism from right-wing army groups and discontent elsewhere and badly needed peasant support. By the late 1960s, a stronger regime was able to ignore or suppress peasant obstructions,[19] but had to yield major concessions to the strikes by workers that virtually shut down France for a month in 1968. Most spectacularly, the strikes and obstructions and demonstrations in Eastern Europe in 1989 and 1990, like the earlier people's power movement in the Philippines, had massive success against regimes that had lost legitimacy.

Finally, terrorism, including deliberate assassination, armed attacks on other groups or government officials, and provocation of bloodshed has been used as an interest articulation tactic in some societies. The use of terrorism typically reflects the desire of some groups to change the rules of the political game. The tragedies in Northern Ireland, the frequent kidnappings, suicide bombings, and attacks by groups in the Middle East seeking to dramatize the situation of the Palestinians, and the assassinations carried out by the Sendero Luminoso (Shining Path) guerrillas in Peru since the mid-1980s demonstrate the continuing use of such tactics.

The use of *political terror tactics* has seldom been successful without large-scale backing of terrorist groups from many citizens, as in some independence movements. Massive deadly violence may destroy a democratic regime, leading to curtailment of civil rights or even military intervention when many citizens and leaders come to feel that any alternative is preferable to more violence. President Fujimori and military leaders in Peru justified their suppression of democratic institutions in April 1992, as necessary to their battle against the Shining Path and cocaine lords. An authoritarian, repressive response often promises quick results against terrorists; however, it is also true that small-group terrorism usually fails when confronted by united democratic leadership.[20] In a democratic society, violence often forfeits the sympathy that is needed if the group's cause is to receive a responsive hearing.

POLICY PERSPECTIVES ON INTEREST ARTICULATION

As we pointed out in Chapter 2, we need to look at the structures performing political functions from both a process and a policy perspective. If we are to understand the formation of policies, we need to know not merely which groups articulate interests, but what policy preferences they express. Many associational interest groups specialize in certain policy areas. The concerns of other interest groups, such as anomic or institutional groups, may be less easily discerned, but they are equally important for the policy process.

Table 5.2 provides an overview of interest articulation. The far left column indicates the types of groups that commonly articulate interests in modern societies. The next columns provide examples of interest articulation by each type in

Table 5.2 PROCESS AND POLICY PERSPECTIVES ON INTEREST ARTICULATION

Types of Interest Groups	Examples of Interest Articulation in Various Policy Areas			
	Domestic Extractive Policy	Domestic Distributive Policy	Domestic Regulative Policy	International Policy
Individual	Peasant family seeks patron's aid with tax law.	Austrian worker asks party official for housing aid.	U.S. family business seeks relief from pollution standards.	British worker writes MP against EC.
Anomic groups	Nigerian women riot over rumor of taxes (1950s).[a]	Polish workers strike to protest bread prices.	Venezuelans strike against dictatorship, 1958.[a]	U.S. students demonstrate against South African policy.
Nonassociational groups	Mexican business leaders discuss taxes with president.	U.S. Black Caucus Congress calls for minority jobs.	Soviet Jews demand freedom to emigrate from USSR.	Saudi royal family factions favor oil embargo.
Institutional groups	American universities urge that charitable contributions remain tax deductible.	U.S. Army Corps of Engineers proposes new river locks.	Anglican church leaders ask an end to apartheid in South Africa.	USSR politburo faction favors withdrawal from Afghanistan, 1986.
Associational groups	French student groups protest government-imposed tuition increases.[b]	British Medical Association negotiates salaries under Health Services.	National Rifle Association lobbies against gun control.	Middle Eastern groups launch terror attacks to protest U.S. and Israeli actions.[a]

[a]Use of coercive, unconstitutional access channels and tactics.

[b]Use of coercion by some elements or subgroups.

respective policy areas: extractive, distributive, and regulative policies in the domestic arena, and a few examples of international policies. Another dimension is provided by the footnotes, which indicate when coercive, illegitimate channels were used, rather than legitimate ones. Careful examination of each case will provide a more precise classification of the access channels, such as elite representation by American black congressmen, use of party channels by the Italian Catholic Church, and use of terror by the Algerian French in the 1950s. In this table we have used examples from many nations in order to suggest the varied possibilities, as well as to fill in all the categories with reasonably obvious cases. If we were studying interest articulation patterns in one nation, of course, we should attempt to build up the table showing the structures, policies, and channels involved during a particular period.

INTEREST GROUP DEVELOPMENT

One of the consequences of modernization is a widespread belief that the conditions of life can be altered through human action. Modernization also usually involves education, urbanization, rapid growth in public communication, and in most cases improvement in the physical conditions of life. These changes are closely related to increases in political awareness, participation, and feelings of political competence. Such participant attitudes encourage more diverse and mass-based interest articulation.

At the same time that participant attitudes emerge in the political culture of societies undergoing modernization, the specialization of labor as people become involved in many types of work beyond agricultural production leads to the formation of large numbers of special interests. The complex interdependence of modern life, the exposure provided by mass communications, and the wide-ranging role of government further multiply political interests. The processes by which these interests and attitudes are organized into associational interest groups are complex. The barriers to coordination and cooperation are overcome in many different ways. The emergent interest group systems, pluralist or corporatist, autonomous or controlled, dominated by the better-off or more equally mobilized, are shaped by the history of interest group development during modernization.

Successful democratic development requires that complex interest group systems emerge to express the needs of groups and individuals in complex modern societies. Yet, this process is by no means automatic. The problems of organizing large groups for collective action are very large. Societies vary widely in the extent to which people engage in associational activity. One element is the trust that is generally shared among members of the society. Edward Banfield pointed to the extreme case of an Italian village within which almost no associational activity occurred, with people unwilling to trust anyone outside their immediate families.[21] Robert Putnam and his colleagues found evidence that such attitudes show continuity over long time periods and have strong effects on the political successes of regional governments in Italy.[22] Ronald Inglehart has shown similar continuity in political trust levels over a decade in the national political cultures of Western

Europe.[23] Thus, in some societies, modernization may weaken traditional structures but fail to foster the development of effective associational groups because of the inhibition of social attitudes. Their ability to achieve either stability or democracy will be hindered as a result.

In other cases, as we have noted, authoritarian parties and bureaucracies may control and penetrate associational groups and choke off the channels of political access. Eastern Europe offers a situation in which 40 years or more of authoritarian domination suppressed autonomous interest groups. On one hand, the processes of economic modernization had put great pressure on these authoritarian systems to allow more open organization and expression of political interests. On the other hand, the opening of these societies has led to an explosion of interest articulation activity and a great need for associational groups to provide regular and organized expression for citizens' interests. They are also needed to counterbalance the demands from institutional groups in the civilian and military bureaucracies.

The explosive development of organized interest groups should not, however, lead us to conclude that every conceivable group now has equal standing in Central European interest group systems. We noted above the caution, based on American experience, that the articulation of interests is frequently biased toward the goals of the better-off, who are also often better organized.[24] It is often pointed out that the American Association of Retired Persons (AARP) is an effective group that is not counterbalanced by a "Young Taxpayers Group," and that the traditional labor-management competition leaves consumers unrepresented.

We might test this notion more broadly by evaluating systems in terms of their *inclusiveness:* What proportion of the population is represented to what degree in national-level politics? In South Africa we have had the extreme case where the majority were prevented outright from forming associational groups. In the Third World competing interests in the capital rarely involve the interests of rural peasants; sometimes, as in Peru, the situation is not unlike that in South Africa: Peasant organizations are brutally suppressed, while urban middle- and upper-class groups are able to petition authorities. It seems to be no coincidence that the bias in group inclusion appears greatest where the gap in income and education is widest. We have postulated above that, pushed to the extreme, those excluded from the process will engage in anomic activity or resort to violence, a conclusion supported by statistical studies of inequality and violence.[25] Even in less extreme cases, the presence of different levels of political awareness means that every interest group system is somewhat biased. Democratization involves not only the provision of competitive elections, but also the reduction of the bias in interest representation.

Some observers have argued that even the free postindustrial societies of Western Europe and North America need more innovation among interest group organizations.[26] Many interests may be based on social values or on material interests that no longer correspond to occupational categories. Citizens interested in the environment, peace, consumer protection, and participatory values may be too scattered and too mobile to be easily mobilized by traditional associational groups. Some of these citizens believe that the challenge they want to pose to society cannot be expressed through ordinary associational organizations using conventional channels of access.

On the organizational side, the new social movements in Western Europe have sought more fluid and dynamic organizations, with constantly changing leadership and members who move in and out of organizational involvement. Some of the parties and organizations have made great efforts to ensure continuing turnover of leaders to avoid becoming like the bureaucratic society they wish to alter. Where participation and self-expression are themselves among the most important values being articulated, the group structure must be always in change.

On the tactical side, the new social movements have used a wide range of approaches and often disagree over the value of partisan campaigning, conventional lobbying, and radical protest. The "green" or environmental movements in several nations, especially West Germany, have sometimes acted as or sponsored political parties, if only to gain a better forum for protest. Some of these parties have had striking success. It is too soon to say if the new social movements will add a new category, with elements of anomic, nonassociational, and associational groups all intertwined, to our classification of interest groups. But their efforts remind us that political change is the theme of our time.

KEY TERMS

anomic interest groups

associational groups

channels of political access

coercive access channels

collective action problems

controlled interest group systems

democratic corporatist interest
   group systems

government bureaucracies

inclusiveness

institutional groups

interest articulation

legislatures

legitimate access channels

mass median

pluralist interest group systems

political parties

political terror tactics

protest demonstrations

relative deprivation

riots

strikes

END NOTES

1. See the data on riots (1948–1977) in Charles Taylor and David Jodice, *World Handbook of Political and Social Indicators*, 3rd ed., Vol. 1 (New Haven, CT: Yale Univ. Press, 1983), Chs. 2–4.
2. Studies of these problems were stimulated by the now classic work of Mancur Olson *The Logic of Collective Action* (Cambridge, MA: Harvard Univ. Press, 1965). See also Mark Lichbach, *The Rebel's Dilemma* (Ann Arbor: Univ. of Michigan Press, 1994); Mancur Olson, "Dictatorship, Democracy and Development" *American Political Sci-*

ence Review, 87:3 (Sept. 1993), pp. 567–76; Todd Sandler, ed., *Collective Action: Theory and Applications* (Ann Arbor: Univ. of Michigan Press, 1992).

3. See Charles Sabel, *Work and Politics* (New York: Columbia Univ. Press, 1982), p. 162.

4. Evelyn P. Stevens, "Protest Movements in an Authoritarian Regime," *Comparative Politics,* 7:3 (April 1975), pp. 361–82.

5. See G. F. Skilling and F. Griffiths, eds., *Interest Groups in Soviet Politics* (Princeton, NJ: Princeton Univ. Press, 1971); the essays by Frederick C. Barghoorn and Skilling in Robert A. Dahl, *Regimes and Oppositions* (New Haven, CT: Yale Univ. Press, 1973); and Roman Kolkowicz, "Interest Groups in Soviet Politics," *Comparative Politics,* 2:3 (April 1970), pp. 445–72.

6. E. E. Schattschneider, *The Semi-Sovereign People* (Hinsdale, IL: Dryden Press, 1960), p. 30; also see Grant McConnell, *Private Power and American Democracy* (New York: Knopf, 1966).

7. Sidney Verba and Norman H. Nie, *Participation in America* (New York: Harper & Row, 1972), Ch. 11; Sidney Verba, Norman H. Nie, and Jae-on Kim, *Participation and Political Equality: A Seven-Nation Study* (New York: Cambridge Univ. Press, 1978), Chs. 6, 7.

8. Gabriel A. Almond and Sidney Verba, *The Civic Culture* (Princeton, NJ: Princeton Univ. Press, 1963), pp. 300–22; William Kornhauser, *The Politics of Mass Society* (Glencoe, IL: Free Press, 1959).

9. Mancur Olson, *The Logic of Collective Action* (Cambridge, MA: Harvard Univ. Press, 1965).

10. For cross-national comparisons, see the essays by Gerhard Lembruch and by David R. Cameron in John Goldthorpe, ed., *Order and Conflict in Contemporary Capitalism* (Oxford: Oxford Univ. Press, 1984); Peter J. Katzenstein, *Small States in World Markets* (Ithaca, NY: Cornell Univ. Press, 1985); Philippe Schmitter, "Interest Intermediation and Regime Governability," in Suzanne Berger, ed., *Organizing Interests in Western Europe* (New York: Cambridge Univ. Press, 1981), Ch. 12; Arend Lijphart and Markus Crepaz, "Corporatism and Consensus Democracy in 18 Countries," *British Journal of Political Science,* 21:2 (April 1991), pp. 235–46.

11. On the relative success of the corporatist systems in economic performance in the 1970 and early 1980s, see Cameron, *Order and Conflict* and the review and analysis in Miriam Golden, "The Dynamics of Trade Unionism and National Economic Performance," *American Political Science Review,* 87:2 (June 1993), pp. 439–54.

12. K. Newton and D. S. Morris, "British Interest Group Theory Reexamined," *Comparative Politics* 7 (July 1975), pp. 577–95; also see J.J. Richardson and A.F.G. Jordan, *Governing Under Pressure* (Oxford: Martin Robinson, 1979).

13. James Q. Wilson, "The Strategy of Protest," *Journal of Conflict Resolution,* 5:3 (Sept. 1961), pp. 291–303; Michael Lipsky, "Protest as a Political Resource," *American Political Science Review,* 62:4 (Dec. 1968), pp. 1144–58.

14. See the essays in Russell J. Dalton and Manfred Kuechler, *Challenging the Political Order: New Social and Political Movements in Western Democracies* (New York: Oxford Univ. Press, 1990).

15. Ted Robert Gurr, "A Comparative Study of Civil Strife," in Hugh David Graham and Ted Robert Gurr, eds., *The History of Violence in America* (New York: Bantam Press, 1969), pp. 462–63; more generally, see Ted Robert Gurr, *Why Men Rebel* (Princeton, NJ: Princeton Univ. Press, 1970).

16. See James F. Short and Marvin E. Wolfgang, eds., *Collective Violence* (Chicago: Aldine-Atherton, 1972); and see Anthony Oberschall, *Social Conflict and Social Movements* (Englewood Cliffs, NJ: Prentice-Hall, 1973).

17. Ann Ruth Wilner, "Public Protest in Indonesia," in Ivo K. Feierabend, Rosalind Feierabend, and Ted Robert Gurr, eds., *Anger, Violence, and Politics* (Englewood Cliffs, NJ: Prentice-Hall, 1972), pp. 355–57.
18. James Payne, "Peru: The Politics of Structured Violence," in Feierabend, Feierabend, and Gurr, eds., *Anger, Violence, and Politics*, p. 360.
19. Suzanne Berger, *Peasants Against Politics* (Cambridge, MA: Harvard Univ. Press, 1972).
20. On violence and democratic survival, see G. Bingham Powell, Jr., *Contemporary Democracies: Participation, Stability and Violence* (Cambridge, MA: Harvard Univ. Press, 1982), Ch. 8; and the contributions to Juan J. Linz and Alfred Stepan, eds., *The Breakdown of Democratic Regimes* (Baltimore: Johns Hopkins Univ. Press, 1978).
21. Edward C. Banfield, *The Moral Basis of a Backward Society* (New York: Free Press, 1958).
22. Robert Putnam, Roberto Leonardi, Raffaella Y. Nanetti, and Franco Pavoncello, "Explaining Institutional Success: The Case of Italian Regional Government," *American Political Science Review*, 77 (March 1983), pp. 55–74; Robert D. Putnam, *Making Democracy Work: Civic Traditions in Modern Italy* (Princeton: Princeton Univ. Press, 1993).
23. Ronald Inglehart, *Culture Shift in Advanced Industrial Societies* (Princeton, NJ: Princeton Univ. Press, 1990), pp. 34–36. Also see Almond and Verba, *The Civic Culture*, Ch. 11.
24. See Notes 2, and 6–9 above.
25. Many of these studies are reviewed by Mark I. Lichbach, "An Evaluation of 'Does Economic Inequality Breed Political Conflict' Studies," *World Politics*, 41 (1989), pp. 431–70. More recent references and analysis appear in the Controversy by T. Y. Wang, William Dixon, Edward N. Muller, and Mitchell A. Seligson, "Inequality and Political Violence Revisited," *American Political Science Review*, 87:4 (Dec. 1993), pp. 979–93.
26. This discussion of the new social movements and the issues they raise draws heavily on Dalton and Kuechler, *Challenging the Political Order*.

SUGGESTED READINGS

Ash, Timothy Garton. *The Magic Lantern.* New York: Random House, 1990.

Beer, Samuel H. *British Politics in the Collectivist Age.* New York: Knopf, 1965.

Berger, Suzanne, ed., *Organizing Interests in Western Europe.* New York: Cambridge University Press, 1981.

Dalton, Russell J., and Manfred Kuechler. *Challenging the Political Order: New Social and Political Movements in Western Democracies,* New York: Oxford University Press, 1990.

Denardo, James. *Power in Numbers: The Political Strategy of Protest and Rebellion.* Princeton, N.J.: Princeton University Press, 1985.

Ehrmann, Henry W. *Interest Groups on Four Continents.* Pittsburgh: University of Pittsburgh Press, 1958.

Goldthorpe, John H., ed. *Order and Conflict in Contemporary Capitalism.* Oxford: Clarendon Press, 1984.

Katzenstein, Peter. *Small States in World Markets.* Ithaca, N.Y.: Cornell University Press, 1985.

Lichbach, Mark. *The Rebel's Dilemma*. Ann Arbor: University of Michigan Press, 1994.

Olson, Mancur. *The Logic of Collective Action*. Cambridge, Mass.: Harvard University Press, 1965.

Putnam, Robert D. *Making Democracy Work: Civic Traditions in Modern Italy*. Princeton: Princeton University Press, 1993.

Sabel, Charles. *Work and Politics*. New York: Columbia University Press, 1982.

Schmitter, Philippe, ed. "Corporatism and Policy-Making in Contemporary Western Europe." *Comparative Political Studies*, April 1977.

Scott, James C. *The Moral Economy of the Peasant: Rebellion and Subsistence in Southeast Asia*. New Haven, Conn.: Yale University Press, 1976.

Wilson, James Q. *Political Organizations*. New York: Basic Books, 1973.

Chapter
6

Interest Aggregation and Political Parties

*I*nterest aggregation is the activity in which the demands of individuals and groups are combined into significant policy proposals. The proposals become significant as they are backed up by substantial political resources, such as popular votes, commitments of campaign funds, seats in the legislature, positions of executive influence, media access, or even armed force. Political parties are particularly important in interest aggregation. They nominate candidates who stand for a set of policies, and then they try to build support for those candidates. Modern political parties first took shape as excluded groups strove to compete for power and dominant groups sought public support to sustain themselves.

In a democratic system two or more parties compete to mobilize the backing of interest groups and voters. In authoritarian systems only one party tries to mobilize citizens' support for its policies and candidates. In both systems interest aggregation may well take place within the parties, as party conventions or party leaders hear the demands of different groups—unions, consumers, party factions, business organizations—and create policy alternatives. In authoritarian systems, however, the process is more covert and controlled.

The structural-functional approach draws our attention to the fact that parties may perform many different functions and that many different structures may perform interest aggregation. Parties frequently affect political socialization, shaping the political culture as they organize thinking about political issues and strive to build support for their ideologies, specific issue positions, and candidates. Parties affect political recruitment as they mobilize voters and are involved in selecting would-be officeholders. They articulate interests of their own and transmit the demands of others. Governing parties are also involved in making public policy and even overseeing its implementation and adjudication. But the distinctive and defining goal of a political party, its mobilization of support for policies and candidates, is especially related to interest aggregation.

Even a single individual can evaluate a variety of claims and considerations in adopting a policy position. If he or she controls substantial political resources, as an influential party leader or a military dictator, his or her personal role in interest aggregation may be considerable. But large national political systems usually develop more specialized organizations for the specific purpose of aggregating interests and resources behind policies. Political parties are just such organizations. In this chapter we compare the role of parties with that of other structures in interest aggregation.

INTEREST GROUPS AND INTEREST AGGREGATION

A well-nigh universal political structure is the *patron-client network*. It was the defining principle of feudalism. The king and his lords, the lord and his knights, the knight and his serfs and tenants—all were bound by ties of personal dependence and loyalty. The American political machines of Boss Tweed of New York, John F. ("Honey Fitz") Fitzgerald of Boston, Richard Daley, Sr., of Chicago, and the like, were similarly bound together by patronage and loyalty. But clientelism is not confined to relationships cemented by patronage only. Every president of the United States has had his circle of personal confidants, his "brain trust," his California or Georgia or Arkansas "mafia," bound to their chief by ideological and policy propensities as well as by interests in jobs and power.

Indeed, the patron-client network is so ubiquitous in politics that it seems to be like the cell in biology or the atom in physics—the primitive structure of all politics, the human interactions out of which larger and more complicated political structures are composed. Students of politics in all countries report such networks.

Contemporary patron-client theory was pioneered by students of East, Southeast, and South Asia, where this phenomenon seems often to dominate the political processes of such countries as the Philippines, Indonesia, Thailand, Japan, and India.[1] It is related to recruitment to political office, interest aggregation, policymaking, and policy implementing. Such domination of interest aggregation by patron-client ties implies more than the appearance of these basic "cells" of politics. It typically means a static pattern of overall policy formation. In such a political system, the ability to mobilize political resources behind unified policies of social change or to respond to crises will be difficult, because doing so depends on ever-shifting agreements between many factional leaders (patrons).

In modern societies, as citizens become aware of larger collective interests and have the resources and skills to work for them, personal networks tend to be regulated, limited, and incorporated within broader organizations. As we see in Table 6.1, extensive performance of interest aggregation by personal patron-client networks is confined mainly to the less economically developed countries.

The subtle dividing line between interest articulation and aggregation can easily be crossed by organizations with powerful resources. Although often operating

Table 6.1   STRUCTURES PERFORMING INTEREST AGGREGATION IN SELECTED
CONTEMPORARY NATIONS[a]

Country	Extensiveness of Interest Aggregation by Actor				
	Patron-Client Networks	Associational Groups	Competitive Political Parties	Noncompetitive Parties	Military Forces
United States	Low	Moderate	High		Low
West Germany	Low	High	High		Low
Japan	Moderate	High	High		Low
France	Low	Moderate	High		Low
Britain	Low	High	High		Low
Russia	Moderate	Low	Moderate	Moderate	Moderate
Mexico	Moderate	Moderate	Low	High	Low
Nigeria	High	Low	Low		High
Egypt	High	Low	Low	Moderate	Moderate
China	Moderate	Low	Low	High	Moderate
India	High	Moderate	Moderate		Low
Tanzania	High	Low	Low	High	Low

[a]Extensiveness of interest aggregation rated as low, moderate, or high only. Rating refers to broad-level performance and may vary in different issue areas and at different times.

merely to express demands and support major political contenders, such as parties, *associational groups* can occasionally wield sufficient resources to become contenders in their own right. The power of the labor unions within the British Labour party, for example, has rested on the unions' ability to develop coherent policy positions and mobilize the votes of their members to support those positions. In many European nations, national decision-making bodies have been set up outside the normal legislative channels, bodies with substantial authority to make national policies in special areas, such as the Dutch Social and Economic Council or the Austrian chamber system. These bodies incorporate labor unions' and employer associations' representatives.

As we discussed in Chapter 5, the set of arrangements called democratic corporatism has in some countries been especially effective in aggregating the interests of both labor and business groups into economic policies controlling unemployment and inflation. These arrangements include continuous political bargaining among large, relatively centralized labor and business interest groups, political parties, and state bureaucracies. They have often been closely linked to political domination by a democratic socialist political party. Such corporatist systems, then, include and link organizations that in other political systems play very different, often antagonistic, roles.

Institutional groups like bureaucratic and military factions can also be important interest aggregators. Indeed, the bureaucracy acts as a kind of interest aggregator in most societies. Although established primarily for the implementation of policies whose broad outline is set by higher authorities, the bureaucracy may negotiate with a variety of groups to find their preferences or mobilize their support. Agencies may even be "captured" by interest groups and used to support their demands. The desire of bureaucrats to expand their organizations by the discovery of new problems and policies, as well as to increase their ability to solve problems in their special areas, often leads them to create client support.

Military interest groups, with their special control over the instruments of violence, have great potential power as interest aggregators. If the legitimacy of the government breaks down and all groups feel free to use coercion and violence to shape policies, then the united military can usually be decisive. One study showed that in the 1960s around two-fifths of the nations of the world had been confronted with military coup attempts, and these were at least partially successful in changing leaders or policy in about a third of the nations. Less than half of these coup attempts, however, were concerned with general political issues and public policy. Most coups seemed motivated by grievances and fears that the professional or career interests of the military will be slighted or overlooked by civil authorities.[2]

COMPETITIVE PARTY SYSTEMS AND INTEREST AGGREGATION

In analyzing parties it is especially important to keep in mind the critical distinction between *competitive party systems,* seeking primarily to build electoral support, and noncompetitive or authoritarian *party systems.* This distinction does not depend on the closeness of electoral victory, or even on the number of parties. It depends on the primacy of winning votes as a prerequisite for control of policymaking, on one hand, and on the possibility for several parties forming and organizing to seek those votes, on the other. Thus, a party can win most of the votes in a given area or region, or even a given national election, but nonetheless be a competitive party. Its goals involve winning elections, either as a primary objective or as a means for policymaking; its dominance at the polls is always subject to challenge by other parties; its organization thus involves arrangements for finding out what voters want and getting supporters involved.

In analyzing the role of competitive parties in interest aggregation, we need to consider not only the individual party, but also the structure of parties, electorates, electoral laws, and policymaking bodies that interact in a competitive party system. Typically, interest aggregation in a competitive party system takes place at several levels: within the individual parties, as the party chooses candidates and adopts policy proposals; through electoral competition, as voters give varying amounts of support to different parties; and through bargaining and coalition building in the legislature or executive.

Competitive Parties and Elections

At the first level, individual parties develop a set of policy positions. Typically, these positions are believed to have the backing of large or cohesive groups of voters. In systems with only two parties, it is important for a party to win a majority, so targeting the "center" of the electorate is often crucial strategically.[3] In systems with many political parties, where none has much chance of winning a majority, it may be more valuable to seek a distinctive and cohesive electoral base. Party policy positions may well reflect the continuing linkages between the party and interest groups, such as labor unions, business associations, or religious and ethnic groups. Historical issue commitments and ideological traditions also play a role.[4]

In developing their policy proposals and choosing their candidates, parties must anticipate the way that election competition brings together party offerings and voter choices. One important element will be the election laws that determine how the choices that voters make are translated into election outcomes. In the United States, Great Britain, and many countries once influenced by Britain (such as India, Jamaica and Canada), the rules governing legislative elections divide the country into many election districts, each of which chooses a single representative. In each district, the candidate winning more votes than any other—a *plurality*—wins the election in the district. This simple, single-member district plurality system, is often called "first past the post," from horse racing, because the winner need only finish ahead of the others, not win an absolute majority of votes. This system seems obvious and natural to American, British, Canadian and Indian voters, but in fact is rarely used in the democracies on the European continent or in Latin America. (However, American primary elections often require absolute majorities for a candidate to win, with runoffs between the two leaders if no one wins a majority in the first election.)

Among the many possible election rules, the most common alternatives to "first past the post" are various forms of *proportional representation*. In these systems the country is divided into fewer, large districts, or even not divided up at all. Each district elects several representatives, from as few as three or four to the entire legislature. The various competing parties offer lists of candidates, rather than a single candidate. The number of legislative representatives a party wins depends on its proportion of the votes it receives. If the entire country were a single legislative district, as in the Netherlands and Israel, a party receiving 5 percent of the vote would be awarded 5 percent of the seats in the legislature.

One of the best-known and most studied phenomena in political science, called Duverger's Law, after the distinguished French political scientist who stated it generally and forcefully as a theory of election rules, is the tendency for plurality election rules of the American and British type to create "two-party" systems in the legislature.[5] Smaller parties that spread their votes evenly across many districts, while failing to come in first in any of them, are eliminated. This frequent elimination in the district contests both discourages politicians from forming small parties and greatly underrepresents small parties that do compete. In Britain in the 1980s, for example, nearly a quarter of the electorate voted for parties that received only a handful of seats in Parliament. At the same time the German election rules, a special version of proportional representation, gave representation to a party like the FDP, which (with only 7 to 11 percent of the vote) not only achieved a place in the Bundestag, but was a critical element of all government coalitions. The presence of such election rules as plurality or proportional representation shapes party election strategies and the party system.

The procedure for developing policy positions varies greatly from country to country and from party to party. In the United States the national party conventions are the focus of developing policy positions, both through the formation of party platforms and, perhaps more important, through the selection of candidates committed to certain policies. In other countries, more often party platforms or manifestos are issued by centralized party program committees or in speeches by party leaders.[6] Whatever the procedure, the final party position is usually a mixture of strategic electioneering and aggregation of interests expressed within the party.

The parties then offer their chosen candidates and policies to the electorate. They not only present candidates, but they also attempt to publicize them and mobilize electoral support through rallies, mass media promotion, door-to-door campaigning, and systematic efforts to locate sympathetic voters and get them to the polls. In the elections citizens directly participate in interest aggregation by voting for different parties. Such votes are converted into legislative seats and, in presidential systems, control of the chief executive by the electoral rules. In the last 30 years political scientists have done a great deal of research on the dynamics of citizens' voting decisions, including the role played by issue and ideological positions, group-party connections, learned "identification" with parties, and evaluations of the performance of the current incumbents.[7]

Figure 6.1 offers a comparative "snapshot" of interest aggregation by parties and voters in several democratic countries. It uses the device of the left-right scale, which in many countries and for many voters acts as a kind of summary of the issues that voters find most important. Voters are shown a scale of numbers, with 1 identified as left (or liberal in the United States) and 10 identified as right (or conservative in the United States). They are then asked to place the parties and themselves on this continuum. In Figure 6.1 we see the left-right scale and where the voters for each party placed themselves on the scale. The height of the column above the scale shows what percentage of the electorate voted for that party.

Several interesting differences in *party-electoral aggregation* in different party systems are illustrated by Figure 6.1. First, we can see that in the countries at the top of the figure, especially in the United States, most voters support only a few parties. Moreover, the party supporters are fairly close to the center of the continuum, where the bulk of voters place themselves. The left-right "gap" between the average party supporters is rather small. Democrats are somewhat to the left and Republicans somewhat to the right, but on average they are not far apart. If the full distribution of voters were displayed in the figure, rather than just the averages, we would see that there is a lot of overlap in the self-placement of voters supporting different parties. Thus, aggregation implies concentration of political resources behind the "centrist" policies of both parties.

In the countries toward the bottom of the figure, especially in Italy, which had a very elaborate form of proportional representation, many parties receive support from voters. The Communist and the Christian Democratic parties have had the most support, but many other parties receive significant voting support as well.[8] The figure for Italy has many short bars. Moreover, here the bars are spread well across the spectrum. Each party is aggregating the support of a more limited and more cohesive group of voters. The ideological gap between the right-most and

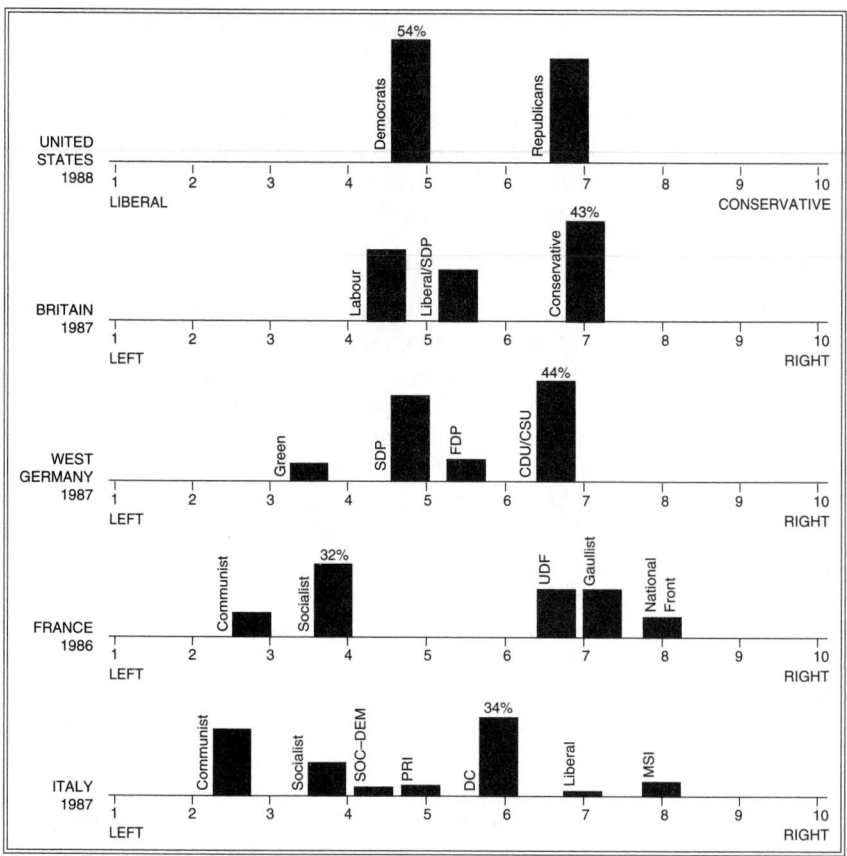

Figure 6.1 Interest aggregation by competitive parties and voters: Percent of voters for each party and their average self-placement on left-right scale in legislative elections in five countries as of 1986. (*Source:* Surveys of voters in Britain, Germany, France, and Italy from *Eurobarometer 25*, April 1986. U.S. data from 1986 Gallup Survey reported in Harold W. Stanley and Richard G. Niemi, *Vital Statistics on American Politics*, Washington, DC: CQ Press, 1988, p. 131; U.S. data uses liberal and conservative instead of left and right; adjusted 9-point scale.)

left-most parties is quite great. The dispersed aggregation of the party-electoral system means that a much more diverse range of ideological interests will be represented in the legislature.

Britain, Germany, and France fall between these more extreme cases. Britain looks more like the United States in its pattern of voter support, but the parties are further apart and the smaller Liberal/Social Democratic Alliance (since 1987, the Liberal Democratic party) falls between them. Germany looks rather like Britain, except that the center party is smaller and there is a notable Green party on the left. France looks more like Italy. But France has one interesting feature that sets it apart from other countries: There is no party whose supporters' average position is near the middle. There are still substantial numbers of French voters whose position is toward the center, although fewer than in the United States, Germany, and Britain, but the party offerings pull them sharply to the right or the left. If we were to look at the offerings of the parties as placed by expert observers on a similar scale, we would see that they gave voters no option of center choice.[9] This aggregation reflects and encourages the confrontation between coalitions of right and left that has been typical of Fifth Republic France.

Competitive Parties in Government

If a competitive party wins control of the legislature and the executive, it will (if unified) be able to pass and implement its policies. Sometimes this control will emerge directly from the electoral process, as a single party wins a majority of the vote. Far more often, no party wins a majority of votes. In many countries the working of the election laws benefits some parties at the expense of others. If these distortions are sufficient, less than 50 percent of the vote may be converted into more than 50 percent of the legislative seats. Such "artificial" legislative majorities have been the rule in countries with "first past the post" (also called plurality) electoral systems, such as Britain and New Zealand.[10]

In Britain, for example, none of the legislature majorities won by either the Labour party or the Conservatives in the 1970s and 1980s were based on support of a majority of voters. For example, Mrs. Thatcher's Conservative party won a solid majority of legislative seats in 1983 and 1987 with the backing of only about 42 percent of the voters. With almost exactly the same level of support in the 1992 elections under John Major's leadership, the Conservatives remained in power, but their parliamentary majority was reduced from 99 to 21 seats. In all these elections, the quarter of the electorate supporting the center parties received only a handful of legislative seats.

In other countries, the combination of parties, voter choices, and election laws does not create single-party majorities, but *party coalitions* formed before the election may still offer the voters a direct choice of future governments. The parties in alliance encourage mutual support from the electorate, often taking advantage of special provisions of voting laws, and agree that if they jointly win a majority of legislative seats they will govern together. In Germany and France, many governments in the 1970s and 1980s came to power in this fashion. Voters are thus given a major role in choosing the direction of government policy through party and electoral aggregation. Single-party and, sometimes, preelection coalition governments also provide voters rather clear targets if they choose to hold the incumbents accountable for their performance in office.

The importance of such aggregation through the election process has been demonstrated by studies showing that very often parties do fulfill their electoral promises when they gain control of government. For example, British parties take pride in carrying out their manifesto promises while in office. When Socialist and Social Democratic governments have come to power in Europe, they have tended to expand the size and efforts of the governmental sector. Studies also suggest that Republicans and Democrats in the United States have been fairly responsible in keeping their promises.[11] However, opposition parties that have been out of office a long time and developed programs of radical change often find these difficult to implement when they come to power, as demonstrated by the experiences of the new left-wing governments that came to power in France and in Greece in 1981. It remains to be seen if the Republicans in the United States, winning control of both houses of Congress in 1994 for the first time in 40 years, will find similar difficulties in implementing their proposals for change in government direction.

If no party or preelection coalition wins control of the legislature and the executive at the election, then the final stage of interest aggregation by parties takes place as parties bargain to form coalitions within the assemblies and the executive. In presidential systems this bargaining between parties may occur when one party gains control of the executive and the other gains control of the legislature, as has been true in the United States in most of the years since 1968. In the United States, as in Japan, the complexity of the bargaining is enhanced by the frequent lack of internal cohesion or discipline of the parties. Aggregation must take place between party factions within and across party lines.

In parliamentary systems, when no party wins a majority, the result is either a minority government or a majority coalition of several parties. In the minority case, the executive must continually bargain with other parties to get policies adopted and even to remain in office.[12] In the case of majority coalitions, the bargaining will be focused primarily on coalition partners, who may divide up the policy areas or develop some other processes of aggregation. Such coalitions tend to be fairly stable in some countries, such as the Netherlands, and much less so in others, such as Finland and Italy, depending on the party makeup of the legislature and other factors.[13] In any case the process of interest aggregation continues through the parties in the legislature and executive. The continuation of interest aggregation at this stage is also enhanced when different parties gain control of different houses of the legislature (as in the United States in 1980–86 or frequently in Germany since the mid-1970s), when parties share power in strong legislative committees, or when internal party factions such as those in Japan's Liberal Democratic party lower the level of party discipline.

The factors that encourage less decisive electoral aggregation and more aggregation within the legislature and the executive have both costs and benefits. On one hand, the connection between voter choice and government policy is made less direct, which can be frustrating and disillusioning to voters. Moreover, the fact that interest aggregation is still going on so "late" in the political process, that new coalitions of interests and resources are constantly emerging on different issues, is confusing to citizens (and even informed observers). It is difficult to assign clear responsibility for government policy when power to shape it is shifting and widely shared. Thus, the value of the vote is lessened as an instrument either directly to shape policy through electing future governments or to punish parties clearly responsible for undesirable policy. Elections as instruments of accountability and manifesto choice are diminished by shifting coalitions after the election.[14]

On the other side, this continuing aggregation can mean that voters for all parties, not only the election winners, will have their elected representatives taking part effectively in interest aggregation and policymaking. Such a representative connection can be especially important for citizen minorities. All citizens are minorities on some issues, and some are notable minorities on many issues. If the rules of election and representation are fair, the possibility of continuing influence on interest aggregation between elections is a valuable protection for minority interests. Finally, even elected governments that won a majority of votes, which few elected governments have, will typically not have majority support for their policy proposals on all issues. British politics offers a number of examples of majority parties implementing manifesto promises that public opinion polls showed were not supported by a majority of voters (most famously the Labour party's renationalization of the steel industry in 1966). So a more flexible pattern of interest aggregation at the legislative level, if based on fair representation, may be helpful to many, and not just the minorities. Bargaining between equitably represented groups may even enhance the possibility that policies will reflect different citizen majorities on different issues. Elections as instruments of representation may be enhanced by postelection aggregation, even though they are diminished as instruments of accountability.[15]

Classifying Competitive Party Systems

In Figure 6.2 competitive party systems are classified by type, with examples given for each. We distinguish between majoritarian party and multiparty systems and rate them according to the relative antagonism between and among parties. The number and strength of parties influences legislative activity and the business of forming government. Either the *majoritarian party systems* are dominated by just two parties, as in the United States, or they have two substantial parties and election laws that usually create legislative majorities for one of them, as in Britain and

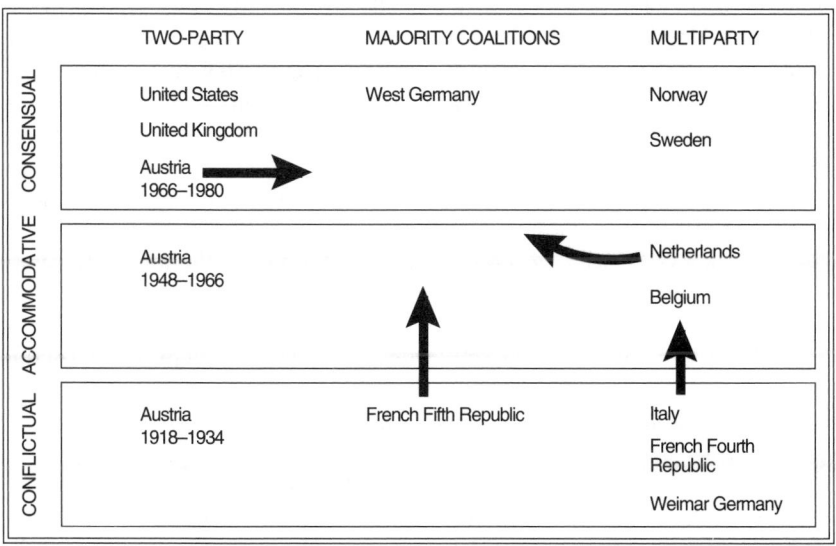

Figure 6.2 Classifying party systems by number of parties and antagonism between parties.

New Zealand. The purely *multiparty systems* have combinations of parties, voter support, and election laws that virtually ensure that no single party will win a legislative majority. Interest aggregation by party bargaining after the election will be critical for shaping policy directions. Germany and France, as we have already mentioned, are among the multiparty systems in which voter support of party coalitions at the electoral level has major impact on forming governments and policies.

A large number of parties does not itself cause government instability. More important is the degree of antagonism or polarization among the parties.[16] We refer to a party system as *consensual* if the parties commanding most of the legislative seats are not too far apart on policies and have a reasonable amount of trust in each other and in the political system.[17] These are typically party systems like those shown toward the top of Figure 6.1. Bargaining may be intense and politics exciting in these systems, as Americans are well aware from observing the charges and countercharges in Washington "gridlock," but it seldom threatens the system itself.

If the legislature is dominated by parties that are very far apart on issues or are highly distrustful and antagonistic toward each other and the political system, we would classify that party system as *conflictual*. If a party system has mixed characteristics of a certain kind—that is, both consensual and conflictual—we classify it as *consociational*, or accommodative. Arend Lijphart in particular has used those terms to describe party systems in which political leaders are able to bridge the intense differences between antagonistic voters.[18]

The United States and Britain are contemporary examples of consensual majoritarian systems, although they differ in the degree of consensus. They are not perfect two-party systems. Britain, in addition to the Labour and Conservative parties, has the Scottish Nationalist party, a smaller Welsh party, and, at the center, the Liberal Democratic party. However, in Britain a single party usually wins a legislative majority and controls the legislature and the executive with disciplined party voting. The United States has had third-party movements and candidates intermittently. (Most recently, in 1992 wealthy businessman Ross Perot formed a new political party, challenged the Republican incumbent George Bush and Democratic party nominee Bill Clinton, and won about a fifth of the vote in the presidential election.) Shifting orientations of presidential party candidates alter the degree of consensus somewhat from election to election. Moreover, the loose cohesion of American parties and the frequently divided control of legislature and executive lead to postelection bargaining that is in some ways similar to consensual multiparty systems. Germany has two large parties, and an alliance between one of those parties and the Free Democrats has usually won legislative control. Good examples of consensual multiparty systems have been found in Norway and Sweden. In these countries there are four or five parties—socialists, agrarian/center, liberals, conservatives, small Communist movements. The three or four larger parties have usually been able to construct long-lived governments, singly or in coalition.

Austria between 1918 and 1934 is the best example of a majoritarian *conflictual party system*. Antagonism between the Socialist party and the other parties was so intense that in the mid-1930s it produced a brief civil war. This conflict resulted in suppression of the Socialist party, the collapse of democratic government, and the creation of an authoritarian one-party system. The case of Austria also illustrates how change can take place in party systems over time. After World War II the leaders of the two major parties negotiated an elaborate coalition agreement of mutual power sharing—and mutual checks and suspicion—as the country sought to control its conflicts while rebuilding its economy and seeking freedom from occupying Soviet forces in the eastern regions. After some 20 years of the consociational "Grand Coalition," party antagonism had declined to the point that more normal majority politics could be tolerated, although some consociational elements remained. In recent years the Austrian party system has appeared to be closer to the more ordinary consensual system, with some single-party majorities and some coalitions.

France, Italy, and Weimar Germany have been good examples of conflictual multiparty systems, with powerful Communist parties on the left and conservative or Fascist movements on the right. Cabinets had to be formed out of centrist movements, which were themselves divided on many issues, thus making for instability, poor government performance, and loss of citizen confidence in democracy. These factors contributed to the overthrow of democracy in Weimar Germany, the collapse of the Fourth French Republic, and government instability and citizen alienation from politics in Italy.

More recently, the French and Italian party systems have become somewhat less antagonistic. Some signs of accommodation appeared in Italy in the 1970s when the Communists rallied together with other parties against Red Brigade terrorism, and in France when the Communist party lost ground to the more moderate Socialist party. In 1993–94 the party system that had dominated Italian politics since the end of World War II experienced a huge series of shocks, beginning with the collapse of international Communism, immediately followed by massive judicial investigations of party corruption and criminal connections that decimated the leadership of most of the non-Communist parties. The elections of March 1994, held under a new electoral system that encouraged coordination between parties, saw a dramatic reshaping of the party system and an electoral victory for a new party coalition. This coalition contained, however, sharp divisions between a brand new party, a formerly neo-Fascist party, and a regional autonomy party; its first government collapsed after less than a year in office and its future remains uncertain.

The mixed system we call consociational can arise in countries in which considerable conflict and antagonism exists on the basis of religion, ethnicity, or social class. Consociational practices are a major hope for deeply divided nations to find a way to peaceful democratic development. Through historical experience the leaderships of competing movements in such countries as the Netherlands have found bases of accommodation that provide mutual guarantees to the various groups. In the consociational systems of Austria and Lebanon after World War II, groups—the socialists and Catholics in Austria, and the Christians and Muslims in Lebanon—worked out a set of understandings making it possible for stable governments to be formed. Austria's accommodation was based on a two-party system, and Lebanon's on many small, personalistic religious parties. These two examples have gone in opposite directions in recent years. Since 1966 Austria has begun to move toward a consensual two-party system, while after 1975 Lebanon was penetrated and fragmented by the Middle Eastern conflict and fell victim to civil war.

South Africa is now attempting consociational practices in its transition to democracy. Leaders of the major political parties of the white minority and two major segments of the black majority negotiated (with great difficulty) arrangements for a democratic election and a multiparty coalition government to follow it. A typically consociational feature of the "Interim Constitution" of the transition was to guarantee a share in power and government—cabinet posts—to all parties winning over five percent of the vote in the election. As the contrasting examples of Austria and Lebanon suggest, such practices (and the ability even agree to attempt them) offer hope, but no guarantees of long-term success to deeply divided democracies.

All this suggests that, although the number of parties is of some importance in relation to stability, the degree of antagonism among parties is of greater significance. Where multiparty systems consist of relatively moderate antagonists, stability and effective performance seem possible. Where systems consist of highly antagonistic elements, collapse and civil war are ever-present possibilities, regardless of the number of parties. When crises develop, the commitment of the leaders of major political parties to work together to defend democracy can be critical for its survival. It may be easier to arrange such commitments in a multiparty, representational setting.[19] Pre–World War II Austria, Chile, the Weimar Republic of Germany, and contemporary Northern Ireland are tragic examples of the absence or failure of such cooperation. Some of the new democracies of Eastern Europe and Latin America and Asia, especially those divided by language or ethnicity, face similar challenges.

AUTHORITARIAN PARTY SYSTEMS

Authoritarian party systems are also specialized interest aggregation structures. They deliberately attempt to develop policy proposals and to mobilize support for them, but they do so in a completely different way from the competitive party systems we have been discussing. With authoritarian party systems, aggregation takes place within the ranks of the party or in interactions with business groups, landowners, and institutional groups in the bureaucracy or military. The citizens have no opportunity to shape aggregation by choosing between party alternatives.

Authoritarian party systems can be distinguished on a range of exclusiveness, according to the tightness of control from the top down within the party and the degree of control over other groups by the party. At one extreme is the *totalitarian party*, which insists on total control over political resources by the party leadership. It recognizes no legitimate interest aggregation by groups within the party nor does it permit any free activity by social groups, citizens, or other government agencies. It penetrates the entire society and mobilizes support for policies developed at the top. These policies are legitimated by an encompassing political ideology that claims to know the true interests of the citizens, whatever their immediate preferences.[20] At the other extreme is the *inclusive governing party* that recognizes and attempts to coordinate various social groups in the society. It accepts and aggregates certain autonomous interests, while repressing others and forbidding any serious challenges to its own control.

Exclusive Governing Parties

Few parties have long maintained the absolute central control, penetration, and ideological mobilization of the totalitarian model. However, the ruling Communist parties of the USSR before 1985, of Eastern Europe before 1989, and of China, North Korea, Vietnam, and Cuba today certainly fall toward the more penetrating and controlling end of the authoritarian party scale. The Chinese regime, for example, has not typically recognized the legitimacy of any large internal groups. Interest articulation by individuals, within bounds, may be permitted; the mobilization of wide support before the top elite has decided on policy is not permitted.[21]

Even at the stage of totalitarian mobilization, the *exclusive governing party* may be the focus of more internal aggregation at various levels than is commonly recognized or legitimately permitted. Internally, various groups may coalesce around such interests as region or industry, or behind leaders of policy factions. Generational differences or differences of temperament may distinguish hard-liners and soft-liners on ranges of policy. Either openly or covertly, beneath the supposedly united front, power struggles may erupt in times of crisis, with different leaders mobilizing backing for themselves and their positions. Succession crises are particularly likely to generate such power struggles, as demonstrated at the death of Stalin in the USSR and at the death of Mao Zedong in China.

Whether thoroughly totalitarian or merely as exclusive governing parties, the penetrating and controlling single parties can play important roles in mobilizing support for policies. An unchallenged ideological focus provides legitimacy and coherence; the party is used to penetrate and organize most social structures in the name of that ideology and in accordance with centralized policies. As these parties have aged, many have seemed to enter a stage of more "mature" totalitarianism that maintains penetration and control, but places less emphasis on mobilization. Finally, as shown by events in the former Soviet Union and Eastern Europe, if and when the party leaders lose faith in the unifying ideology, it may be difficult to maintain party coherence.

As an instrument designed for unified mobilization, the exclusive governing party has seemed attractive to many leaders committed to massive social change. The party that successfully mobilized a colonial people behind independence, for example, might be used to penetrate and change an underdeveloped society. As the experiences of many new nations have shown, however, the creation of an exclusive and penetrating governing party that could be used for social transformation is extremely difficult. The protracted guerrilla warfare that contributed to the development of the Chinese and Cuban parties is not easily replicated. The exclusive governing parties attempted in some African states have had limited penetrative capacity. In Ghana, the Convention People's party of Kwame Nkrumah seemed a successful example of the exclusive governing party in the early years of independence (1960–66), but was easily toppled by a military coup. By 1990 the loss of confidence in Marxist-Leninist ideology and in the Soviet model of totalitarian development led all eight of the African regimes that had once invoked it to abandon that approach.[22] In China the party has been forced several times to rely on the army, even on coalitions of regional army commanders, to sustain its control.

Inclusive Governing Parties

Throughout the pre-industrial areas, especially in nations with notable ethnic and tribal divisions, the more successful authoritarian systems have seemed to be inclusive authoritarian party systems, rather than exclusive. That is, they have recognized the autonomy of social, cultural, and economic groups and have tried to incorporate them or bargain with them, rather than penetrate and remake them. In the more successful African one-party systems, such as Kenya, Tanzania, and Ivory Coast, aggregation around personalistic, factional, and ethnic-based groups was permitted within decentralized party organizations. In recent years, the tightening of control under President Daniel Arap Moi has been coincident with increasing ethnic conflict in Kenya.[23] The indigenous Communism in Yugoslavia took a more decentralized and corporatist form than in other Communist Party states, as a matter of policy and in recognition of the party's linkage to peasant supporters.[24] The successor regime in Belgrade was unable to maintain that formula for integration of the country's constituent states as tragic events there have demonstrated.

These party systems have sometimes been labeled authoritarian corporatist systems. Like the democratic corporatist systems (see Chapter 5), they encourage formation of large organized interest groups whose representatives can bargain with each other and the state. Unlike the democratic corporatist systems, however, these authoritarian party systems provide no political resources directly to the citizens. Efforts at independent protest and mobilization outside the official channels are suppressed. They do permit some autonomous formation of demands within the ranks of the party and by groups associated with it.

The degree of legitimate aggregation permitted below the top leadership in the inclusive authoritarian systems may be substantial and take many forms. The party will typically try to gather various social groups under the general party umbrella and also negotiate with more or less autonomous groups and institutions outside the party. Some of these inclusive parties have attempted aggressive programs of social change. Others have been primarily arenas for aggregating various social and institutional interests. At the extreme of loosest and least exclusive control, such parties may even permit other parties to offer candidates in elections, as long as they have no real chance of winning.

The oldest and one of the most elaborately inclusive authoritarian parties has been the Partido Revolucionario Institucional (PRI) in Mexico. The PRI dominated the political process and gave other parties no realistic chances of winning elections for over 50 years. The PRI maintained general popular support after the creation of a broad coalition within the party by Lázaro Cárdenas in the 1930s; it was also careful to control the counting of the ballots. Its actions were not shaped by electoral competition, at least until the late 1980s. However, the party incorporated many associational groups within it, with separate sectors for labor, agrarian, and popular interests. While some discontent was suppressed, other dissatisfied individuals were deliberately enticed into the party. The party also gave informal recognition to rather distinct and well-organized political factions grouped behind such figures as ex-presidents.

Various Mexican leaders mobilized their factions within the PRI and in other important groups not directly affiliated with it, such as big business interests. Bargaining was particularly important every six years when the party chose a new presidential nominee. The legal provision that the incumbent president could not succeed himself guaranteed some turnover of elites and may have facilitated more legitimate and open internal bargaining. Recently, however, rising discontent has emphasized the difficulties in coordinating all interests through the party. Those of the urban and rural poor who have not shared in Mexico's general growth have joined with others who want a more fully democratic system. An armed uprising of peasant guerrillas in early 1994 shocked the political establishment and led to more promises of genuine democratic competition.

The relative stability of some inclusive authoritarian party systems should not obscure the frequent failures to build stable authoritarian party systems. In many countries the governing authoritarian party coexists in uneasy and unstable coalition with the armed forces and the civilian bureaucracy. In some countries the party has become relatively unimportant window dressing for a military regime or personal tyranny.[25] The loss of confidence in authoritarian party solutions to problems of economic development and ethnic conflict has seriously weakened their ability to aggregate interests. As the memories of a unifying struggle against colonialism have faded, and the leaders of independence movements have departed or been forced from office, the ties of ideology and experience that held such parties together have unraveled. This trend has been encouraged by the general loss of legitimacy of the single-party model. In some cases the failure of authoritarian parties has permitted the emergence of party competition. In others the consequence has been enhanced resort to naked coercion by government agencies or private forces, with the military serving as final arbiter.

MILITARY FORCES AND INTEREST AGGREGATION

In the period after World War II parliamentary and democratic governments were instituted among most of the nations of the Third World. But the lack of effectiveness and authority of these new civil institutions in many cases led to their breakdown and their supplantation by one-party and *military governments*. With its control of instruments of force, and in the absence of a strong constitutional tradition, the military was an effective contender for power. Even in those regimes where civilian authority was reestablished, the military generally constituted a significant power contender, and exercised influence in the political process. In Brazil the military played a crucial interest aggregation role in the democratic processes before 1964 and played the dominant aggregating and policymaking roles for 20 years after. In Nigeria, the collapse of democracy into civil war resulted in military rule until 1979. In 1983 another military coup deposed an elected Nigerian president; in 1993 the military rulers annulled presidential elections, even though they had previously designed the parties and candidates. In Ghana the overthrow of Nkrumah was followed by military rule interspersed with experimentation with competitive parties. In Chile military government ruled for 15 years and has only recently been replaced. And in many other nations, including Syria, Pakistan, Indonesia, Guinea, Zaire, Argentina, Paraguay and Haiti, the military has been the dominant, or at least a major, interest aggregator. (In 1994 the United States sent to Haiti a diplomatic delegation consisting of former President Carter, former Chief of Staff Colin Powell and Senator Sam Nunn, backed up by a large invasion force, which together succeeded in persuading the military leaders to step aside and permit the elected government to resume office.) In fact, the armed forces are the dominant interest aggregation structure in over one-fifth of the world's regimes, including almost half of those in Africa (see Figure 6.3 below).

The military's virtual monopoly of coercive resources gives it great potential power as a political contender. Thus, when agreement fails on aggregation either through democratic or authoritarian party systems, the military may emerge by default as the only force able to maintain orderly government. The soldiers then remain the basic force underpinning the personal tyranny of a civilian president or a military council. Or the armed forces may use coercive power to further institutional or even ideological objectives. Military rulers may use control of the state to attempt to create military and/or bureaucratic versions of authoritarian corporatism, linking organized groups and the state bureaucracy with the military as final arbiter of disagreement. They may undertake "defensive" modernization in alliance with business groups or even undertake more radical restructuring modernization.[26] In Latin America almost all the corporatist versions of authoritarian aggregation have had a strong military component and only rarely a dominating role for the authoritarian party.

The major limitation on the armed forces in interest aggregation is that their internal structures are not designed to mobilize support across a range of issues or outside the coercive arena. The military is primarily organized to facilitate downward processing of commands involving the implementation of coercion. It is not set up to aggregate internal differences and effect a compromise or to mobilize wide support of all components behind policy. Moreover, military organizations are not easily adapted to rally or communicate with social groups outside the command hierarchy. Thus, the military lacks some advantages in mobilizing support held by party systems. These internal limitations may be less serious when the military is dealing with common grievances and putting pressure on—or seizing power from—incumbent authorities. These limitations become a major problem, however, when a military government needs to mobilize backing for, say, economic development policy. Legitimate authority and communication of the regime's political and ideological goals to many social sectors are then needed. For these reasons military governments frequently prove unstable, are forced to share power with other institutions, or encourage the formation of cooperating authoritarian parties.

TRENDS IN INTEREST AGGREGATION

We have noted in Chapter 4 and elsewhere the democratic trend that began in the mid-1970s and gained important momentum with the collapse of authoritarian regimes in Eastern Europe at the end of the 1980s. Figure 6.3 attempts to classify the world's regimes by the predominant interest aggregation structure at three points: the end of the 1970s, the end of the 1980s, and the early 1990s. The percentages we report have to be viewed as estimates, often based on limited information. But the figure provides a rough idea of the frequency of the three major forms: competitive parties and elections, single-party regimes, and military-dominated regimes. The "residual" category of traditional governments consists mostly of small kingdoms in the Middle East, South Asia, and the Pacific.

As shown in Figure 6.3, in 1978 about one-third of the world's 150-plus independent countries were reported to have competitive party and electoral systems as their predominant interest aggregation structures. These regimes were the main form in Western Europe and North America (including the Caribbean), not uncommon in Latin America and Asia, but rare in Africa and the Middle East. Nearly as many countries had one of the versions of single-party regimes. They were the

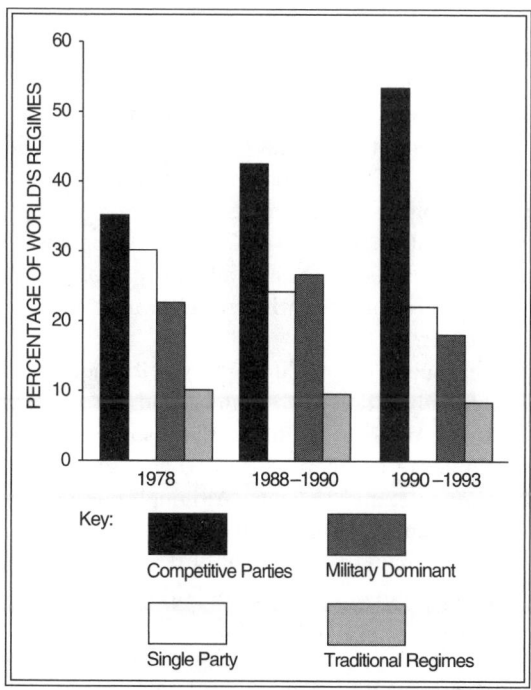

Figure 6.3 Change in predominant interest aggregation structure—moving toward democracy in the world? (*Source:* Adapted from Raymond D. Gastil, *Freedom in the World 1979, 1988–1989, 1990–1991.* New York: Freedom House, 1979, 1989, 1991.)

main form in Eastern Europe and relatively common in Africa and Asia, though rare in the Western Hemisphere and Western Europe. In slightly less than a quarter of the countries the armed forces dominated interest aggregation, either formally (military governments) or in practice (military-dominated civilian governments). The military-dominated regimes accounted for about a third or more of the countries in Africa and Latin America.

A decade later, the trend was obviously away from single-party governments. Across the world they declined from 30 to 24 percent of the regimes, although still accounting for nearly 40 percent of African nations. As we already know, the decline of exclusive governing party regimes was even more striking. As expected, the *democratic trend* toward competitive party and electoral systems was notable, with an increase from 36 to 41 percent of the world's political systems (and more experimenting with some competition). The proportion of military governments actually increased slightly, from 23 to 26 percent of the world's countries.

The trend toward democracy took off beginning in 1989, as shown by the rate of change in 1990–91; it was much more dramatic than what we observed in the prior decade. The proportion of competitive regimes is now over 50 percent, with declines in the proportions of all other forms. The majority of the remaining single-party systems are loosely corporatist, with a few exceptions such as China and Cuba. The decline of ideological underpinnings for authoritarian governments, as well as the withdrawal of support from the Soviet Union, has contributed to this trend, especially in Africa.

The long-time presidents of Zambia and Malawi were replaced through elections, and other authoritarian leaders were forced to open up to at least some degree of competition. Kenya, Nigeria, Sudan and Zaire remain the most prominent holdouts against this trend. In Kenya, President Daniel Arap Moi reluctantly gave in to multiparty elections, but was then re-elected with less than a majority of the vote against a badly split opposition. Nigeria went through almost a decade of democratic transition, only to see the military annul the presidential election of June 1993 and continue in control. Sudan is under a fundamentalist Muslim regime that does not admit to the legitimacy of democratic institutions. In Zaire, Mobutu Sese Seko has held on so far despite the withdrawal of international support and concerted opposition efforts.

Perhaps in deference to the decline in the legitimacy of authoritarianism, the military is now more likely to dominate from behind the scenes than through direct rule, especially in Latin America. Latin America also has seen the genuine replacement of military regimes by competitive party regimes in such important countries as Argentina, Brazil, Chile, and Uruguay. Although one-party systems have been opened up in Africa, the proportion of military-dominated governments increased notably in the 1980s, from 36 to 46 percent of the total, and remains at that level. Of 30 military regimes enumerated in the world in 1990, 24 were in Africa, with the rest scattered through the other regions of the developing world. The recent casualties to military intervention include competitive governments in Suriname and Haiti in Latin America (1991), and Sierra Leone in Africa (1992). (The civilian government in Haiti was later restored by United States intervention.) Although the era of confidence in military government as a solution to development seems to have passed, military domination remains a likely outcome when other types of government are unable to solve internal conflicts.

Where there has been "backsliding" on the road to democracy, such as the temporary shutting down of the Peruvian Parliament by President Fujimori, or the imposition of tight control on political activity in Burma, the military has usually been at least part of the antidemocratic movement. With such examples in mind, we cannot assume that the democratizing trend will continue relentlessly. Multiparty regimes that seem unable to cope with economic and social problems often lose their legitimacy. Such is now the challenge facing the new experimentally competitive regimes of Eastern Europe and the Soviet Union, as well as the Third World.

SIGNIFICANCE OF INTEREST AGGREGATION

How interests are aggregated is an important determinant of what a country's government does for and to its citizens. The factors that most interest us about government and politics—stability, revolution, participation, welfare, equality, liberty, security—are very much consequences of interest aggregation. Through interest aggregation, the desires and demands of citizens are converted into a few policy alternatives. In terms of policy, the consequence is that many possible policies have been eliminated and only a few remain. In terms of process, the consequence is that political resources have been accumulated in the hands of relatively few individuals, who will decide policy. The remaining policy alternatives are serious or major alternatives because they have the backing of numerous political resources. Policy alternatives such as the government taking over the steel industry production in the United States have never been "serious," because no set of leaders commanding major political resources has favored them, even though such policies have been implemented elsewhere (twice in Britain).

Narrowing and combining policy preferences can be seen easily in the working of competitive party systems. Of the many possible policy preferences, only a few are backed by parties after the parties choose leaders and establish platforms to run on. In the elections, voters give backing to some of these parties and thus shape the strength of party representation in the legislature. Even at the legislative stage, some further consolidation and coalition building takes place between party factions or party groups. At some point, however, most of the policy possibilities have been eliminated. Either they were never backed by parties or parties supporting them did badly in the elections. In noncompetitive party systems, military governments, and monarchies, aggregation works differently, but with the similar effect of narrowing and combining policies and resources. It may be that on some issues, aggregation will virtually determine policy, as when power is held by a military government, a faction of an authoritarian party, or a disciplined party majority in a competitive system. In other cases the legislative assembly, military council, or party politburo may contain several factions of similar strength.

One characteristic of interest aggregation in all systems is its degree of polarization. In Chapter 3 we discussed consensual and conflictual or polarized political cultures. We mentioned that the United States, West Germany, and Britain were consensual, with most citizens preferring moderate positions. Italy, France, and Greece were more polarized cultures, with larger concentrations of citizens on the left and fewer in the center.

Ordinarily, we expect polarization in the policymaking body to look pretty much like polarization in the political culture. In a relatively consensual society like Germany, the Bundestag is made up of mainly moderate and tolerant parties. In more conflictual Italy, the stalemated Parliament was long dominated by two parties very distant from each other—the Communists and the Christian Democrats.

But politics shapes its environment as well as reflecting it. Interest aggregation often alters the amount of polarization that the political culture might be expected to project into policymaking. That is one reason politics is so fascinating. Well-organized and well-led accommodative political parties might, at least for a while, be able to dominate politics and limit the strength of extremist groups in the legislature, as in the consociational model we mentioned earlier. Conversely, well-organized extremists might be able to appeal to the fears and prejudices of some groups and get them more effectively to the polls, thus gaining more legislative strength in an otherwise consensual country.

Of course, authoritarian interest aggregation structures tend to create a political power balance that does not reflect popular opinion. In a highly divided and conflict-ridden society, such unrepresentativeness may be viewed as a great virtue. Leaders of military coups in many nations have justified their overthrow of party governments by claiming to depolarize politics and rid the nation of conflict it cannot afford. Similarly, heads of authoritarian parties typically claim that their nation must concentrate all its energies and resources on common purposes and that to allow party competition would be too polarizing.

One justification for democracy is that it leads political leaders to act as the people wish. In a polarized political culture, the cost of interest aggregation that reflects division and uncertainty may be seen as too high a price to pay for citizen control. As the frequent instability in authoritarian and military governments indicates, however, it may be easier to do away with the appearance of polarization than the reality. Cultural divisions may end up being reflected through military factions or intraparty groups, instead of through party competition, and the citizens may end up without either freedom and participation or stability.

KEY TERMS

association groups	democratic trends
authoritarian party systems	exclusive governing party
competitive party systems	inclusive governing party
conflictual party systems	institutional groups
consensual party systems	interest aggregation
consociational party systems	majoritarian party systems

military government

multiparty systems

party coalitions

party-electoral aggregation

patron-client network

plurality election rules

proportional representation

totalitarian party

END NOTES

1. Steffan Schmitt, James Scott, Carl Lande, and Laura Guasti, *Friends, Followers and Factions* (Berkeley, CA: Univ. of California Press, 1977); S. Eisenstadt and Rene Lemarchand, *Political Clientelism, Patronage and Development* (Beverly Hills, CA: Sage, 1981); John W. Lewis, *Political Networks and the Chinese Policy Process* (Stanford, CA: Northeast Asia Forum, 1986); Lucian W. Pye, *Asian Power and Politics* (Cambridge, MA: Harvard Univ. Press, 1985). Also see the studies of the personal networks of leaders in the politics of the former Soviet Union, such as T. H. Rigby and Rokdan Harasimin, *Leadership Selection and Patron Client Relations in the USSR and Yugoslavia* (Beverly Hills, CA: Sage, 1981).

2. William Thompson, *The Grievances of Military Coup-Makers* (Beverly Hills, CA: Sage, 1973).

3. The large literature on party strategies owes its largest debt to Anthony Downs, *An Economic Theory of Democracy* (New York: Harper & Row, 1957). More generally, see Dennis C. Mueller, *Public Choice* (Cambridge: Cambridge Univ. Press, 1979).

4. Seymour Martin Lipset and Stein Rokkan, eds., *Party Systems and Voter Alignments* (New York: Macmillan, 1967); Richard Rose, ed., *Electoral Behavior: A Comparative Handbook* (New York: Free Press, 1974); Russell J. Dalton, Scott C. Flanagan, and Paul Allen Beck, eds., *Electoral Change in Advanced Industrial Societies* (Princeton, NJ: Princeton Univ. Press, 1984).

5. Maurice Duverger, *Political Parties: Their Organization and Activity in the Modern State*, trans. Barbara and Robert North (New York: John Wiley, 1963); *Les Partis Politiques*, originally published in Paris in 1951. For a discussion of the historical development of the idea and the "law," see William H. Riker, "The Two-party System and Duverger's Law: An Essay on the History of Political Science," *American Political Science Review*, 76 (Dec. 1982), pp. 753–66.

6. Ian Budge, David Robertson, and Derek Hearl, *Ideology, Strategy and Party Change: Spatial Analyses of Post-War Election Programmes in 19 Democracies* (New York: Cambridge Univ. Press, 1987).

7. In addition to the references in note 4 above, see for example, Ian Budge, Ivor Crewe, and Dennis Farlie, *Party Identification and Beyond* (London: John Wiley, 1976); Russell J. Dalton, *Citizen Politics in Western Democracies* (Chatham, NJ: Chatham House, 1988); Philip E. Converse and Roy Pierce, *Representation in France* (Cambridge: Harvard Univ. Press, 1986); Elisabeth R. Gerber and John E. Jackson, "Endogenous Preferences and the Study of Institutions," *American Political Science Review*, 87:3 (1993), 639–56; Michael Lewis-Beck, *Economics and Elections: The Major Western Democracies* (Ann Arbor: Univ. of Michigan Press, 1988); John Zaller, *Elite Discourse and Public Opinion* (New York: Cambridge Univ. Press, 1991).

8. The data in Figure 6.1 are a fair picture of the party system that dominated Italy from the 1950s until the shattering upheavals of the 1990s, which are discussed briefly below.

9. For example, the survey of "experts" by Castles and Mair in 1982 shows a center gap of over three points between the Socialist party and the nearest conservative party (UDF),

although between a quarter and a third of voters regularly place themselves at the center. See Francis G. Castles and Peter Mair, "Left-Right Scales: Some 'Expert' Judgments," *European Journal of Political Research*, 12 (1984), pp. 73–88. Also see Dalton, *Citizen Politics in Western Democracies*, p. 196.

10. For analyses of the implications of election laws for party representation and government majorities, see Douglas Rae, *The Political Consequences of Election Laws* (New Haven, CT: Yale Univ. Press, 1967, 1971) and Arend Lijphart, "The Political Consequences of Electoral Laws, 1945–85," *American Political Science Review*, 84 (June 1990), pp. 481–96. (Also see note 5 above.)

11. For Britain, see Richard Rose, *Do Parties Make a Difference?* (Chatham, NJ: Chatham House, 1984), Ch. 5; also see Colin Railings, "The Influence of Election Programmes: Britain and Canada, 1945–79," in Budge, Robertson, and Hearl, *Ideology, Strategy, and Party Change*, pp. 1–14. More generally, see Michael J. Laver and Ian Budge, eds., *Party Policy and Government Coalitions* (New York: St. Martin's Press, 1992), and the review in Michael Gallagher, Michael Laver, and Peter Mair, *Representative Government in Western Europe* (New York: McGraw-Hill, 1992), Ch. 8. For the United States, still useful is Gerald Pomper, *Elections in America* (New York: Dodd, Mead, 1968), Chs. 7–10.

12. See Kaare Strom, *Minority Government and Majority Rule* (New York: Cambridge Univ. Press, 1990).

13. On cabinet stability, see Lawrence C. Dodd, *Coalitions in Parliamentary Government* (Princeton, NJ: Princeton Univ. Press, 1976); G. Bingham Powell, Jr., *Contemporary Democracies* (Cambridge, MA: Harvard Univ. Press, 1982), Ch. 7; Gary King, James E. Alt, Nancy E. Burns, and Michael Laver, "A Unified Model of Cabinet Dissolution in Parliamentary Democracies," *American Journal of Political Science* 34 (pp. 846–71; Paul Warwick, "Economic Trends and Government Survival in Western European Parliamentary Democracies, *American Political Science Review,* 86:4 (1992), pp. 875–87.

14. On these issues of citizen control, see G. Bingham Powell, Jr., "Constitutional Design and Citizen Electoral Control," *Journal of Theoretical Politics*, 1 (April 1989), pp. 107–30. Some empirical evidence is offered in G. Bingham Powell, Jr., and Guy Whitten, "A Cross-National Analysis of Economic Voting," *American Journal of Political Science,* 37:2 (1993), pp. 391–444.

15. For further analysis and some empirical evidence of greater congruence between citizens, governments and policymakers created in postelection bargaining, see John Huber and G. Bingham Powell, Jr., "Congruence between Citizens and Policymakers in Two Visions of Liberal Democracy," *World Politics*, 46:3, (1994), pp. 291–326.

16. For simplicity's sake, we here assume that polarization in the sense of policy distance goes together with antagonism and distrust between parties. This seems to be generally, but not universally, true. The analysis in G. Bingham Powell, Jr., "Extremist Parties and Political Turmoil: Two Puzzles," *American Journal of Political Science* 30 (May 1986), pp. 357–78, suggests both the relationship and the importance of antagonism as the more important factor.

17. This classification is adapted from Arend Lijphart's *Democracy in Plural Societies* (New Haven, CT: Yale Univ. Press, 1977) and *Democracies* (New Haven, CT: Yale Univ. Press, 1984). Also see Powell, *Contemporary Democracies*, and Powell, "Constitutional Design and Citizen Electoral Control."

18. Lijphart, *Democracy in Plural Societies.*

19. On the role of parties in the defense of democracy, see Powell, *Contemporary Democracies*, Chs. 8, 10; and the contributions in Juan J. Linz and Alfred Stepan, eds., *The Breakdown of Democratic Regimes* (Baltimore: Johns Hopkins Univ. Press, 1978).

20. On totalitarian parties see, for example, C. F. Friedrich and Z. K. Brzezinski, *Totalitarian Dictatorship and Autocracy* (Cambridge, MA: Harvard Univ. Press, 1956); Juan

Linz, "Totalitarian and Authoritarian Regimes," in Fred Greenstein and Nelson Polsby, eds., *Handbook of Political Science* Vol. 3 (Reading, MA: Addison-Wesley, 1975), pp. 175–412; Amos Perlmutter, *Modern Authoritarianism: A Comparative Institutional Analysis* (New Haven, CT.: Yale Univ. Press, 1981), especially, pp. 62–114.

21. See Franz Schurman, *Ideology and Organization in Communist China* (Berkeley: Univ. of California Press, 1966).

22. On the efforts in Africa, see Crawford Young, *Ideology and Development in Africa* (New Haven, CT: Yale Univ. Press, 1982), Ch. 2.

23. See Henry Bienen, *Kenya: The Politics of Participation and Control* (Princeton, NJ: Princeton Univ. Press, 1974), and Jean-Francois Medard, "The Historical Trajectories of the Ivorian and Kenyan States," in J. Manor, ed., *Rethinking Third World Politics* (London: Longman, 1991).

24. See Bogdan Denis Denitch, *The Legitimation of a Revolution: The Yugoslav Case* (New Haven, CT: Yale Univ. Press, 1976).

25. See Robert H. Jackson and Carl G. Rosberg, *Personal Rule in Black Africa* (Berkeley: Univ. of California Press, 1982) and Young, *Ideology and Development in Africa.*

26. Perlmutter, *Modern Authoritarianism*, pp. 114 ff.; see also Alfred Stepan, *The State and Society: Peru in Comparative Perspective* (Princeton, NJ: Princeton Univ. Press, 1978) and the essays in David Collier, ed., *The New Authoritarianism* (Princeton, NJ: Princeton Univ. Press, 1979).

SUGGESTED READINGS

Converse, Philip E., and Roy Pierce. *Political Representation in France.* Cambridge, Mass.: Harvard University Press, 1986.

Dalton, Russell, Scott Flanagan, and Paul Allen Beck, eds. *Electoral Change in Advanced Industrial Societies.* Princeton, N.J.: Princeton University Press, 1984.

Dodd, Lawrence C. *Coalitions in Parliamentary Government.* Princeton, N.J.: Princeton University Press, 1976.

Downs, Anthony. *An Economic Theory of Democracy.* New York: Harper and Row, 1957.

Duverger, Maurice. *Political Parties.* New York: Wiley, 1955.

Gallagher, Michael, Michael Laver, and Peter Mair. *Representative Government in Western Europe.* 2nd ed. New York: McGraw-Hill, 1995.

Gastil, R. D., ed. *Freedom in the World: Political Rights and Civil Liberties 1987-88.* New York: Freedom House, 1988.

Jackson, Robert H., and Carl G. Rosberg. *Personal Rule in Black Africa.* Berkeley: University of California Press, 1982.

Laver, Michael, and Norman Schofield. *Multiparty Government.* New York: Oxford University Press, 1990.

Lijphart, Arend. *Democracy in Plural Societies.* New Haven, Conn.: Yale University Press, 1977.

Lijphart, Arend. *Electoral Systems and Party Systems.* N.Y.: Oxford University Press, 1994.

Linz, Juan J., and Alfred Stepan, eds. *The Breakdown of Democratic Regimes.* Baltimore: Johns Hopkins University Press, 1978.

Lipset, Seymour M., and Stein Rokkan. *Party Systems and Voter Alignments.* New York: Free Press, 1967.

Michels, Robert. *Political Parties.* New York: Collier, 1962.

Nordlinger, Eric A. *Soldiers in Politics: Military Coups and Governments.* Englewood Cliffs, N.J.: Prentice-Hall, 1976.

O'Donnell, Guillermo, Philippe C. Schmitter, and Laurence Whitehead. *Transitions from Authoritarian Rule: Prospects for Democracy.* Baltimore: Johns Hopkins University Press, 1986.

Ostrogorski, M. J. *Democracy and the Organization of Political Parties.* New York: Anchor, 1964.

Perlmutter, Amos. *Modern Authoritarianism: A Comparative Institutional Analysis.* New Haven, Conn.: Yale University Press, 1981.

Powell, G. Bingham, Jr. *Contemporary Democracies: Participation, Stability and Violence.* Cambridge, Mass.: Harvard University Press, 1982.

Rae, Douglas. *The Political Consequences of Electoral Laws.* New Haven, Conn.: Yale University Press, 1971.

Riker, William H. *Liberalism Against Populism.* San Francisco: W. H. Freeman, 1982.

Rokkan, Stein. *Citizens, Elections, Parties.* New York: McKay, 1970.

Sartori, Giovanni. *Parties and Party Systems.* Cambridge: Cambridge University Press, 1976.

Strom, Kaare. *Minority Government and Majority Rule.* New York: Cambridge University Press, 1990.

Von Beyme, Klaus. *Political Parties in Western Europe.* New York: St. Martin's, 1985.

Ware, Alan. *Citizens, Parties and the State.* Princeton, N.J.: Princeton University Press, 1988.

Chapter 7

Government and Policymaking

*P*olicymaking is the pivotal stage in the political process, the point at which bills become laws passed by parliaments, or edicts are issued by the ruling council of an authoritarian regime. At a later stage policies are implemented and enforced. To understand how policies are made, we must know what the decision rules are. What kind of power is effective in different political systems? Is it a simple majority vote in the legislature or does such a vote require approval by an independently elected executive? Or is it a decree issued by the monarch, a signed agreement by military commanders, or the official backing of the politburo? Or is it merely the whim of the military dictator?

We must also recognize the central importance of the agencies of government in policymaking. The demands of interest groups for tax decreases or for the protection of endangered species cannot become effective unless they are transformed into laws by the legislative authorities and implemented by government officials according to some accepted decision rule. Economic, societal, and personality influences become important when they impinge on or manifest themselves within the institutions of government: parliaments, cabinets, ministries and executive departments, and courts. The flow of governmental action is multidirectional. While the needs and demands of societal and interest groups are very much in the minds of political leaders, most of the actual initiation and formulation of policy proposals goes on at the governmental level, by governmental officials and by legislators and their staffs.

This chapter focuses on decision rules and on the policymaking role of governmental agencies such as legislatures, executives, and bureaucracies. Many scholars feel that in the 1960s and 1970s political science neglected the importance of governmental institutions while concentrating on public opinion, pressure groups, and party politics.[1] Needless to say, we ought not neglect either the upward flow of influence and demands from the society or the downward flow of decisions from the government.

DECISION RULES FOR POLICYMAKING

All governments must have some set of rules for making decisions. They must have a constitution, whether it is a specific written document, a set of customs or practices, or, as is usually the case, both. Even a military government or a dictatorship based on coercion, attempts to have a working set of arrangements for having decrees proposed, considered, and adopted. *Decision rules* are the basic rules governing how decisions are made, setting up agencies and offices with specific powers, assigning them territorial and functional jurisdiction, and the like. Individuals and groups seeking to influence policy have to operate within the framework of these rules. In a federal system such as the United States, a pressure group may have to be active at the state and federal level. If the working constitution merely requires a decree from the commander of the armed forces, or a declaration by the politburo, a different approach will be needed to influence these crucial policymakers.

The decision rules shape political activity because they determine what political resources to seek—whether legislative seats or the support of military commanders—and how to acquire and use them. It is important that these decision rules be calculable and stable. The importance of the calculability of decision rules was suggested in a comment by Thomas Jefferson in his introduction to the first Manual of the House of Representatives: "A bad set of rules is better than no rules at all." In the absence of a legitimate set of arrangements for formulating issues, deliberating and debating them, and deciding among points of view, government breaks down and issues may be decided by force.

Making Constitutions

Constitution making is a fundamental political act: It creates or transforms the decision rules. These decision rules lay out the system, process, and policy arrangements of a political system. Thus constitution making may affect structure and recruitment in establishing a two-chambered legislature, or culture and socialization through prohibiting the governmental "establishment of religion." It may organize the policy process, for example, by giving a particular chamber the power of initiating appropriation measures, or empowering the executive to initiate treaty making. It may restrict the scope of public policy by protecting private property, free speech, and assembly.

Basic changes in constitutional rules usually take place in the aftermath of defeat in war, the success of independence movements, or significant social or revolutionary change. Thus, the defeated powers and the successor states of World Wars I and II all adopted new constitutions or had new constitutions imposed on them. Most of the constitutions that are in force today were formed as the result of some break, often violent, with the past—war, revolution, colonial rebellion. In these situations decision rules have to accommodate new internal power distributions or external power contexts. Britain is unusual in not having a formal written constitution, but rather only a long-accepted and highly developed set of customs, buttressed by major statutes. This practice reflects the gradual, incremental, and, on the whole, peaceful record of political change in Britain. Nevertheless, the major changes in British decision rules, such as the shifting of power from the Crown to Parliament in the seventeenth century, and the Reform Acts of 1832 and 1867, which established party and cabinet government based on broad electorates, followed on periods of civil war, mass mobilizations, and disorder.

Perhaps the greatest exception to the association between disruptive upheavals and constitution creation is the peaceful development over the last 40 years of the constitution of the European Community, an emergent political unit whose growing powers are altering the decision rules affecting almost 400 million Europeans in 15 countries. But while there has been no violence associated with the formation and growth of the European Community, its origins cannot be separated from the bitter lessons of World Wars I and II.

The decades since World War II have seen much constitutional experimentation. Japan, Germany, and Italy—the defeated powers—introduced new political arrangements under the active supervision of the victorious powers; and these arrangements have proven to be durable. France has had two constitutions in this period, and it appears that its second effort—the Fifth Republic, embarked on in 1958—will be successful. Both Germany and France have undertaken some interesting constitutional engineering intended to overcome the weaknesses of their earlier constitutional arrangements—the Weimar Republic and the Fourth Republic. The German constitutional framers sought to overcome the political fragmentation and instability of the Weimar Republic by combining proportional representation with single-member district plurality voting and by eliminating splinter parties with less than 5 percent of the vote. These arrangements encourage the German voters to make their choices among the larger political parties, hence reducing party fragmentation. They also introduced a novel arrangement intended to cope with problems of cabinet instability. A government may be overthrown after the loss of a vote of confidence in the Bundestag only if it is a "constructive" vote of no confidence. That is, a vote of nonconfidence in the incumbent government must be accompanied by presentation of an alternative majority in the Bundestag. The French experiment is a combination of parliamentary and presidential government, and it also appears to have been successful. The Fifth Republic introduced a separately elected powerful presidency, along with the institutions normal to a parliamentary system, that is, a prime minister and cabinet responsible to the National Assembly.

In the last two decades the worldwide trend toward democracy, the ending of the Cold War and the dissolution of the Soviet Union has precipitated a new debate about the properties and virtues of differing governmental systems. The new constitutional arrangements adopted by democratizing countries such as Spain and Portugal, and the more recent efforts at constitutional crafting in Eastern Europe, Russia, and the other successor countries of the Soviet Union, in South Africa, and elsewhere, has reignited old polemics about the virtues and faults of presidentialism and parliamentarism, federalism and centralism, the different kinds of electoral arrangement, and the like. Some scholars are skeptical about constitutional engineering and tinkering. March and Olsen have argued, "The contemporary record with respect to intentional change does not encourage boundless confidence in the possibilities for deliberate controlled change."[2] They point out that it is possible to "shock" institutions into change, but the outcome of the shocks may turn out to be quite different from what was intended. On the other hand, Giovanni Sartori has long affirmed the importance of institutional "crafting" and "constitutional engineering."[3] We will have the occasion to discuss some of the recent constitutional engineering literature at appropriate points below.

Geographic Distribution of Government Power

The basic decision rules or constitutions of political systems differ along three dimensions: (1) geographic distribution of authority; (2) structural-processual separation of authority; and (3) limitations on governmental authority.

Classifying systems according to the geographic division of power gives us *confederal systems* at one extreme, *unitary systems* at the other extreme, and *federal systems* in the middle (see Table 7.1). The United States under the Articles of Confederation was a confederal system. The central government had authority over foreign affairs and defense, but it had to depend on financial and other support from the states to implement this power. Under the Constitution, adopted in 1787, the American government changed from confederal to federal, that is, both central and state governments had spheres of authority and the means to implement their power. Today, the United States, Germany, Russia, India, Mexico, and Brazil are federal systems in which central and local units each have autonomy in particular spheres of public policy. These policy areas and powers are, however, divided among central and local units in varying ways. Britain, France, China, Japan, and Egypt are unitary governments with power and authority concentrated at the center. Regional and local units have those powers specifically delegated to them from the central government, which may change or withdraw the powers by central decision.

In comparing confederal, federal, and unitary systems, however, we must keep in mind the distinction between formal and actual distribution of power. In unitary systems, in spite of the formal concentration of power at the center, regional and local units may acquire authority that the central government rarely challenges. In the American federal system over the last century, power has steadily moved from the states toward the center. In recent years there has been a reverse effort to move power from the federal government to the states. Even in unitary systems there have been efforts to shift some power to provincial and local governments. This has been a response to democratic pressures, demands for greater scope to grass-roots influences. Thus, the real differences between federal and unitary systems may be considerably less significant than their formal arrangements suggest. An example of the discrepancy between formal and actual federalism was the case of Mexico. Here until recently the Partido Revolucionario Institucional (PRI) had centralized control in a system that is formally federal. Recent developments in Mexico, with oppositional parties winning ground in some states, and the PRI power monopoly under challenge, has produced some 'real' federalism to go along with the formal variety.

Table 7.1   DIVISION AND LIMITATION OF GOVERNMENTAL AUTHORITY

Geographic Distribution of Authority		
Centralized ◀──────────────────────────────────▶ Decentralized		
Unitary Confederal	Federal	
France	United States under Constitution	United States under Articles of Confederation
Japan	Germany	European Economic Community
United Kingdom	India	
China	Nigeria	
Egypt	Russia	
	Brazil	
	Mexico	

Structural Separation of Authority			
Concentrated ◀──────────────────────────────▶ Separated			
Authoritarian	Parliamentary	Mixed	Presidential
China Mexico	Germany	France	United States
Egypt	United Kingdom	Russia	Brazil
Nigeria	Japan		
	India		

Judicial Limitations on Governmental Authority		
Unlimited ◀──────────────────────────────▶ Limited		
Nonindependent Courts	Independent Courts	Judicial Review
China	United Kingdom	United States
Egypt		Germany
Nigeria	Russia	Japan
Mexico	Brazil	France
		India

Separation of Governmental Powers

The theory of *separation of powers* has a long and venerable history going back at least to the work of Locke and Montesquieu.[4] Separation of power had the virtue of preventing the injustices which might result from an unchecked executive or an unlimited legislature. Madison and Hamilton elaborated this theory in *The Federalist*,[5] which described and defended the institutional arrangements proposed by the Constitutional Convention of 1787.

Political theorists in the course of the nineteenth and first part of the twentieth centuries reflecting on the two successful historical cases of representative democracy—Britain and the United States—gradually codified what we may call the "classic" separation of powers theory which dominated the political science of the pre–World War II period. This theory argued that there are essentially two forms of representative democratic government—the presidential and the parliamentary. The *democratic presidential regime* provides two separate agencies of government separately elected by and deriving authority from the people—the executive and the legislative. The *parliamentary regime* combines the executive and legislative authority in a single institution. The executive (the Cabinet) is the agent of parliamentary authority and in many parliamentary systems consists largely of members of parliament. In the debate over which system of representative democracy was better British and American political theorists usually favored the British-style parliamentary system. This version of parliamentarism, coupling plurality voting rules that usually created clear party majorities in Parliament with a Cabinet and prime minister responsible to Parliament, was said to result in governments clearly responsible to the public will, periodically expressed. The U.S. presidential system was a divided system, periodically resulting in stalemate or "gridlock" at times when the executive and the legislative branches were controlled by different parties. Another strand of this "classic" theory of separation of powers explained the crisis prone version of the parliamentary system—exemplified by the Weimar Republic of Germany, and the French Third Republic—largely in terms of proportional representation that accentuated ideological fragmentation resulting in cabinet instability and breakdown.

This "classic" theory of separation of powers ran into complications and anomalies in the decades after World War II. The Scandinavian countries demonstrated that the parliamentary system with proportional representation could work quite stably when ideological conflict between the political parties remained moderate. The political parties in the parliaments could form congenial majority coalitions, and there would be responsible and responsive government. Where cultural and ideological cleavage and conflict were intense (as in the Low Countries and Austria), party leaders mindful of the costs of democratic breakdown and civil war, could agree to disagree on some intractable questions (such as the official language, or religious toleration). This produced another version of stable parliamentary system called "consociational" democracy by Arend Lijphart,[6] which emphasized representation in policymaking by all major social groups and achieved stability by adopting protective and limiting rules on what could and could not be debated and altered.

Research on continental European forms of parliamentary democracy produced a further refinement in the discovery of "corporatist democracy" by Philippe Schmitter, Gerhard Lehmbruch, and others,[7] who pointed to arrangements primarily in the smaller European democracies—the Low Countries, Austria, Norway, and Sweden—where the "class struggle," so threatening to democratic stability, could be abated by the introduction of a formal "corporatist" system of deliberating and bargaining over wages, benefits, and prices by labor, capital, and government. These became technical rather than ideological questions, resolvable by deliberation and compromise. Thus, the Anglo-American bias of early separation of powers theory was overcome when it was demonstrated that continental European parliamentary democracies could reconcile proportional representation with its advantage of providing better group representation with stable and effective government.

The Third Wave of democratization (see Chapters 1 and 3) beginning in the mid-1970s in southern Europe, and then spreading to Latin America, Eastern Europe, and the Soviet Union, has reopened this parliamentary-presidential debate. With countries all the way from the Russian Federation to South Africa engaged in constitutional deliberation about which type of regime is most suitable to democratic transitions, political theorists have been challenged to come up with persuasive evidence and prudent argument. One side of this debate, dominated by European specialists and led by Juan Linz, Arend Lijphart, and Giovanni Sartori favors parliamentarism particularly of the continental European variety since it provides a consensual framework in which different ethnic and religious groups can find representation.[8] Since many of the transitional democracies of the present day are taking shape in societies which are divided by ethnic and religious differences, Lijphart argues that the parliamentary, proportional representation system should be the preferred regime. The other side of this debate, led by Matthew Shugart, John Carey, and Donald Horowitz, among others,[9] makes the telling argument that while the world of scholarship seems to be ranged on the side of the parliamentary solution of the democratic transition dilemma, practical politics seems to be coming out on the side of elected presidents having differing degrees of political power. Even in the domain of the former British empire, in such African countries as Nigeria and Zimbabwe and in most of the Eastern European and the successor countries of the Soviet Union, the constitutions provide for presidents with some political power. The Latin American area has been largely dominated by presidential regimes for more than a century. In 1993 a popular referendum in Brazil reaffirmed its commitment to a presidential regime.

The Shugart and Carey study is the first major empirical investigation of the phenomenon of presidentialism. And its findings require that we modify our treatment of the structural separation of authority to recognize that features of parliamentarism and presidentialism are blended in a number of hybrid systems of partial separation of powers. In John Carey's words, "The easiest way to understand the classification of different regimes with presidencies is that the hybrid regimes all compromise the basic principle of separate origin and survival of the branches. That is, in pure presidential systems, the branches originate in entirely separate elections and cannot threaten the survival of the other branch throughout their respective terms. In pure parliamentary regimes, there is no separate origin—the premier and cabinet are chosen by the assembly which is elected. In the hybrids there may be separate origin, but the separation of survival is compromised."[10] In such systems, the prime minister may be appointed by the president, but subject to dismissal by the legislature, for example, or the president may be able to dissolve the legislature.

In the middle rows of Table 7.1 we classify governments according to the degree of concentration and separation of power. *Authoritarian governments* in the left-hand column are those in which executive, legislative, and judicial power are concentrated and in which the agents of government are not chosen in popular competitive elections. Three of the twelve countries included in this book have authoritarian governments not chosen in competitive elections—China, Nigeria, and Egypt. Mexico is a transitional system moving from a one-party noncompetitive system to increasing multiparty competition. Britain, Germany, Japan, and India are parliamentary systems in which executive and legislative power are concentrated in cabinets representing majorities in popularly elected lower houses of the parliaments. As noted above, Shugart and Carey identify several subtypes of mixed (or "hybrid") systems that have independently elected presidents with substantial policymaking power, but which also must share control over the executive branch with the legislature. A variety of arrangements exist for such shared control; their consequences are often sharply affected by the balance of party or coalition control of the presidency and legislature. Current examples of such mixed systems are Fifth Republic France, Russia, and a number of the new Eastern European systems.

At the extreme right of Table 7.1 is the pure presidential category with the United States and Brazil as examples. The main characteristics of this system are that the chief executive is popularly elected, can appoint and dismiss the members of his cabinet and government, and has some constitutionally granted lawmaking authority, and both he and the assembly hold office for fixed terms.

Contrary to the judgment of many reputable political theorists, most of the new constitutions of transitional democracies of Eastern Europe and the Third World are of this *presidential-parliamentary* and *mixed presidential-parliamentary* regimes. What seems to make them attractive is that they offer a popular choice of the chief executive who has both substantive and ceremonial powers and can serve as a symbol of natural unity. Such presidential or mixed regimes can be combined with proportional election of the assembly as in many Latin American and Eastern European cases and in Russia, thus providing for the "consensual" feature that parliamentary-favoring scholars consider so important in binding ethnic and religiously heterogeneous societies to the support of new democratic constitutions. With proportional representation relatively small groups can gain representation in the parliament and participate in the bargaining and coalition-making process.

These new constitutional ideas, projects, and experiments are being tried out in a relatively large number of cases, involving a great variety of cultures and social structures as well as mixtures of separation of powers arrangements. We will be learning in the next years and decades which of these experiments prove out in fact and which of them fail. Will our experience vindicate the optimism of Giovanni Sartori about the effectiveness of institutional engineering or the skepticism of James March?

Limitations on Government Powers

Unlike authoritarian regimes, parliamentary, presidential, and mixed democratic regimes are characterized by some form of legal or customary limitation on the exercise of power. Systems in which the powers of various government units are defined and limited by a written constitution, statutes, and custom are called *constitutional regimes*. Civil rights—such as the right to a fair trial and freedom to speak, petition, publish, and assemble—are protected against government interference except under unusual and specified circumstances. The courts are crucial institutions in the limitations on governmental power. Governments may be divided into those, at one extreme, in which the power to coerce citizens is relatively unlimited by the courts, and those, at the other extreme, in which the courts not only protect the rights of citizens but also police other parts of the government to see that their powers are properly exercised. The United States is the best example of a system in which political power is limited by the courts. Its institution of *judicial review* allows federal and state courts to rule that other parts of the government have exceeded their powers. Most other constitutional regimes have independent courts that protect persons against the improper implementation of laws and regulations but cannot overrule the assembly or the political executive. The substantive rights of persons in these systems are protected by statute, custom, self-restraint, and political pressure. The constitutional courts of Germany and Japan have limited powers of judicial review of the decisions of other agencies of government. A limited form of judicial review has been in place in France since 1958, in which the Fifth Republic Constitution provided for a *constitutional council* chosen by the president of the republic and of the two legislative chambers. These three officials plus the prime minister were given the power to submit legislation to the council for a ruling as to its conformity to the constitution. In 1974 this power to submit legislation to the council was granted to 60 senators or deputies. In the last decades this "review" power in France has grown into a significant constitutional check on legislative action.

All written constitutions provide for amending procedures, since it is generally recognized that there must be some adaptability and flexibility in basic decision rules, as problems arise with existing institutions, or as social structure changes and new groups demand access. Those procedures can be an important limitation on governmental power. Many constitutions provide that certain arrangements may not be amended, as, for example, the provision in the U.S. Constitution granting each state equal representation in the Senate.

Amending procedures vary widely, ranging from the complex to the simple. Perhaps the simplest case is that of the United Kingdom where a simple parliamentary statute may alter the constitutional arrangements. Thus since the Parliament Act of 1911 the power of the House of Lords has been reduced to that of proposing amendments and delaying legislation for one parliamentary session. Some constitutions prescribe an absolute majority of all legislators, or a special majority such as three-fifths, rather than the majority of a quorum which is sufficient for ordinary statutes. Others require that an amendment be approved twice with an interval of time between passages. Brazil requires its legislature to vote an amendment in two separate occasions with a three-fourths vote each time. In some cases a popular referendum is added on to the legislative action. The U.S. Constitution has the most difficult formal procedure, requiring initiation by two-thirds of both houses of the Congress (or by the never-employed procedure of a national convention called by two-thirds of the states), and approval by three-fourths of the state legislatures, or three-fourths of specially elected conventions held in the states. Constitutions that have more complicated amending procedures, such as the American, are called "rigid" constitutions; the simpler ones are said to be "flexible." Here again, however, we have to distinguish between law and practice. Some flexible constitutions such as those of Norway and Denmark have rarely been amended, while rigid ones like the American and Swiss have frequently been changed.[11]

Table 7.1 emphasizes very general differences and tends to obscure significant differences within categories, as, for example, among democratic political systems. Arend Lijphart, in an important study of types of democracy, divides democratic regimes into two major categories: majoritarian and consensual.[12] The institutions of the majoritarian type of democracy are relatively simple, designed to give power to the representatives of the majority of the voters. The political executive—the cabinet—is chosen from among the leaders of a unicameral legislature, or from the dominant of two chambers in a bicameral legislature. Hence, power is concentrated at a single point, not divided as in a separation of powers system. The party systems of these majoritarian democracies tend to follow a simple left-right division, and their electoral arrangements are of the single-member district, plurality variety. According to Lijphart, consensual democracies are designed to break up and limit the exercise of power. They typically provide for power sharing in the executive, often requiring that ethnic and religious groups be represented in the cabinet. They are also characterized by bicameral legislatures in which one of the chambers is representative of regional and ethnic groups. Switzerland, Belgium, and the Netherlands are good examples of consensual democracies; New Zealand, Britain, and Sweden are good examples of majoritarian systems. The United States falls in between with a majoritarian electoral and party system, a majoritarian executive, a federal distribution of power among the central government and the states, and a consensual bicameral legislature with a powerful Senate, representative of the states. Clearly, majoritarian systems are typical of homogeneous, culturally unified societies, as in Britain, New Zealand, and Sweden, while consensual democracy is more typical of religiously and linguistically heterogeneous societies such as Switzerland, Belgium, and the Netherlands where democratic survival has turned on accommodative arrangements protective of minorities.

ASSEMBLIES

In addition to interest groups and political parties, which we discussed in Chapters 5 and 6, three important types of institutions are involved in policymaking: the executive, whether elective or appointive; the higher levels of bureaucracy; and the assembly. The distribution of policymaking predominance among these three institutions varies from country to country and from issue area to issue area. Almost all contemporary political systems have *assemblies,* variously called *senates,* chambers, diets, houses, and the like. Their formal approval is usually required for major public policies. They are generally elected by popular vote, and hence are at least formally accountable to the citizenry. Today more than 80 percent of the 185 independent countries belonging to the United Nations have such governmental bodies. The almost universal adoption of legislative institutions suggests that in the modern world a legitimate government must formally include a representative popular component. Nonetheless, we refer to them as "assemblies" rather than "legislatures" because in most countries their role in formulating laws—in legislating—is quite small.

The Functions of Assemblies

All assemblies[13] have many members—ranging from fewer than a hundred to more than a thousand—who deliberate, debate, and vote on policies that come before them. Most important policies and rules must be considered and at least formally approved by these bodies before they have the force of law. Although legislative approval is needed to give authority to policy, in most countries legislation is actually formulated elsewhere, usually by the political executive and the upper levels of the bureaucracy. When we compare assemblies on the basis of their importance as political and policymaking agencies, the U.S. Congress, which plays a very important role in the formulation and enactment of legislation, is at one extreme. The other extreme is represented by the National People's Congress of the People's Republic of China, which meets infrequently and does little more than listen to statements by party leaders and legitimize decisions made elsewhere. Roughly midway between the two is the House of Commons in Britain. There legislative proposals are sometimes initiated or modified by ordinary members of Parliament, but public policy is usually made by the Cabinet or ministers (who are, to be sure, chosen from the members of the parliamentary body). The typical assembly primarily provides a deliberating forum, formally enacts legislation, and sometimes amends it.

A recent study of European legislatures[14] classifies them according to power in the decision-making process and popular perception of their importance. The judgment of power is that of academic experts; estimates of citizen perception are based on samples of popular opinion made through recent surveys. It is of interest that, while the Italian legislature is rated first in terms of expert estimates of power (see Table 7.2), among the European populations surveyed, popular Italian opin-

Table 7.2   THE ROLE OF ASSEMBLIES IN SELECTED EUROPEAN COUNTRIES

Policy Influence Ranking	Importance to Citizens Ranking
Italy	Britain
Holland	Ireland
Sweden	West Germany
West Germany	Holland
Britain	France
France	Italy
Ireland	

Source: Adapted from Philip Norton, "Conclusion: Legislatures in Perspective," *West European Politics*, 13 (July 1990), p. 146; and *Eurobarometer*, 19 (April 1983), p. 110.

ion rates its legislative body lowest in importance. Britain, on the other hand, is third from the bottom in expert judgment of influence in the policymaking process, but comes out on top in terms of "importance" in popular opinion. Ireland moves from the lowest expert evaluation to a high public ranking. The legislature's prestige in a nation does not accurately reflect its policymaking influence; it is more a reflection of the general esteem in which governmental institutions are held. Thus, frequent cabinet crises and changes in Italy reduce popular respect for government in general, but they create opportunities for policy initiatives by groups in the legislature and a more important role in the making and unmaking of cabinets. Assemblies perform a wide variety of functions other than policymaking. Debates in assemblies can contribute to the socialization process, shaping citizens' and elites' perceptions not only of political issues, but also of the appropriate norms and procedures of the political system. Assemblies can also play a major role in elite recruitment, especially in parliamentary systems where prime ministers and cabinet members typically serve their apprenticeships in the assembly. The committee hearings and floor debates in legislative assemblies may be important sites for interest articulation and interest aggregation, especially if majority party control is absent or loosely exercised. However, as in policymaking, the assemblies of different nations play very different roles in their respective political systems. The British House of Commons is ordinarily of little importance in policymaking, because it is controlled by the ruling party's majority, but the Commons and its debates are central to socialization and elite recruitment. The U.S. Congress and its committees play a major role in interest aggregation and policymaking; they must share other functions with many other institutions in the decentralized American system. Thus far, at least, the People's Congress in China has played only a limited socialization role in China's political process.

This brief comparison of the functions performed by assemblies should set to rest the simplified notion that assemblies are simply to be viewed as legislative bodies. All assemblies in democratic systems do have an important relationship to legislation, but not a dominant one. Their political importance is based not just in this function, but also in the great variety of other political functions they perform.

Differences in the Structure of Assemblies

Assemblies differ in their organization as well as in their powers and functions. About half the parliaments or congresses in the world consist of two chambers, which have different powers and different ways of selecting members. In Europe, the chambers of parliaments developed out of "estates" (social status groups), bodies intermittently called together by kings or other hereditary rulers for consultation and revenue. In France there were three estates: the clergy, the higher aristocracy, and the so-called third estate, representing other classes. In England in the early period, estates were organized in two chambers—the lords spiritual (the bishops) and temporal (the "barons") in the House of Lords, and knights and burgesses elected from the counties and boroughs to the House of Commons. Today this basis of parliamentary organization persists only in England, where the House of Lords (its powers greatly diminished) is still dominated numerically by the hereditary aristocracy. Most of the democratic countries, and some of the authoritarian ones, have bicameral (two-chamber) assemblies. Federal systems normally provide simultaneously for two forms of representation: one chamber for constituencies based on population and the second for constituencies based on geographic units. Even in unitary systems such as France, *bicameralism* is a common practice, but the purpose of the second chamber is to break up the process of policymaking and provide for longer and more cautious consideration of legislation. The emphasis in these systems is on separation of power rather than distinct representation of special geographic entities. The bicameral U.S. Congress grew out of both federalism and separation of powers. The House of Representatives directly represents the citizens, with districts roughly equal in population size, giving a voice to various local interests and, in the aggregate, the popular majority. The 50 U.S. states are equally represented in the Senate; thus, federal units have special access to one of the two legislative chambers and are in a position to protect their interests. The U.S. congressional system is also connected with the other branches of government through checks and balances. Thus, the Senate must approve treaties and executive appointments as a way of checking the executive; both the Senate and the House must vote on a declaration of war; and all measures involving taxation and appropriations must be initiated in the House.

The American system, in which the two chambers seem practically equal in power, is unusual. In most bicameral systems one chamber is dominant, and the second (the British House of Lords and the French Senate) tends to play a primarily limiting and delaying role. As we have pointed out, cabinets in parliamentary systems are usually chosen from the majority party or parties' leadership in the more popularly representative chamber. Governments in parliamentary systems depend on majority support to continue in office. If the cabinet is chosen from among the majority party in one of the chambers, then the cabinet is responsible to that chamber, which will consequently acquire a more important position in policymaking than the second chamber.

Assemblies also differ in their internal organization, in ways that have major consequences for policymaking and implementation. There are two kinds of internal organization in assemblies and parliaments: party organization and formal organization (presiding officers, committees, and the like). A party system in a presidential government may function differently from that in a parliamentary government. Parliamentary parties in Britain, as in most parliamentary systems, are disciplined in that members of Parliament rarely vote in opposition to the instructions of party leaders. Because cabinets generally hold office as long as they can command a majority of the assembly, deviating from party discipline means risking the fall of the government and new elections. In presidential systems, the executive and members of the assembly are elected for definite terms of office, and the fate of the party and of its members is less directly and immediately involved in voting on legislative measures. In American legislatures, party discipline operates principally with respect to procedural questions, like the selection of a presiding officer or the appointment of committees. On substantive legislative and policy issues, Democratic and Republican legislators are freer to decide whether or not to vote with party leaders. A comparison of roll call votes in the U.S. Congress and the British House of Commons would show much more consistency in party voting among British members of Parliament.

All assemblies have a committee structure, some division of labor permitting specialized groups of legislators to deliberate on particular kinds of issues and recommend action to the whole assembly. Without such a sublegislative organization, it would be impossible to handle the large flow of legislative business. As we have seen, however, the importance of committees varies. The committee systems of some countries, such as the United States, tend to be very influential in the legislative process, highly specialized and matching the executive departments in subject matter, and tending to dominate the legislative process. Strong committees having a clear legislative division of labor, and matching the ministerial departments, are to be found in systems in which legislatures are powerful, and in which the opposition can be influential.[15]

POLITICAL EXECUTIVES

Political executives have many names and titles, and their duties and powers also vary enormously.[16] Some political executives are called presidents, others are called prime ministers, chancellors, premiers, and still others chairmen or chairs. There are even a few surviving kings who have genuine power. In the remaining Communist regimes, some of the top leaders are called president as in Cuba and North Korea, or may as in the case of Deng Xiaoping in China be the supreme arbiter without reference to formal offices. In most other authoritarian regimes the top leaders are called president.

Titles may be misleading in telling us what functions these officials perform. Political executives tend to be the main formulators of public policy. Table 7.3 distinguishes among executives according to whether they are *individual* or *collective, effective* or *ceremonial*. Political executives are effective only if they have genuine powers in the enactment and implementation of laws and regulations. If they do not have these powers, they are symbolic or ceremonial. In presidential systems the ceremonial and effective roles are almost always held by the same person, the president. The two roles are almost always separated in parliamentary systems, where a distinction is made between the "head of state," who is primarily a ceremonial official, and the "head of government," who makes and implements the decisions.

Individual effective executives include the U.S. presidency, an office with very substantial powers affecting all processes of government. Although the U.S. executive includes collective bodies such as the cabinet and the National Security Council, they advise the president instead of acting as collective decision makers. The French president is also a powerful individual executive, who appoints the premier and may dissolve the assembly and call for new elections. Saudi Arabia is a traditional kingship in which a large concentration of power in the monarch is regulated and limited only by custom and tradition. There is a ministerial council but it tends to be dominated by the monarch. The general secretary of the Central Committee of China's Communist Party is also an individual political executive and tends to be an important political figure.

Table 7.3   TYPES OF POLITICAL EXECUTIVES; EXAMPLES FROM SELECTED
COUNTRIES

Effective	Ceremonial
Individual	
U.S. President	German President
French President	British Queen
French Prime Minister	Japanese Emperor
German Chancellor	Indian President
British Prime Minister	President PRC
General Secretary, PRC	
Mexican President	
Indian Prime Minister	
Russian President	
Brazilian President	
Collective	
British Cabinet	
Japanese Cabinet	British Royal Family
Chinese Politburo	
Swiss Federal Council	

Sorting out political systems on the individual-collective scale is a bit more complicated. In Britain the prime minister tends to dominate the Cabinet in time of war or emergency. Strong prime ministers even in less troubled times may dominate their Cabinets, but for the most part the British executive is a collective unit. The Cabinet meets regularly, makes important decisions, and acts on the basis of group deliberation. The Federal Council of Switzerland is an extreme example of a collective executive. The chair of the Federal Council is elected annually and seems to be little more than a presiding officer.

Although we may speak of the political executive as being individual or collective, we are talking about the distribution of power and authority in it, not simple numbers. All executives have many members. They consist of elective and appointive officials who have policymaking power. A British prime minister makes some 100 ministerial and junior ministerial appointments; a German chancellor may make a similar number. In the United States, on taking office an incoming president may have to make as many as 2,000 political appointments, of which 200 are key policymaking positions in the executive branch.

A word or two about ceremonial executives is appropriate. Monarchs like the British queen and Scandinavian kings are principally ceremonial and symbolic officers with very occasional political powers. They are living symbols of the state and nation and of their historical continuity. Britain's queen opens Parliament and makes statements on important holidays and anniversaries. When there is an election, or when a government falls, the queen formally appoints a new prime minister. She is the symbol and the transmitter of legitimacy. With a stroke of her wand she may create a knight or a duke. Normally she has no choice in selecting a prime minister, since she picks the candidate likely to have a majority in the House of Commons, but if there is doubt about which leader has a majority or who leads the party, the queen's discretion may be an important power. In republican countries with parliamentary systems, presidents perform the functions that fall to kings and queens in parliamentary monarchies. German and Italian presidents issue statements, make speeches on important anniversaries, and designate prime ministers after elections or when a government has resigned.

A system in which the ceremonial executive is separated from the effective executive has a number of advantages. The ceremonial executive tends to be above politics and symbolizes unity and continuity. The U.S. presidency, which combines both effective and ceremonial functions, risks the likelihood that the president will use ceremonial and symbolic authority to enhance political power or that involvement in politics may hamper presidential performance of the symbolic or unifying role. Communist countries have tended to separate the ceremonial and the effective executives. The president of the People's Republic of China, elected by the congress, is a ceremonial officer. He greets distinguished visitors, and opens and presides over meetings of the People's Congress.

Britain's royal family is an example of a collective ceremonial executive. So many occasions call for the physical presence of the monarch that members of the royal family share appearances. The activities of the royal family are reported daily in the press, giving legitimacy to a great variety of events. There is much riding in carriages, parading, and ritual in British public life. In contrast, the Scandinavian and low country monarchies are more humdrum, and, because members of the royal families have occasionally been seen using the more humble means of transportation, the Scandinavian and low countries are sometimes called "bicycle monarchies." In recent decades scandals in the British royal family have lessened its prestige, and reduced its capacity to create a sense of cohesion and dignity.

Functions of the Executive

Political executives typically perform important system functions. The executive is the locus of leadership in the political system. Kemal Ataturks, Roosevelts, de Gaulles, Reagans, and Adenauers may hold the chief executive positions, and their energy, ideas, imagination, and images may provide stabilizing and adaptive capacity to the political system. Studies of childhood socialization show that the first political role perceived by children tends to be the top political executive—the president, prime minister, and king or queen. In early childhood the tendency is to identify the top political executive as a parent figure; as the child matures he or she begins to differentiate political from other roles, as well as to differentiate among various political roles (see Chapter 3). The conduct of the political executive affects the trust and confidence that young people feel in the whole political system and that they carry with them into adulthood. People who experienced Roosevelt, Churchill, de Gaulle, or Adenauer in their childhoods bring expectations into their adult political lives that are different from those of people who were children under Carter, Reagan, Clinton, or Thatcher, Major, Mitterand, or Kohl.

The role of the political executive in recruitment is obviously important. Presidents, prime ministers, and first secretaries have large and important appointive powers, not only of cabinet and politburo members and government ministers, but of judges as well. Typically, political executives are the source of honors and distinctions to members of the government and private citizens—they give distinguished service medals, knighthoods and peerages, and prizes of various kinds.

The political executive plays a central role in political communication, the top executive having the crucial one. Presidents' press conferences, prime ministers' speeches in parliament, cabinet members' testimony in committees, and the party leaders' speeches at the party congress may communicate important information about domestic and foreign policy. These high-level communications may be appeals for support or for improved performance in various sectors of the society and economy, or they may outline new policies.

The executive is of primary significance in the performance of the process functions. The executive may serve as an advocate of particular interests, as when a president supports the demands of minority groups or the business community or a prime minister supports the interests of pensioners or depressed regions. Cabinet members typically speak for particular interests, such as labor, business, agriculture, children, and minority groups. They may play a crucial role as interest aggregators as they seek to build coalitions favoring legislation.

Typically, the executive is the most important structure in policymaking. The executive normally initiates new policies and, depending on the division of powers between the executive and the legislature, has a substantial part in their adoption. The political executive also oversees the implementation of policies and can hold subordinate officials accountable for their performance. Whatever dynamism a political system has tends to be focused in the executive. The U.S. system is unique in the extent to which the legislative initiative is shared between the Congress and the executive. The central decisions in a foreign policy crisis are generally made by the top executive: the president (George Bush in the Gulf crisis, Bill Clinton in the Haitian and second Gulf crisis) or the prime minister (Margaret Thatcher in the Falklands crisis). In domestic policy, too, a bureaucracy without an effective executive tends to implement past policies, rather than to initiate new ones. Without the direction of politically motivated ministers, bureaucracies tend toward inertia and conservatism.

The decision of a president, prime minister, cabinet, or politburo to pursue a new course in foreign or domestic policy will usually be accompanied by structural adaptations—the appointment of a vigorous minister, an increase in staff, the establishment of a special cabinet committee, and the like. Where the political executive is weak and divided, as in Fourth Republic France or contemporary Italy, this dynamic force is missing. Initiative then passes to the bureaucracy, legislative committees, and powerful interest groups, and general needs, interests, and problems may be neglected.

In a separation-of-powers system when the presidency and the congress are controlled by different parties, even a strong president may be hampered in carrying out an effective policy. Although the executive consists of the cabinet heads for all the policy areas, its policy thrust will be reflected by its composition. New departures in foreign policy or welfare policy may be reflected in new appointments or rearrangements, and sometimes by the direct assumption of responsibility for a policy area by the chief political executive.

THE BUREAUCRACY

Modern societies are dominated by large organizations, and the largest organizations in these societies are the government *bureaucracies*. As governments have increased their efforts to improve the health, productivity, welfare, and security of their populations, the size of government organizations has increased over the years. But in recent decades there has been a movement to reduce government budgets, and downsize the bureaucracy.

Structure of the Bureaucracy

The most important officials in bureaucracies are the experienced and expert personnel of the top governmental service. Students of policymaking in Britain point out that the British "government" consists of approximately 100 "frontbench" members of Parliament, some 20 of whom serve in the Cabinet, with the remainder named as ministers, junior ministers, and parliamentary secretaries in charge of the government departments. This relatively small group of political policymakers confronts some 3,000 permanent *higher civil servants* largely recruited from the universities directly into the higher civil service. They spend their lives as an elite corps, moving about from ministry to ministry, watching governments come and go, and becoming increasingly important as policymakers as they rise into the top posts. The importance of the permanent higher civil service is not unique to Britain, though perhaps it has been most fully institutionalized there. In France, too, the higher civil service is filled with powerful generalists who can bring long tenure, experience, and technical knowledge to their particular areas. In the United States, many top positions go to presidential appointees rather than to permanent civil servants. Despite this difference and despite a greater emphasis on technical specialization, there are permanent civil servants in the key positions just below the top appointees in such agencies as the Internal Revenue Service, the Federal Bureau of Investigation, the Central Intelligence Agency, the National Institutes of Health, and all the cabinet departments. These people tend to be specialists, such as military officers, diplomats, doctors, scientists, economists, and engineers, and they exert great influence on the formulation and execution of policies in their specialties.

Bureaucracies may present special problems in revolution, and other periods of major social change. When the Bolsheviks originally took power in Russia in 1917, they had to depend on some of the military officers and officials of the Czarist regime until they could train their own. The secretariat of the Communist Party attempted to oversee their loyalty. In the 1990s with the dissolution of the Soviet Union and the disestablishment of the Communist parties in the successor countries, and in Eastern Europe, the resistance and inertia of the old bureaucracies have hampered the implementation of new policies.

Although bureaucracies are supposed to be politically and ideologically neutral agencies, in fact they are influenced by the dominant ideologies of the time and tend to have conservative propensities and institutional interests of their own.[17]

The Functions of the Bureaucracy

A functional analysis of the bureaucracy may suggest why this governmental organization has acquired such great significance in most contemporary societies. We have often stressed that most political functions are performed by more than one agency or organization. Thus policymaking is performed by the political executive, the assembly, even by the courts as in the American political system. But the bureaucracy is almost alone in carrying out its function—enforcement or implementation of laws, rules, and regulations. In a sense bureaucracies monopolize the output side of the political system. Occasionally, of course, policymakers "take the law into their own hands." The "plumbers unit" in the Nixon White House, the Colonel Oliver North operations in the Reagan White House, and their performance of what are normally policy, security, and other operational functions are examples of policymakers attempting directly to enter into implementation.

In addition to this near monopoly of enforcement, bureaucracies greatly influence the processes of policymaking. Most modern legislation is general and can be effectively enforced only if administrative officials work out regulations elaborating the policy. The extent to which a general policy is carried out usually depends on bureaucrats' interpretations of it and on the spirit and effectiveness with which they enforce it. Moreover, much of the adjudication in modern political systems is performed by administrative agencies with power to hold hearings and enforce regulations whether organized as independent regulatory bodies or as units in regular operating departments.

In Chapters 5 and 6 we discussed how bureaucratic agencies may serve as articulators and aggregators of interests. Departments like those for agriculture, labor, defense, welfare, and education may be among the most important voices of interest groups. And when an agriculture department obtains agreement on policy among different agricultural interest groups or a labor department draws together competing trade unions around some common policy, bureaucrats are performing a significant interest-aggregating function.

Finally, bureaucracies are involved in performing the communication function. News reporters are constantly knocking at the doors of top administrative officials in search of the latest information on all spheres of foreign and domestic policy. And with the increasing power of the media in modern societies top government executives are eager to get their versions of events into "prime time" television and popular talk shows. "Classification" of information—designating it as "secret" or "confidential," and so on—is largely disregarded by the modern media. What used to be viewed as improper "leaks" of information and intelligence, has become a veritable flood. The journalistic professions have developed strong investigative traditions which they justify on the basis of "a public right to know" which refuses to recognize any limits on the publication of private as well as political information. Thus, control over information no longer plays the role in the power of the political executive and the bureaucracy that it formerly played. Top administrators now must have more complex strategies and professional assistance in dealing with the media. The new art of "spin control" has replaced classification and "executive privilege" in the modern media world in a never-ending struggle for access, visibility, and impact, constantly evaluated by opinion polls.

The decisions made by political elites, whether executives or legislators, are based to a considerable extent on the information they obtain from the administrative side of government. Similarly, interest groups, political parties, the business elites, and the public depend on such information. In modern societies each day sees the publication by government agencies of important "indicators," "indices," "trends," or reports which resonate through the public and private sector, affecting the calculations and decisions of politicians, the value of money, the fluctuations in the securities markets, the production strategies and employment decisions of business firms, and the like.

Public exasperation with bureaucracy, its propensities for inefficiency and lack of responsiveness is one of the central themes of political discourse. It is reflected in the cynical "go ask City Hall" in the popular vernacular, in Aaron Wildavsky's book titled *Implementation: How Great Expectations in Washington Are Dashed in Oakland*,[18] and in Vice President Gore's project on "reinventing government." But if it is impossible to get along with bureaucracy it is also impossible to get along without it. Public policies, without bureaucratic implementation, are simply statements of intent enacted by the executive and the assembly. They allocate resources and designate responsibility for the realization of these goals. But realization depends on the bureaucracy. Policies may be lost in the thicket of bureaucratic misunderstanding or opposition. Creating and maintaining a responsive and responsible bureaucracy is one of the intractable problems of modern and modernizing society—capitalist or socialist, advanced or backward. It is a problem that can never be solved thoroughly, but only mitigated or kept under control by a variety of countervailing structures and influences.

Mark Nadel and Francis Rourke suggest the variety of ways that bureaucracies may be influenced and controlled externally or internally, through government and societal agencies and forces (see Table 7.4).[19] The major external government control is, as we have suggested, the political executive. Although presidents, prime ministers, and ministers formally command subordinate officials and have the power to remove them for nonperformance of duty, there is actually mutual dependence and reciprocal control between executives and bureaucracies. The power of the executive is typically expressed in efforts at persuasion; rarely does it take the extreme form of dismissal or transfer. Centralized budgeting and administrative reorganization are other means by which the executive controls bureaucracy. The reallocation of resources among administrative agencies and changing lines of authority may bring bureaucratic implementation into greater conformity with the aims of the political executive.

Assemblies and courts also exercise significant external controls over the bureaucracy. Committee investigations, questions put to administrative agencies by assembly members, judicial processes controlling administrative excesses—all may

Table 7.4   TYPOLOGOY OF CONTROLS FOR BUREAUCRATIC RESPONSIBILITY

Formal	Informal
External	
Directly or indirectly elected chief executive: president, prime minister, governor, etc.	Public opinion
	Press
Elected assembly: congress, parliament, city council, etc.	Public interest groups
	Constituencies
Courts	Competing bureaucratic organizations
Ombudsman	
Internal	
Representative bureaucracy where legally required	Perception of public opinion (anticipated reaction)
Citizen participation where legally required	Professional standards
Decentralization	Socialization in the norms of responsibility

Source: Taken from Mark V. Nadel and Frances E. Rourke, "Bureaucracies," in Fred I. Greenstein and Nelson W. Polsby, eds., *Handbook of Political Science*, vol. 5. (Reading, MA: Addison-Wesley, 1975), p. 418. Reprinted with permission.

have some effect on bureaucratic performance. The invention and rapid diffusion from Sweden of the institution of the *ombudsman* is another indication of the problem of controlling the bureaucracy from the perspective of injury or injustice to individuals.[20] In the Scandinavian countries, Britain, Germany, and elsewhere the ombudsman investigates claims of injury or of damage to individuals as the result of government action, offering a procedure more expeditious and less costly than court action. Ombudsmen report to the legislative body for remedial action.

Among the extragovernmental forces and agencies that attempt to control bureaucracies are public opinion and the mass media, interest groups of various kinds, particularly public interest groups like "Nader's Raiders," and affirmative-action groups watchful over the interests of minorities and women.

Bureaucratic responsiveness and responsibility are affected by internal controls, such as advisory committees composed of members of the various political parties, and of different interest groups, appointed to oversee the impartiality of bureaucratic performance. Another way of controlling bureaucracy is to decentralize it, thereby bringing agencies closer to the groups they are affecting.

Finally, the attitudes and values of the bureaucrats themselves affect their responsiveness and responsibility. There are different bureaucratic "cultures." The permanent secretaries of the British civil service have been vividly caricatured in the popular BBC series, *Yes, Minister.* The norms and values that bureaucrats bring with them as they are recruited into public service, and the standards and obligations they are taught to respect within public service, have an important bearing on bureaucratic performance.

The variety and kinds of controls we have been discussing operate in the advanced industrial democracies. Authoritarian systems lack many of these controls, particularly the external ones of elected political executives and legislators, independent courts, mass media, and interest groups. Authoritarian systems are particularly prone to bureaucratic inefficiency and conservatism in the absence of free and competitive elections, autonomous interest groups, and a free press. And in most nonindustrial countries the agents of control are not well developed, the proportion of participants among the population is low, and lower-level government employees are poorly trained and poorly paid—all conditions that encourage bribery and extortion as a frequent mode of interaction between citizens and public officials whether the system is authoritarian or not.[21]

"Bureaucracy," in the sense of inefficiency and inertia, is pandemic. It is truly a dilemma because we are unlikely to invent any schemes for carrying out large-scale social tasks without the organization, division of labor, and professionalism that bureaucracy provides. Its pathologies can only be mitigated. The art of modern political leadership consists not only in the prudent search for appropriate goals and policies, but also in the attempt to learn how to interact with the massive and complex bureaucracy—how and when to press and coerce it, reshuffle it, terminate its redundant and obsolete parts, flatter and reward it, teach it, and be taught by it.

KEY TERMS

assemblies	higher civil service
authoritarian regime	individual executive
bicameralism	judicial review
bureaucracy	mixed parliamentary-presidential
ceremonial executive	regime
civil service	ombudsman
collective executive	parliamentary regime
confederal systems	political executive
constitutional council	presidential-parliamentary regime
constitutional regime	policymaking
decision rules	senates
democratic presidential regime	separation of powers
effective executive	unitary systems
federal systems	

END NOTES

1. Peter Evans, Jurgen Rueschemeyer, and Theda Skocpol, *Bringing the State Back In* (Cambridge: Univ. of Cambridge Press, 1985); Alfred Stepan, *State and Society: Peru in Comparative Perspective* (Princeton, NJ: Princeton Univ. Press, 1978); Eric Nordlinger, *On the Autonomy of the Democratic State* (Cambridge, MA: Harvard Univ. Press, 1981).

2. James G. March and Johann P. Olsen, *Rediscovering Institutions: The Organizational Basis of Politics* (New York: Free Press, 1989), pp. 171–72.

3. Giovanni Sartori, *Comparative Constitutional Engineering* (New York: New York Univ. Press, forthcoming).

4. John Locke, *Two Treatises of Government* ed. Peter Laslett (Cambridge: Cambridge Univ. Press, 1960); Charles de Secondat, Baron de Montesquieu, *The Spirit of the Laws* (London, Hafner, 1960).

5. *The Federalist: A Commentary on the Constitution of the United States* (Washington, DC: National Home Library Foundation, 1937).

6. Arend Lijphart, "Typologies of Democratic Systems," Institute of International Studies, University of California, Berkeley, CA Reprint No 298, 1968 and "Consociational Democracy," *World Politics* 1969, 21:2, 207–25.

7. Philippe Schmitter and Gerhard Lehmbruch, *Trends Toward Corporatist Intermediation* (Beverly Hills, CA: Sage, 1979).

8. Juan Linz and Arturo Valenzuela, eds., *The Failure of Presidential Democracy: Comparative Perspectives* (Baltimore: Johns Hopkins Univ. Press, 1994).

9. Matthew Shugart and John Carey, *Presidents and Assemblies: Constitutional Design, and Electoral Dynamics* (Cambridge: Cambridge Univ. Press, 1992); Donald Horowitz, "Comparing Democratic Systems," in *The Global Resurgence of Democracy* ed. Diamond and Plattner (Baltimore: Johns Hopkins Univ. Press, 1993), pp. 127 ff.

10. Personal communication from John Carey, Nov. 8, 1994.

11. On amending rules in constitutions, see Ivo Duchachek, *Power Maps; Comparative Politics of Constitutions* (Santa Barbara, CA: ABC Clio Press, 1973), pp. 210 ff.

12. Arend Lijphart, *Democracies: Patterns of Majoritarian and Consensus Government in Twenty-One Countries* (New Haven, CT: Yale Univ. Press), Chs. 1 and 2. G. Bingham Powell *Contemporary Democracies* (Cambridge, MA: Harvard Univ. Press, 1982), pp. 212 ff. anticipates some of Lijphart's arguments. Robert Dahl *Democracy and Its Critics* (New Haven, CT: Yale Univ. Press, 1989), particularly Ch. 11, reviews and evaluates Lijphart's classification.

13. On the functions of assemblies, see Robert Packenham, "Legislatures in Political Development," in *Legislatures in Developmental Perspective*, ed. Arthur Kornberg and L. D. Musolf (Durham, NC: Duke Univ. Press, 1979); Jean Blondel, *Comparative Legislatures* (Englewood Cliffs, NJ: Prentice-Hall, 1973); Gerhard Loewenberg and Samuel Patterson, *Comparing Legislatures* (Boston: Little, Brown, 1979); Michael Mezey, *Comparative Legislatures* (Durham, NC: Duke Univ. Press, 1979); Philip Norton, "Parliaments: A Framework for Analysis" and "Legislatures in Comparative Perspective," *West European Studies*, July 1990, pp. 1–9, 143–55.

14. See Philip Norton, "Parliament."

15. Kaare Strom, *Minority Government and Majority Rule* (Cambridge: Cambridge Univ. Press, 1990), pp. 43–44

16. For detailed information about the organization and recruitment of the modern political executive, see Jean Blondel, *World Leaders: Heads of Government in the Post-War Period* (Beverly Hills, CA: Sage, 1982); Jean Blondel, *Government Ministers in the Contemporary World* (Beverly Hills, CA: Sage, 1985).

17. See Joel Aberbach, Robert D. Putnam, and Bert A. Rockman, *Bureaucrats and Politicians in Western Democracies* (Cambridge, MA: Harvard Univ. Press, 1981).

18. Jeffrey Pressman and Aaron Wildavsky, *Implementation* (Berkeley, CA: Univ. of California Press, 1973).

19. Mark V. Nadel and Francis E. Rourke, "Bureaucracies" in *Handbook of Political Science*, Vol. 5, eds. Fred Greenstein and Nelson Polsby (Reading, MA: Addison Wesley, 1975), pp. 373–440.

20. See Frank Stacey, *The British Ombudsman* (Oxford: Clarendon Press, 1971); Roy Gregory and Peter Hutchesson, *The Parliamentary Ombudsman; A Study in the Control of Administrative Action* (London: Allen and Unwin, 1975).
21. On the difficulties involved in reducing administrative corruption in developing countries, see Robert Klitgard, *Controlling Corruption* (Berkeley, CA: Univ. of California Press, 1989).

SUGGESTED READINGS

Aberbach, Joel, Robert Putnam, and Bert Rockman. *Bureaucrats and Politicians in Western Democracies.* Cambridge, Mass.: Harvard University Press, 1981.

Dahl, Robert A., *Polyarchy; Participation and Opposition.* New Haven, Conn.: Yale University Press, 1971.

Evans, Peter, Jurgen Rueschemeyer, and Theda Skocpol. *Bringing The State Back In.* Cambridge: University of Cambridge Press, 1985.

Linz, Juan, and Arturo Valenzuela, Eds. *The Failure of Presidential Democracy; Comparative Perspectives.* Baltimore: Johns Hopkins Press, 1994.

Lijphart, Arend. *Democracies: Patterns of Majoritarian and Consensus Government in Twenty One Countries.* New Haven, Conn.: Yale University Press, 1989.

March, James G., and Johann P. Olsen. *Rediscovering Institutions; the Organizational Basis of Politics.* New York: The Free Press, 1989.

North, Douglass. *Institutions, Institutional Change and Economic Performance.* Cambridge: Univerity of Cambridge Press, 1990.

O'Donnell, Guillermo, and Philippe Schmitter. *Transitions from Authoritarian Rule.* Baltimore, Md.: Johns Hopkins Univerity Press, 1986.

Powell, G. Bingham. *Contemporary Democracies.* Cambridge, Mass.: Harvard University Press, 1982.

Sartori, Giovanni. *Comparative Constitutional Engineering.* New York: New York University Press, 1995.

Secondat, Charles de, Baron de Montesquieu. *The Spirit of Laws.* London: Hafner, 1960.

Schmitter, Philippe, and Gerhard Lehmbruch. *Trends Toward Corporatist Intermediation.* Beverly Hills, CA: Sage Publications, 1979.

Shugart, Matthew, and John Carey. *Presidents and Assemblies: Constitutional Design and Electoral Dynamics.* Cambridge: Cambridge University Press, 1992.

Strom, Kaare. *Minority Government and Majority Rule.* Cambridge: Cambridge University Press, 1990.

Weaver, Kent, and Bert Rockman, Eds. *Do Institutions Matter? Government Capabilities in The United States and Abroad.* Washington D. C.: The Brookings Institution, 1993.

Chapter
8

Public Policy

I n the past century Western nations have been transformed from authoritarian, or oligarchic regimes with limited suffrage, to democracies. The power of the state has increasingly been used to meet popular needs and demands. The last century of political development in the West has produced *welfare states* with programs of social insurance, health, public education, and the like. As the level of expenditures has grown to between one-third and one-half of the national product in most industrialized democratic countries, a number of problems have arisen. In some countries the increasing cost of the welfare state in taxes has produced a backlash or tax rebellion in efforts to prevent further increases in programs and to roll back those already in effect. The size of the government budget and its effects on savings, investment, inflation, and employment have been the central issue in the politics of advanced industrial societies in recent years. Thus, the simple relationship between democratization and welfare broadly defined, characteristic of the earlier decades of the twentieth century has given way to a more problematic situation.

The study of *public policy* has become a growth industry in the social sciences. Among the interesting themes being explored in this growing field of study are the varieties of welfare states and their causes. The United States is an example of a welfare pattern that stresses equality of opportunity through public education. In contrast, on the European continent, social security and health programs have taken precedence over educational programs.[1] The crisis of the welfare state has provoked a conservative reaction that stresses setting limits on public expenditures and labor costs.[2] An alternative corporatist approach, which has had some success in small European countries, involves regular bargaining relationships among labor, business, and government over issues of wage, price, and investment policies.[3] The data we present in this chapter are intended to provide background for understanding these and other contemporary controversies over public policy. We will compare in general the policy performance of countries with differing characteristics in different parts of the world.

The public policies of nations may be summarized and compared according to *outputs* (see Chapter 2) that is, the kinds of actions governments take in order to accomplish their purposes. We can classify these actions or outputs under four headings. First we have the *extraction* of resources—money, goods, persons, and services—from the domestic and international environments. Second there is *distributive* activity—what money, goods, and services are distributed, and to whom? Third there is the *regulation* of human behavior—the use of compulsion and inducement to enforce extractive and distributive compliance or otherwise bring about desired behavior. Last, we speak of *symbolic performance*—the political speeches, holidays, rites, public monuments and statues, and the like—used by governments to exhort citizens to desired forms of conduct, to provide inspiring examples, to edify the population, and to socialize the young.

EXTRACTIVE PERFORMANCE

All political systems, even the simplest, extract resources from their environments. When simple societies go to war, specific age groups may be called on to fight. Such direct extraction of services is still found in the most complex of modern states, in the form of military duty, other obligatory public service like jury duty, or compulsory labor imposed on those convicted of crime. The most common forms of resource extraction in contemporary nations are taxation and borrowing. *Taxation* is the extraction of money or goods from members of a political system for governmental purposes, in consideration for which they receive no immediate or direct benefit. Figure 8.1 shows the *central government revenues*—revenue extracted by the central government—as a percentage of the *gross national product (GNP)*, defined as the total value of goods and services produced by a country's residents in a year, for most of the nations included in this book. Data are not available for China, the Russian Federation, and Nigeria. We include data on Hungary as representative of patterns of extraction in the former Communist countries, recognizing that this is a very rough approximation.

Hungarian central government revenues as a proportion of the GNP were the largest for our selection of countries. The state extracted 55.6 percent of the GNP from its economy in 1992, down slightly from the 58.2 percent of the GNP it took in 1988, the last full year of the Communist regime. It is of interest that the size of government revenue in some countries of the advanced capitalist world is not radically smaller than that of Hungary and other Eastern European countries when they were under Communist control. Not included in Figure 8.1, Norway as of 1992 extracted more than 47 percent of its GNP, and the Netherlands more than 49 percent. In Figure 8.1 France and the United Kingdom among the advanced industrial societies are shown to extract revenue at around the 40 percent level of GNP, while the United States and Japan are under 20 percent.

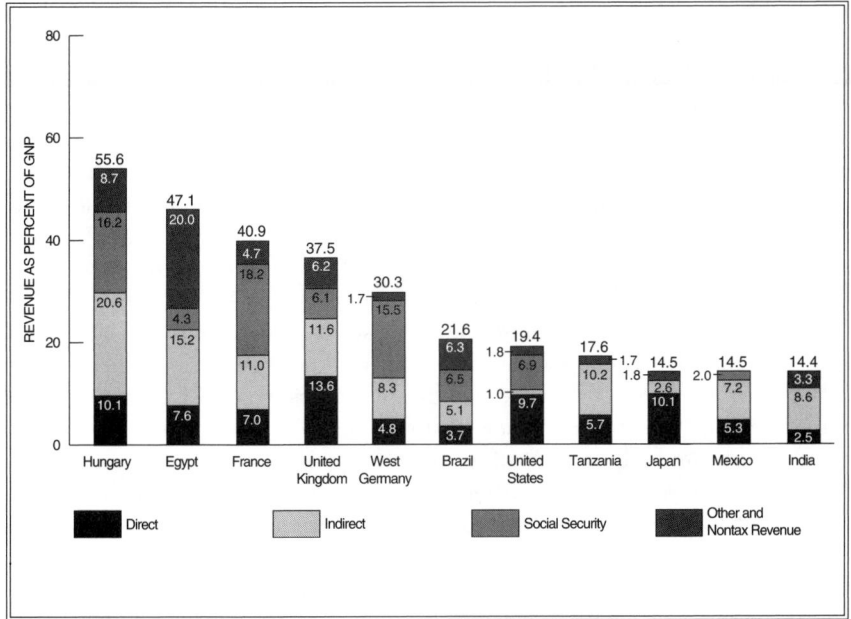

Figure 8.1 Central government revenue as a percent of GNP and by source of revenue. (*Source:* Adapted from World Bank *World Development Report*, New York: Oxford University Press, 1994, Table 11, pp. 152–53. (Data are for 1992, except in the cases of Egypt, Mexico, and Tanzania when they are for 1980.))

We should observe that Figure 8.1 reports central government revenues only. In such federal systems as the United States and Germany we would have to add the state and local revenues to the central revenues to get an accurate picture of the extractive burden borne by these countries. A substantial proportion of government revenue in the United States is collected by states and localities. The total for all revenues for the United States would run to more than 30 percent. Similarly for Germany, the states (called *länder*) and municipalities collect substantial amounts of revenue, which would raise the total to more than 40 percent. Japan's extraordinarily low central government revenue at 14.5 percent in 1992 strikes the eye. Factors contributing to Japan's ability to keep extraction low include a very small defense budget and limited government participation in welfare programs (although the difference between Japan and other industrialized countries has greatly decreased recently), as well as reliance in recent years on deficit financing through the sale of government bonds to financial institutions.[4]

Outside the European–North American area the size of central government revenue rarely exceeds 20 percent. Egypt, with its substantial public sector, is an exception. The figure for 1980 was 47.1 percent of GNP. Much of this was in the form of revenue from publicly owned and operated enterprises and foreign aid. The central government revenue of Mexico is under 15 percent, as is that of India.

Figure 8.1 also reports the sources of revenue as proportions of GNP for each country. Sources of revenue are important because they determine who pays how much of the taxes. Personal and corporate income taxes and taxes on capital gains and wealth are called *direct taxes*, in that they are directly levied on persons and corporations. They tend to be *progressive* in character, that is, the tax rates are higher for richer than for poorer citizens. *Indirect taxes* such as sales and value added taxes, excise taxes, and customs duties are levied on transactions or services, and their welfare distributive effects depend on who purchases the commodities and services. General sales taxes or value added taxes that affect necessities such as food and clothing are *regressive*, that is, those who are less able to afford them share an equal burden with those who can. But direct taxes on luxury goods may not be regressive, since the poor rarely purchase them. Social security contributions often are regressive because they are usually paid disproportionately by the less economically advantaged, although this need not be the case. Also, it may be argued that in many countries, the poor are the principal recipients of the sums thus raised. In 1988 Hungary received almost half of its revenue in indirect taxes— taxes on turnover in the process of manufacture, sales, excises, and customs duties. Nine percent of its GNP was extracted in direct taxes primarily on income, and 14 percent was taken in transfers from firms and employees for social services. By 1992, as Hungary's transition to a market system took off, the share of revenue from indirect taxes had declined a bit, while direct and social security taxes had increased somewhat. As former Communist regimes move toward capitalist economies, we observe their tendency to adopt the extractive patterns common to that system.

In Germany and the United Kingdom most of the revenue comes from social security and income taxes, but Germany relies far more heavily on social security payments and Britain more on income taxes. India, Mexico, and Tanzania receive most of their revenue from indirect taxes.

The composition of the revenues of nations is quite complex, depending on the kinds of taxes imposed, the distribution of income and wealth, the consumption patterns of different strata of the population, and deliberate government efforts at distributive equity. Heidenheimer, Heclo, and Adams classify the tax systems of the *Organization for Economic Cooperation and Development (OECD)* countries into three categories. The OECD includes some 26 free-market economies, primarily in Europe and North America. They divide these countries first into heavy social security tax systems including Germany, Austria, the Netherlands, France, and Italy, which receive one-third to one-half of their revenue from social security, which is imposed more or less equally on both employers and employees. In the second category, the United States and Japan are farthest below average in total tax burden, and they rely heavily on direct taxes rather than on sales and consumption taxes. Finally, countries such as Sweden and Norway impose the highest tax burdens of all the OECD countries, and they rely on all three types of taxation—direct, indirect, and social security payments. Both countries impose the greatest burden of social security payments on the employers, with Sweden levying the entire social security tax on employers and Norway taking three-quarters of it from these sources.[5]

Tax rates have been decreasing in all Western countries in the last decade, and there has been a shift from the more visible direct income taxes to less visible indirect consumption taxes and a sharp decrease in higher income tax rates. From 1975 to 1990 British top marginal rates declined by 43 percent, the U.S. rates by 42 percent, Swedish by 35 percent, and Japanese by 25 percent. The average decline in top tax rates for all OECD countries in the last 15 years has been 18 percent.[6] These trends in revenue policy have been associated with the spread of economic views which stress the importance of entrepreneurial incentives for productivity. This change in patterns of taxation is increasing income inequality in the advanced industrial countries.

DISTRIBUTIVE PERFORMANCE

The *distributive performance* of the political system is the allocation by governmental agencies of various kinds of money, goods, services, honors, and opportunities to individuals and groups in the society. It can be measured and compared according to the quantity of whatever is distributed, the areas of human life touched by these benefits, the sections of the population receiving these benefits, and the relationship between human needs and governmental distributions intended to meet these needs. Government expenditures do not measure all these distributions, but they give us a quantitative measure of this distributive effort. Although these figures are drawn from a variety of sources especially from data released by the governments, and their accuracy cannot be guaranteed, they are rough indicators of the countries' efforts.

Figure 8.2 reports *central governmental expenditures* as a percentage of the GNP, and as proportions of total expenditures for defense, welfare, and other purposes, for most of the countries included in this book. Data were not available for Japan, Russia, China, and Nigeria. Since data were available for Hungary, that country was included in order to have at least one country from the former Soviet bloc, and Tanzania was substituted for Nigeria.

As we glance across the figure, it is clear that the level of central government expenditures varies substantially from country to country—depending primarily on level of economic development. Central government expenditure accounts for more than 54 percent of Hungary's GNP; but it is notable that Egypt has a public sector almost as large proportionally as Hungary. France and England approach 40 percent, and the United States, if we were to add in state and local expenditures, would rise to more than 30 percent. Germany, with high Lander expenditures, would reach 40 percent.

The height of the bar for each country represents the proportion of central government expenditures of total gross national product; and the length of each segment of the bar represents the proportion of the GNP spent by the central government on defense, welfare, and other purposes. The neutral shaded part of the bars represents defense expenditures, the lighter shaded segment represents expenditures on education, health and welfare added together, and the dark shaded part of the bar represents other expenditures such as those associated with economic enterprises operated by the state, expenditures to foster domestic business, interest payments on the public debt, and expenditures on public services of one kind or another. The United States is by far the heaviest spender in the military field, with over one-fifth of total expenditure spent on defense, as compared with about one-tenth for the British and the Egyptians.

The developed countries listed in Figure 8.2—France, Germany, England, and the United States—all allocate from one-half to two-thirds of their central government expenditures to education, health, and welfare. France, Germany and Britain allocate more than two-thirds of their expenditures, while the United States allocates just under one-half of its state and local education expenditures to these purposes. Among Third World countries, India allocates the smallest proportion of its expenditures to education, health and welfare.

The "other" category accounts for from one-half to two-thirds of the expenditures of Third World countries, and from a fifth to one-third of the budgets of developed countries. This category includes expenditures on the public debt, a significant amount in the budgets of all of our countries, developed and developing. It also reflects the large state enterprise components in such economies as those of Brazil, Hungary, India, and Tanzania.

Table 8.1 provides a somewhat more vivid impression of the impact of government expenditures on the economies and societies of the 12 selected countries included in our book. Expenditures are reported as percentages of GNP and in

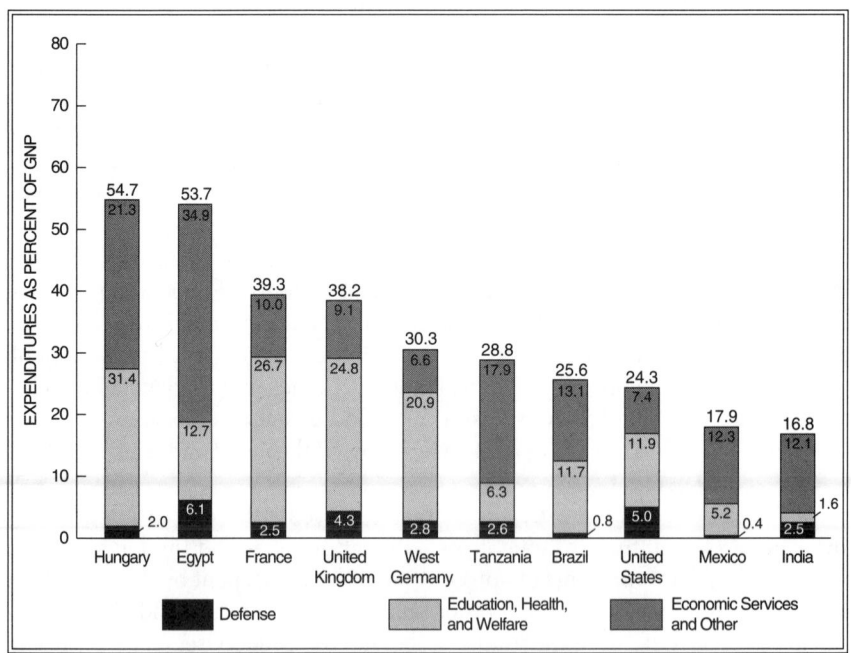

Figure 8.2 Central government expenditures as a percentage of GNP for selected nations. (Data are for 1992, except in the cases of Egypt, Mexico, and Tanzania when they are for 1980.) (*Source:* Adapted from World Bank, *World Development Report, 1994* New York: Oxford University Press, 1994, Table 10, pp. 180–81.)

Table 8.1 EXPENDITURES ON MILITARY, EDUCATION AND HEALTH FOR SELECTED NATIONS 1980–1990 AS PERCENTAGE OF GNP AND IN U.S. DOLLARS PER CAPITA

	GNP Per Capita ($)	Military		Education		Health	
		Percent GNP	Amount Per Capita ($)	Percent GNP	Amount Per Capita ($)	Percent GNP	Amount Per Capita ($)
Brazil	$1,837	1.7%	$32	3.5%	$64	2.5%	$48
China	$317	3.5%	$11	2.5%	$8	1.3%	$4
Egypt	$675	5.1%	$34	6.0%	$40	1.1%	$7
France	$17,317	3.6%	$622	5.4%	$942	6.6%	$1,140
Germany	$17,419	3.0%	$520	4.1%	$714	5.5%	$959
India	$360	3.1%	$11	3.1%	$11	1.0%	$3
Japan	$23,053	1.0%	$224	4.8%	$1,107	4.8%	$1,101
Mexico	$1,719	0.4%	$7	4.1%	$71	0.4%	$6
Nigeria	$269	0.8%	$2	1.5%	$2	0.2%	$1
Former USSR	$2,981	8.7%	$260	5.6%	$166	3.0%	$89
United Kingdom	$12,797	4.0%	$509	3.6%	$601	5.2%	$663
United States	$19,492	5.6%	$1,097	5.6%	$1,095	5.2%	$1,012

Source: These data are taken from Ruth Seger Sivard, *World Military and Social Expenditures, 1993* (Washington, DC: World Priorities, 1993). Sources cited by Sivard include *The World Bank World Development Report, World Development Indicators*, and publications of the International Monetary Fund (IMF), the Arms Control and Disarmament Agency (ACDA), the U.S. Agency for International Development (USAID), the UN Food and Agriculture Organization (FAO), the UNESCO *Statistical Yearbook*, all for various years.

U.S. dollars per capita. A country such as Nigeria seems hardly to touch its people. It spends only $2 per capita on education, and $1 on health; India spends $11 per capita on education, and $3 on health. At the other end the United States spends more than $1,000 each, on defense, education, and health. France and Japan are not far behind the United States in education and health, and Germany and the United Kingdom follow in order. Japan, while equal to the Western countries in education and health (actually Japan is highest of all in education expenditures per capita), is very much on the bottom in defense expenditures. It is a bitter irony that the countries that "need" it the most have the least to spend for education and health. But we ought not conclude that there is a one-to-one relation between expenditures for education and health and the knowledge, skills, and bodily well-being of the people of these countries. Just as our measures of GNP fail to include the subsistence productivity of households, our measures of educational and health expenditures do not include self improvement, and the different and less costly kinds of health care such as those provided in China (for a critique of the GNP index see Chapter 2).

Our tables show the tragic quandary for low-income countries: While they are confronted with the urgent challenge of upgrading the skills and improving the vitality and performance of their work forces, their resources in education and health are insufficient to make rapid headway. The striking differences in these rankings and in the economic and governmental performance which they reflect are not reported in the mood of winners or losers in a contest, but rather to emphasize the great differences in the conditions of material life that prevail in the world today.

Levels of expenditure on national security, particularly among less developed countries, vary with the condition of the international environment. Nations locked in tense international confrontations as in the Middle East, or undertaking efforts at widespread influence, make extraordinary defense efforts, even at the cost of the education and health of their inhabitants.

In his study comparing the welfare efforts of some 64 countries representing different regions and developmental levels and historical patterns, Harold Wilensky confirms our point that poor nations, with their limited budgets and many demands, cannot easily spare the resources for these programs.[7] In both absolute and relative terms expenditure on social security in poor nations tends to be limited. But he makes the point that in these societies the aged, the infirm, and the elderly receive some care through the extended family. There is in most Third World societies a traditional version of a welfare safety net.

All the wealthier nations make efforts to assist the aged, the disabled, and the unemployed; however, differences in expenditures reflect policy and historical experience. The United States made a much greater effort, and much earlier, in mass education than did most European nations; on the other hand, Americans began spending on social insurance and public services much later, and still do less in this area. Americans have historically put much more emphasis on equality of opportunity and less on welfare obligations than Europeans. Wilensky also found that centralized governments, well-organized working-class parties and movements, and low military expenditures were all associated with stronger efforts in welfare.

Prior to the watershed year of 1989, the Soviet Union, and the Communist countries of Eastern Europe spent less on education, health, and welfare than the welfare democracies of Western Europe. In addition, in the last decades their growth rates fell substantially behind. It is easy in retrospect, to see how confidence in the future of socialism dissipated in these countries even within the inner circles of the Communist parties.[8] It is impossible to predict the rates and patterns of change among the successor countries of the former Communist bloc, but in all of these countries we observe the emergence of larger private economic sectors. As they succeed in introducing market economies we may anticipate that levels and objects of government revenue and expenditure will become more similar to Western patterns.

REGULATIVE PERFORMANCE

Regulative performance is the exercise of control by a political system over the behavior of individuals and groups in the society. Although we usually associate regulation with legal coercion or its threat, political systems commonly control behavior by material or financial inducements and by exhortation as well.

The *regulative policies,* or activities, of modern political systems have proliferated enormously over the last century or so. Industrialization and urban concentration have produced interdependence and problems in traffic, health, and public order. Growth in industry has created problems with monopolies, industrial safety, labor exploitation, and pollution. At the same time, the growth of science and the development of the attitude that humanity can harness and control nature have led to increased resort to governmental action.

Recent history has been particularly marked by the proliferation of regulatory activities. The pattern of regulation varies not only with the broad socioeconomic and cultural changes associated with industrialization and urbanization, but also with changes in cultural values. Thus, in recent years regulation in the United States has extended to include protection of voting rights, correction of racial segregation, prohibition of discrimination against minority groups and women in employment, control of pollution, and the like. At the same time, in most modern nations regulation of birth control, abortion, divorce, and sexual conduct has lessened.

In characterizing the regulative performance of a political system, we answer these questions:

1. What aspects of human behavior and interaction are regulated and to what degree? Does the government regulate such domains as family relations, economic activity, religious activity, political activity, geographic mobility, professional and occupational qualifications, and protection of person and property?
2. What sanctions are used to compel or induce citizens to comply? Does the government use exhortation and moral persuasion, financial rewards and penalties, licensing of some types of action, physical confinement or punishment, and direction of various activities?

3. What groups in the society are regulated, with what procedural limitations on enforcement and what protections for rights? Are there rights of appeal? Are these sanctions applied uniformly, or do they affect different areas or groups differently?

All modern nations use sanctions of these various kinds in varying degrees. But the variety of patterns is great and reflects different values, goals, and strategies. Governments have taken over various industries in many nations, but the range is very different. In recent decades, one study shows, governments in the United States employed only 1 percent of the persons engaged in mining and manufacturing and 28 percent of those working for public utilities supplying gas, water, and electrical power; in France, the corresponding figures were 8 percent and 71 percent.

Although we must treat the critical area of regulative performance briefly, one more aspect must be emphasized: government control over political participation and communication. We saw in earlier chapters that the presence or absence of political competition was a defining characteristic of political systems. Countries vary all the way from authoritarian ones that prohibit party organization, the formation of voluntary associations, and freedom of communication, to democratic ones, where such rights are protected. Government regulatory performance in this area has a crucial effect on political processes.

Table 8.2 shows the political rights and civil liberties ratings for the countries included in this book. Political rights refer to the opportunities people have to participate in the choice of political leaders—voting rights, the right to run for office, and the like. Civil liberties refer to the protection of substantive areas of human behavior, such as freedom of speech, press, assembly, and religion, as well as procedural protections, such as those of trial by jury and against arbitrary and cruel governmental action. Those countries receiving rankings of 7 in the second column of Table 8.2 are assumed to exercise comprehensive control over the communications media and to set no limits on government regulatory activity vis-à-vis the individual. The rankings made by Freedom House, *Comparative Survey of Freedom* are based on the judgments of a number of expert referees. There is an important correspondence between rankings for political and civil rights. No country that scores high on participatory rights is very low on civil liberties, and no country low on participatory rights is high on civil liberties, suggesting that there is a strong relationship between popular participation and the rule of law and equitable procedure.

The democratic industrial countries all have ratings of 1 or 2 for both political and civil rights. At the other extreme are China, Egypt, and Nigeria which come out high on suppression of political rights and civil liberties. Brazil, Mexico, and Russia were rated in the middle, tolerating but limiting political competition, and providing some protection of civil liberties. These rankings, of course, vary over time. Nigeria's ratings rose and fell over the decades as military regimes replaced civilian ones. Ratings for the United States have improved since the civil rights movement of the 1960s.

In a cross-national study of governmental repression which analyzed the behavior of 153 countries during the 1980s, Steven C. Poe and C. Neal Tate con-

Table 8.2   POLITICAL RIGHTS AND LIBERTIES RATING FOR SELECTED COUNTRIES, 1994

	Political Rights	Civil Rights
Brazil	3	4
China	7	7
Egypt	6	6
France	1	2
Germany	1	2
India	4	4
Japan	2	2
Mexico	4	4
Nigeria	7	5
Russia	3	4
United Kingdom	1	2
United States	1	1

Source: Freedom House, *The Comparative Survey of Freedom, 1994, Freedom Review,* January–February 1994, pp. 14 ff. These annual ratings of political rights and civil liberties have been administered by Freedom House in one form or another since 1955. In recent years they have been conducted by an experienced staff and knowledgeable consultants from the various regions of the world.

cluded that the major variables explaining positive civil and political rights records among nations were democratic political institutions and conditions of peace and social order. Authoritarian nations and those involved in internal or international war were the most frequent civil rights violators. Other variables such as level of economic development had some limited explanatory power.[9]

Lest the impression be given that regulation is only negative in value, as in the suppression of rights, we should be reminded that our civilization and our amenities are dependent on governmental regulation. Such matters as safety of persons and property, prevention of environmental pollution, provision of adequate sanitation, safe disposal of toxic wastes, maintenance of occupational safety, and equal access to housing and education are commonly covered by governmental regulation and implementation. The revolt against overregulation in the last decades should not be permitted to obscure this fundamental point.[10]

SYMBOLIC PERFORMANCE

A fourth category of political system outputs is *symbolic performance.* Much communication by political leaders takes the form of appeals to history, courage, boldness, wisdom, and magnanimity embodied in the nation's past; or appeals to values and ideologies, such as equality, liberty, community, democracy, communism, liberalism, religious tradition, or promises of future accomplishment and rewards. Political systems differ in citizens' confidence in their leaders and faith in their political symbols. Symbolic outputs are also intended, however, to enhance other aspects of performance: to make people pay their taxes more readily and honestly, comply with the law more faithfully, or accept sacrifice, danger, and hardship. Such appeals may be especially important in times of crisis. Some of the most magnificent examples are the speeches of Pericles in the Athenian Assembly during the Peloponnesian War or those of Franklin Delano Roosevelt in the depths of the Great Depression, or Winston Churchill during the dangerous moments when Britain stood alone after the fall of France in World War II. But symbolic performance is also important in less extreme circumstances. Political leaders seek to influence citizens' behavior in energy crises or in times of drought, famine, and disaster. "Jawboning"—exhorting business executives and labor leaders to go slow in raising prices and wages—is a frequently employed anti-inflation measure. Public buildings, plazas, monuments, holidays with their parades, and civic and patriotic indoctrination in schools all attempt to contribute to the population's sense of governmental legitimacy and its willingness to comply with public policy.

OUTCOMES OF POLITICAL PERFORMANCE

Our comparisons of the levels and composition of taxation, governmental expenditures, and regulation in different countries do not tell us how these measures really affect welfare and order. The functioning of the economy and the social order as well as international events may frustrate the purpose of political leaders. Thus, a tax rebate to increase consumption and stimulate the economy may be nullified by a rise in the price of oil. Increases in health expenditures may have no effect because of rising health costs, or health services may be so distributed as not to reach those most in need. Consequently we have to look into the actual welfare *outcomes* as well as governmental policies and implementation, in order to estimate the effectiveness of public policy.

DOMESTIC WELFARE OUTCOMES

In Table 8.3 we compare our selection of countries on a number of welfare and health indicators. The first two columns of Table 8.3 report measures of economic well-being—GNP per capita, and GNP growth rate in 1980–92. In column 3 we give the fertility rate, from which we can forecast the degree to which the growth rate really measures per capita improvement, or fails to keep up with population increase. The assumption is that a fertility rate of 2.1 results in a steady-state population, replacing both parents with a bit left over for mortality. Anything over that rate results in population increase, and reduces the impact of the absolute growth rate. Column 4, population per physician, is a measure of health care availability in terms of level of economic development. Columns 5, 6, 7, and 8, show the connections between level of economic development and the incidence of morbidity and mortality in the population. Table 8.4 tells us about infrastructural aspects of welfare, the relationship between such material conditions as the availability of electricity, telephones, roads, and safe water supplies, and level of economic development. Finally in Table 8.5 we compare countries at various levels of economic

Table 8.3   WELFARE OUTCOMES IN SELECTED COUNTRIES (1990–92)

	GNP per Capita (U.S. $)	Average Annual Growth in GNP (1980–92)	Fertility Rate	Population per Physician	Infant Mortality per 1,000 Live Births	Percentage of Low-Birth Weight Babies	Prevalence of Malnutrition Under Age 5	Life Expectancy at Birth
Japan	$28,640	3.6%	1.5	310	5	6%	—	79
United States	$23,240	1.7%	2.1	160	9	7%	—	77
Germany	$23,030	2.4%[a]	1.3	370[a]	6	—	—	76
France	$22,260	1.7%	1.8	270	7	5%	—	77
United Kingdom	$17,790	2.4%	1.8	810[b]	7	7%	—	76
Hungary	$2,970	0.2%	1.8	340	15	9%	—	69
Brazil	$2,770	0.4%	2.8	2,030[b]	57	11%	7.1	66
Mexico	$3,470	−0.2%	3.2	1,480[b]	35	12%	13.9	70
Egypt	$640	1.8%	3.8	1,320	57	10%	10.4	62
China	$470	7.6%	2.0	1,520[b]	31	9%	21.3	69
India	$310	3.1%	3.7	2,460	79	33%	63.0	61
Nigeria	$320	−0.4%	5.9	19,830[b]	84	15%	35.7	52

[a]Before unification.

[b]Figures are for 1970.

Source: World Bank, *World Development Report 1994* (New York: Oxford University Press, 1994), Tables 1 and 27, pp. 162–63, 214–15.

development in terms of their educational policies, the efforts they make to raise educational levels, and the extent to which they succeed.

Our purpose in presenting these socioeconomic data is to show how governmental and private efforts, in societies at different levels of economic development and of differing social structures and cultures, affect human life chances—the availability of economic opportunity, the equity of income distribution, the health and longevity, the skill, creativity, and productivity of their populations. Although the natural resources, the socioeconomic structure, and the cultural and historical backgrounds of these countries constitute constraints and opportunities, politics and government are the purposive and collective goal-setting and problem-solving institutions in the pursuit of economic growth, social welfare, and equity.

In Chapter 2 we have already shown that comparison according to Gross National Product seriously exaggerates the differences between rich and poor countries, since it compares them according to the official exchange rates of the currencies. If we compare income per capita according to the purchasing power of the national currencies these differences turn out to be smaller than what the GNP figures suggested, though still quite substantial. Thus, Japanese income per capita would be more, twenty times that of India, fifteen times that of Nigeria, ten times that of China, six times that of Egypt, and four times that of Brazil (see Figure 1.2).

Part of the explanation for these disparities is reported in columns 2 and 3 of Table 8.3, which give the rate of growth in *gross domestic product (GDP)* for the 1980s,[11] and the fertility rate. Japan has been running a strong and steady economic development race since its rise from defeat in World War II. As of 1992, it still had the highest rate of growth among all the advanced industrial societies; and its fertility rate of 1.5 was producing a declining population thus accentuating the impact of its high growth rate. Currently (as of 1994) its growth rate has declined, even moving into minus territory for a while. For the long term, the secular pattern of growth in Japan has resulted in the best record in life expectancy and infant mortality (columns 5 and 8). Its children show the benefits of material welfare, with the lowest percentage of low-birth weight babies.

The relationship between economic level, and health is dramatically demonstrated in the figures for Nigeria, where with a low GNP per capita, a negative growth rate, and high birth rate of 5.9, life expectancy is now about age 50 (compared with well over 70 years in advanced industrial countries) and where almost one out of ten infants fails to survive the first year of life. On the average there is only a single physician per 20,000 inhabitants, and more than one-third of its children under five years of age suffer from malnutrition.

The importance of culture and public policy is suggested by the figures for China and India. With a similarly low GNP per capita. Chinese average life expectancy is 69 years and infant mortality is 31 per 1,000 live births, while those of India are 61 years and 79 per 1,000, respectively. One-third of India's new-born infants had low birth weights, and two-thirds of those under five were suffering from malnutrition. The corresponding figures for China are 9 percent low birth weight babies, and 21 percent undernourishment of children under five.

The effect of level of economic development on health expenditures, health facilities, sanitation, availability of potable water, access to the outside world through telephone and roads is dramatically reported in the most recent *World Development Report,* which focuses on infrastructure.[12] During the 1980s the average public expenditure per capita for health for the economically developed countries was $469 compared with $11 for the developing countries. The average number of persons per physician in the developed world was 398, as compared with 2,043 for the developing world. While 97 percent of the people of the developed world had access to safe water, this was true for only 53 percent of the population of the less advantaged areas.

Table 8.4 provides a brief picture of the availability of infrastructure in the countries included in our book. The differences in the availability of facilities supportive of welfare, health, convenience and access to the outside world, at different levels of economic development is striking. In the developed countries practically all of the people can count on safe supplies of water. In the middle- and low-income countries from one-fifth to one-quarter of the population lack this minimal necessity. In the case of Nigeria more than one-half lack access to safe water supplies. Almost all of the people of developed countries live in households with access to electricity; in countries such as India and Egypt only around half the households have access to electricity. In the developed countries on the average there is a telephone for one of every two persons; in the poorer countries there may be as few as three to a thousand. High road density assures access to products and ideas in the developed countries; low density reduces this access in such countries as India, Nigeria, and China.

While the incidence of infant mortality, low birth weight babies, and malnutrition is much lower in advanced economies, these problems are still serious among the poorer strata in advanced industrial countries such as the United States. A comparison of health care expenditures as a percentage of GNP, and the male

Table 8.4   AVAILABILITY OF INFRASTRUCTURE IN SELECTED COUNTRIES (1992)

	Households with Electricity (percent)	Telephone (per 1,000 population)	Road Density (km per million population)	Population with Access to Safe Water (percent)
Japan	—	441	6,007	96%
United States	100%	545	14,172	100%
West Germany	100%	483	—	100%
France	99%	495	14,406	100%
United Kingdom	N.D.	442	6,174	100%
Hungary	96%	96	5,804	98%
Brazil	79%	63	704	86%
Mexico	75%	66	820	81%
Egypt	46%	33	302	90%
China	N.D.	—	—	72%
India	54%	6	893	73%
Nigeria	81%	3	376	42%

N.D. No data

Source: World Bank, *World Development Report 1994* (New York: Oxford University Press, 1994), Table 32, pp. 224–24.

infant death rates for the United States, Sweden, France, Netherlands, West Germany, and Britain in 1985, showed the United States while spending the largest proportion of its GNP for health care, at the same time had the highest male infant death rate.[13]

Data on income distribution are not easy to come by, but the data in Table 2.1 (Chapter 2) gave us some impression of how income distribution varies in four kinds of nations: (1) advanced market societies, (2) former Communist societies, (3) medium-income developing societies, and (4) low-income developing societies. Looking back at Table 2.1, we can see that in advanced capitalist societies the top 10 percent of households get around one-fourth of the income and the bottom 40 percent get about 15 to a little more than 20 percent. Hungary has the most equal distribution of all the countries in Table 2.1. More than one-fourth of the income goes to the poorest 40 percent of the households and only 18.7 percent to the top 10 percent of the households.

The two Third World patterns are particularly interesting and illustrate the operation of the Kuznets curve. In his studies of European economic history, Simon Kuznets pointed out that in the early stages of industrialization income distribution became more unequal as the more advanced industrial sector outpaced the rural agricultural sector. In the later stages of industrialization, income distribution came closer to equality.[14] The data in Table 2.1 tend to support this theory. Brazil and Mexico with GNPs per capita of around $3,000, roughly at a midpoint in economic developmental level, have the most unequal income distribution among the countries in the table. India at the bottom in terms of per capita income, has a more equal distribution. The Ivory Coast, rich by African standards with a GNP of $770, has a distribution pattern much like that of Mexico.

The Kuznets curve is explained by the common trends of economic and political modernization. In the early stages of modernization the large, traditional rural sector is left behind as industry and commercial agriculture begin to grow. At higher levels of economic attainment, the rural agricultural sector is penetrated and reduced in size by comparison with the growing industrial and service sectors of the economy. In addition, the development of trade unions and political parties in democratic countries results in legislation that affects income distribution through taxation, wage policy, and social security, health, and other benefits.

In turning to education, our data provides a more complete sense of the way policy outputs interact with current conditions to shape policy outcomes. Table 8.5 provides us with such a perspective. In the first column we see each country's educational goals, as reflected in the number of years children are required to attend school. The next three columns describe the implementation of educational policy. First, we see the expenditure on public education as a percentage of the GNP, a rough measure of what proportion of total productive output goes into education, in other words, of the "priority" given to education by the nations's leaders. Then we see how this converts into dollars per pupil, a rough measure of the impact of this educational effort on these age cohorts. Countries such as Egypt devote similar percentages of their GNP to education as do the advanced industrial societies. Hence we may say they are making proportionally similar efforts to educate their populations. But if you examine the per capita expenditure column you will

Table 8.5   EDUCATION AND LITERACY IN SELECTED COUNTRIES: POLICY, OUTPUT, OUTCOMES (1991)

	Years of Required Education	Percent of GNP for Public Education	Amount Per Student ($)	Primary Total	Primary Female	Secondary Total	Secondary Female	Tertiary Total	Literacy Male	Literacy Female	Female of Shares of Labor Force
Brazil	7–14	3.5%	$321	106%	82%[b]	39%	26%	12%	83%	80%	28%
China	7–16	2.5%	$52	123%[a]	118%[a]	51%	45%	2%	84%	62%	43%
Egypt	6–14	6.0%	$185	101%	93%	80%	73%	19%	63%	34%	10%
France	6–16	5.4%	$6,369	107%	106%[a]	101%	104%	43%	99%	99%	40%
Germany	6–18	4.1%	$6,473	107%	107%[a]	—	103%	36%	99%	99%	39%
India	6–14	3.1%	$62	98%	84%	44%	32%	—	62%	34%	25%
Japan	6–15	4.8%	$7,171	102%[a]	102%[a]	97%	98%	31%	99%	99%	38%
Mexico	6–14	4.1%	$300	114%[a]	112%[a]	55%	55%	15%	90%	85%	27%
Nigeria	6–12	1.5%	$29	71%	62%	20%	17%	4%	62%	40%	34%
Russia	6–17	5.6%	$1,097	—	—	—	—	—	99%	98%	—
United Kingdom	5–16	5.2%	$4,144	104%	105%	86%	88%	28%	99%	99%	39%
United States	6–16	5.2%	$6,580	104%	104%	90%	90%	76%	99%	99%	41%

[a]For some countries with primary education the gross enrollment ratios may exceed 100% because some pupils are younger and older than the country's standard primary school age.

[b]Figures are for 1970.

Source: UNESCO Statistical Yearbook, 1993; World Bank, *World Development Report 1994* (New York: Oxford University Press, 1994), Table 28, pp. 216–17, Table 29, pp. 218–19; Ruth Seger Sivard, *World Military and Social Expenditures, 1993* (Washington, DC: World Priorities, 1993), Table 111, pp. 46–48.

observe that the differences in dollar expenditures per student are very large. A lower economic development level converts the same level of effort into a far smaller output, and we may assume, less effective transmission of knowledge and skills.

A few comparisons may make these points clearer. The government of Nigeria only requires children from ages 6 to 12 to attend school, and only allocates 1.5 percent of its GNP to education. This translates into an average annual expenditure of $29 per pupil or student. Egypt requires eight years of education, and spends 6 percent of its GNP for these purposes, amounting to a per student expenditure of $185. At the other end Japan has a nine-year obligatory education from 6 to 15, invests 4.8 percent of its GNP in education, amounting to an annual expenditure of $7171 per student. The outcomes are what we might predict from these differences in output. Nigeria has 71 percent of the appropriate age cohorts in primary school, 20 percent in secondary, and 4 percent in postsecondary education of all kinds. The figures for Egypt are better—100 percent in primary schools, 80 percent in secondary schools and 19 percent in colleges, universities, and other postsecondary educational and training institutions. At the high end in terms of educational outcomes, France has all of its primary and secondary school age children in schools, and almost one-half of its college-age population are in some form of advanced education.

The figures on literacy are a crude measure of the skill and competence of a population. Here the payoffs of development and investment in education are clear. Less than two-thirds of the Indian, Egyptian, and Nigerian population are literate. China with a similarly low GNP and small investment in education is 84 percent literate. Most of the women in developing countries tend to be illiterate—only a third to two-fifths are literate in Egypt, India, and Nigeria; but, surprisingly, almost two-thirds of Chinese women are literate according to these figures. Ideology and culture may explain educational as well as health outcomes in China, where larger results are obtained with similar or even lower investments. These figures must, of course, be treated with caution. The figure of 99 percent literate in the United States conflicts with studies showing substantial functional illiteracy among American adults, probably because such literacy figures are based on the number of school years completed, not on actual tests of reading ability.

The discrepancy between male and female literacy rates tells us something of the status of women in these societies. If we glance down the last column of Table 8.5 we observe Egypt with 10 percent women in the labor force, India with 25 percent, and Nigeria with more than one-third, even though all three had similarly low female literacy rates. Other variables such as culture, and the character of the economy enter into the role of women in the various sectors of the society.

In Chapter 2 we presented the argument of the economist, Amartya Sen, on the interaction between the education of women and their entry into the labor force on the one hand, and the reduction of the birth rate on the other. Modernizing the status of women had the effect of bringing demography and economic development into a favorable equilibrium, in contrast to the vicious circle reflected in demographic and economic developments in many third world countries. The interest of parents in third world countries with its prevalence of poverty, disease, and the absence of a safety net, lies in having many children, to counteract the death rate and insure support in old age. The self interest of parents in having large families comes into conflict with the national interest in population control and economic development. As women are educated, and/or enter the labor force the advantages of smaller families become evident.

Table 8.5 reveals the sobering difficulties of trying to change societies, even in an area such as literacy, where modern methods and technology are available. It is hard for a poor country to spend a high percentage of its GNP on education, because to do so means that sacrifices must be made elsewhere. In any case, the country's revenue is limited, because much of its productive effort simply goes to feed the producers. No matter how large the country's percentage of effort may be, it does not translate into much per child, because the resource base is small and the population is growing rapidly, pouring children into the new schools. The older population is mostly illiterate, so that the net effect on literacy is slow.

DOMESTIC SECURITY OUTCOMES

Maintaining order and national security and protecting persons and property are the most basic responsibilities of government. Without them the conduct of personal, economic, and civic life are impossible. Crime rates have been on the increase in recent decades in the advanced industrial countries, as well as in the developing world. Thus in the United States the crime rate increased in the decade between 1982 and 1991 by almost 15 percent. In France in 1990 the incidence of crimes against persons and property was almost twice that of 1975. In Russia the crime rate doubled between 1985 and 1993, reflecting the fact that that country is experiencing the collapse and remaking of a moral and legal order.[15] There is evidence that these trends may have peaked in the United States. But this may only be a short run blip; the problem of crime in the United States is at the top of the political agenda.

The rising crime rate is primarily a problem of the larger urban areas where much of the population of modern countries resides, where its economy is conducted and managed, and where its cultural amenities are concentrated. What these figures suggest is that in modern and modernizing societies, despite increasing expenditures on law enforcement, that part of the quality of life which is contributed by the physical safety of our persons and possessions, has been attenuating. We might put it in these terms: Wealth and income may be rapidly increasing in these countries, but we must subtract from its absolute value, the anxiety over personal safety which is a familiar attribute of urban life, and the decline in freedom of movement and ready access to our private and collective possessions.

In a sense the inner cities hold the outer cities in a state of siege. The reasons for this are complex, involving material, structural, cultural, and moral changes. The United States is the primary example here, though safety and public order have declined throughout the advanced industrial world. Greatly increased migration in the last decades into the inner cities of advanced industrial countries, or in the rapidly developing ones, either from the domestic countryside, or from foreign countries at lower levels of economic development, has increased the incidence of cultural difference and conflict in the larger cities of the developed world. The cultural and moral changes of the 1960s and 1970s involving the lifting of sexual inhibitions and restraints, and the weakening and even breakdown of the nuclear family, have impaired the capacity of modern cultures to transmit effective standards of conduct to the young. But perhaps most decisively, the increasing inequality of income and wealth, and the hopelessness of life prospects in the inner city, lie behind this general decline in public order and safety. In the former Communist countries the situation is compounded by the fact that while experiencing these larger cultural trends, they have simultaneously undergone or are undergoing a major legal and moral revolution.

Despite this general rise of crime in modern and modernizing societies, we have relatively little in the way of comparative data. And what data we have leave much to be desired from the point of reliability. Much depends on the accuracy of the reporting agencies. Murder rates are usually considered the most reliable statistics. *The United Nations Demographic Yearbook* for 1994 reports deaths per 100,000 population "by homicide or other injury leading to death inflicted by other persons". The data for individual countries is for various years from 1987 to 1991. Figure 8.3 tells us that the two Latin American countries—Brazil (1987) and Mexico (1990)—are highest in homicides with more than 16 cases per 100,000 population. From other sources we know that the Russian Federation has equalled these rates in the early 1990s.[16] They are followed by the United States with more than

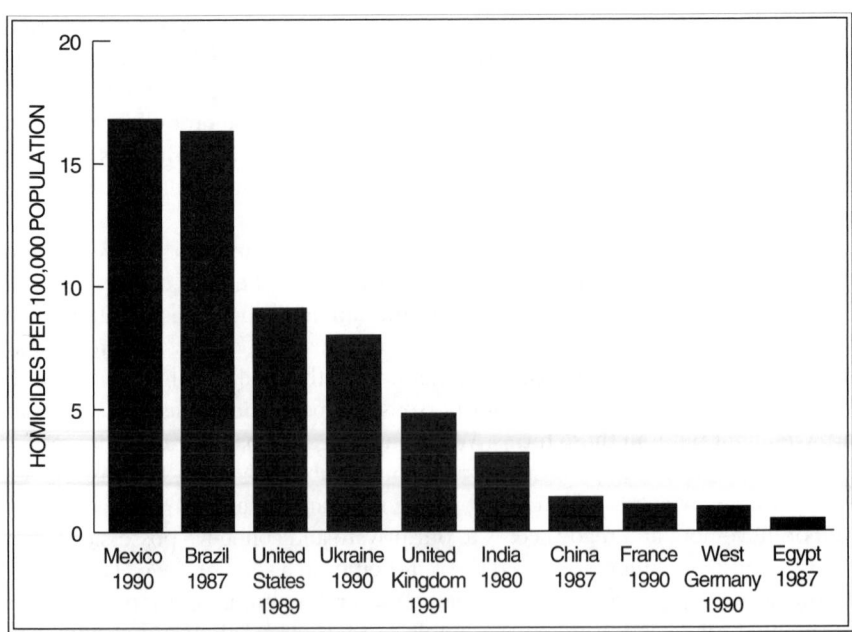

Figure 8.3 Homicides per 100,000 Population in Selected Countries (1987–1991) *Source:* United Nations, *Demographic Yearbook* (New York: UN, 1994), Table 24, pp. 688 ff. National Crime Records Bureau, Ministry of Home Affairs, New Delhi, 1991, p. 8.

9 per 100,000. Ukraine, another successor country of the Soviet Union, had a similarly high murder rate—8 per 100,000.

Surprisingly enough the figure for the United Kingdom—long known as an orderly country—was quite high, almost 5 per 100,000. This reflects the situation in Northern Ireland, as well as the migration into Britain's inner cities of people from the Caribbean and South Asian parts of its former empire. India had 3.2 homicides per 100,000 population in 1980. The remaining countries included in Figure 8.3—China, Egypt, France, West Germany, and Japan—have homicide rates ranging around 1 per 100,000 population.

Reliable current data for political violence as an indicator of the regulatory performance of our countries is not available. The last available figures for riots for the period 1948–77 show the United States with the largest number of such events (the disorders of the 1960s and 1970s), with India (language and religious riots) next in frequency, followed by the United Kingdom (primarily Northern Ireland), and with France, Japan, Nigeria, Mexico, and Egypt in that order. In more recent decades, though we are lacking in exact numbers, we know that such events in China (the Tienanmen Square disorders), Egypt (Islamic fundamentalism), India (Hindu-Islamic clashes), Mexico (the Chiapas disorders) and the countries of the former Soviet Union (ethnic, religious, and secession clashes in Georgia, Armenia, Azerbaizan, and most recently in Chechnya), have claimed the lives, and destroyed the property of large numbers of people.[17]

Some impression of the different levels of effort in policing crime and disorder is reflected in the figures for the number of police officers in proportion to population for the countries included in this book. The range is from the high of one police officer for every 350 persons in the United States, to 820 in India, and 1,140 in Nigeria. Comparative budgetary figures for police and law enforcement were unavailable for most of our countries.[18] Public expenditures on law enforcement have been on the steady increase in the United States in the last years; and the last figure we have for the rate of increase in the prison population in the United States for a single year from 1990 to 1991, was more than 5 percent. In France the increase in prison population from 1983 to 1990 almost amounted to a doubling.[19]

OUTPUTS AND OUTCOMES IN THE INTERNATIONAL ARENA

Nations typically engage in a great variety of international activities in order to enhance their welfare and security—economic, diplomatic, and military—and these activities affect prosperity and depression, war and peace, stability and change in the international political economy. These developments in turn affect the internal politics and policies of nations in a never-ending process. The interplay of international political and economic conditions and the political processes and public policy outputs of nations has been described and analyzed in a series of studies by Peter Gourevitch. He traced the political and policy responses of five Western industrial nations—Great Britain, France, Germany, Sweden, and the

United States—to the three world depressions of 1870–90, 1930–40, and 1975–85. Gourevitch also shows how these crises affected business, labor, and agriculture differently in each country, tracing the preferences and responses of interest groups, their interaction with political parties in each country, through to changes in political structure and policy. These changes in political structure and policy in individual countries are attributable to the impact of international depression and can be seen as creating the basis for equilibrium or breakdown in the last century of Western international relations. Thus, the world depression of the 1930s resulted in a conservative reaction in England, a moderate left (the New Deal) reaction in the United States, a polarization and paralysis of public policy in France ("Immobilisme"), and a radical polarization, a breakdown of democracy, and the emergence of National Socialism and an aggressive nationalism in Germany. While the causes of World War II were complex and in considerable part resulted from international interactions, the pacifism of Britain, the demoralization and defeatism of France, the isolationism of the United States, and the nihilism and aggression of Germany were fed by the economic devastation of the world depression of the 1930s.[20]

The most important and most costly outcome of the interaction among nations is warfare. Table 8.6 reports the incidence of warfare for a variety of nations since the conclusion of the Napoleonic Wars in 1816—reporting the number of wars and battle deaths incurred by each country. Russia has averaged more than 127,000 military and civilian deaths per year in international warfare alone in the last century and a half, and Germany more than 46,000. These costs of international warfare have gradually escalated. Most of the deaths are concentrated in the twentieth century, and civilian deaths have risen even more rapidly, especially in those countries the location of which has made them likely battlefields. According to one authority, more than 90 percent of the deaths in war since 1700 have occurred in the twentieth century.

Wars have occasioned as many civilian as military deaths. The number of concurrent wars peaked in 1987 at 27, the highest number since 1700, with a death toll in that year of over 2 million, more than 80 percent of them civilian. These included the wars in Afghanistan, Angola, Cambodia, Colombia, El Salvador, Ethiopia, Guatemala, India, Iran, Iraq, Lebanon, Nicaragua, Sri Lanka, the Sudan, Vietnam, and others. By 1989, the number of ongoing wars had dropped to 15, but in that year alone there were 300,000 war deaths in the world. The number of wars rose rapidly again in 1991; and in 1992 there was a new record with 29 concurrent wars, most of them in the Third World.[21]

These contemporary Third World wars are the result of the territorial and power changes of the post–Cold War period, ethnic conflicts, the rise of religious fundamentalism, conflicts between power factions and war lords. Five of the ongoing wars in 1992 were taking place in parts of the former Soviet Union—in Georgia there were two separate wars, between the Ossetians and Abkhazians versus the government; a religious territorial war was going on between the Armenians and the Azerbaijanis; there was ethnic conflict in Moldova, and an Islamic rebellion in Tajikistan. There were ethnic, clan, and "warlord" wars in the African countries of Rwanda, Burundi, Nigeria, Somalia, and others. In the Middle East in 1992

Table 8.6   INTERNATIONAL SECURITY OUTCOMES IN SELECTED NATIONS, 1816–1990

Country	Years in International System	Number of Wars[a]	Battle Deaths[a]	Civilian Deaths[a]	Total Deaths per Year
Russia	175	19	9,700,000	12,500,000	127,000
Germany[b]	166	6	5,353,500	2,293,000	46,000
China	131	11	3,128,500	2,086,000	40,000
France	173	22	1,965,000	490,000	14,000
Japan	124	9	1,371,000	501,000	15,000
United Kingdom	175	19	1,295,000	131,000	8,600
United States	175	8	665,000	201,000	4,900
Egypt	54	5	25,000	53,000	1,440
India	44	5	14,000	16,000	680
Mexico	160	3	19,000	5,000	150
Tanzania	30	1	1,000	0	30

[a]Does not include civil wars.

[b]Figures are for Prussia before unification in 1871.

Sources: Calculated from data made available by the Inter-University Consortium for Political and Social Research. The data up to 1980 were collected by J. David Singer and Melvin for their book, *The Wages of War, 1816–1965* (New York: John Wiley & Sons, 1972), pp. 275 ff. Data on civilian deaths and all data from 1980–1990 are from Ruth Leger Sivard, *World Military and Social Expenditures 1991* (Washington, DC: World Priorities, 1991) pp. 22–25.

there was ongoing warfare between the Iraqi government, the Kurds, and the Shi-ite Muslims; in Afghanistan there was warfare between the Islamic factions; in India there was intermittent violence involving the Sikhs and government forces, radical nationalist Hindus and Muslims; in Sri Lanka the Tamils and Buddhists were locked in a bloody embrace.[22]

We suggested in Chapter 7 that in the post–Cold War period the UN has the opportunity of acquiring legitimacy as a major world peacekeeping force in a situation in which super powers were no longer confronting each other all around the globe, unwilling to tolerate the intervention of the UN. Whether or not the UN becomes an effective peacekeeping agency depends on the maintenance of a consensus among the great powers. Such a consensus helps explain the success of the Iraq-Kuwait Desert War of 1990 and the Haitian intervention of 1994; and the absence of consensus among the NATO powers, and Russia and the United States explains the failure of international control in the Bosnian wars of the 1990s. If the international political system of the Cold War period could be described as a relatively stable, though sharply antagonistic bipolar structure, what kind of structure will emerge in the post–Cold War world is still an open question.

Since the development of nuclear weapons the world has been under a cloud of doubt and anxiety over the availability of these destructive instruments in the hands of powers pursuing incompatible goals. Half a century of maneuvers, deployments, and diplomatic negotiations between the United States and the Soviet Union produced a relatively stable balance of terror. In the late 1980s both sides began to recognize the unacceptable dangers of this continued accumulation of nuclear arsenals, and a process of "stand down" from active deployment, and "draw down" of stockpiles has begun.

This process of nuclear disarmament has been complicated by the breakup of the Soviet Union, leaving three successor nuclear powers—Ukraine, Tadjikistan, and Russia. The larger so-called "Nuclear Club" includes these heirs of the former Soviet arsenal, China, the older Western members—the United States, Britain and France—and the newer members—Israel, India, and Pakistan. Efforts on the part of such nations as Libya, Iraq, and North Korea to acquire nuclear weapons have thus far been contained, but the threat of nuclear proliferation, and of the destabilization and catastrophes that might ensue if these efforts were successful, is an ever-present component in the security policymaking of modern nations, and a drain on their welfare.

The costs of national security policy, and foreign policy in the broader sense are quite high. Table 8.1 showed that expenditures for military purposes in many nations are typically as high as those for education and health. The federal government in the United States spent the very same amount and proportion of GNP on these three objects. While military expenditures have been declining since the collapse of the Soviet Union, security prospects do not promise that this reduction will continue, or that the sense of international safety which began to spread in the late 1980s and the 1990s will be justified by events.

POLITICAL GOODS AND POLITICAL PRODUCTIVITY: A SYSTEM, PROCESS, AND POLICY APPROACH

Our approach to political analysis leads us from process to performance to evaluation. If we are to compare and evaluate the working of different political systems, we need to direct our attention to the variety of desired goals that can be implemented by political action. One society or one group of citizens may value order and stability; another may value participation and liberty. They may value these political "goods" with different intensity, and their preferences and the intensity of their preferences may change with time and circumstances.

Judgment and evaluation of political performance is inescapable, even when we think we are being completely unbiased. A long tradition in political analysis has emphasized order, predictability, and stability. We call these "system values" since they are judgments of the functioning of the whole set of political institutions and their effectiveness. Some may want them to change, to adapt to new circumstances. Others may dislike change and prefer stability. Political instability—constitutional breakdowns, frequent cabinet changes, riots, demonstrations, and the like—upset most people. On the other hand there are crises in the economy or in international affairs when citizens demand positive and adaptive measures to cope with these crises.

Another school of thought has emphasized goods associated with process—citizens' participation and freedom of political competition. Democracy is good and authoritarianism is bad, according to this school of thought, which directs research to maintaining democracy. Systems rejecting it or failing to sustain it are considered unsuccessful. Recent interest in human needs, in the quality of life, and in the tremendous problems of economic development has led to concentration on policy goods, such as economic welfare, quality of life, and personal security. A political system that improves welfare, decreases inequalities, enhances public safety, and cleans up its environment becomes the model. All these schools of thought are preoccupied with important practical goods valued by most people in varying degrees and under varying circumstances. Without accepting any particular theory about basic human needs and values, we can say that each of these goods, and others listed here, have been valued by many people in many societies.

Table 8.7 draws on our three-level analysis of political systems and on the work and thought of a number of scholars and thinkers in order to present a checklist of goods or values that are produced by political systems. We cannot deal with these items at great length, but we can emphasize a few of the ideas involved. System goods have to do with the regularity and predictability with which political systems work and with the ability of systems to adapt to environmental challenges and changes. Regularity and adaptability are typically somewhat in conflict. On the one hand, most people feel anxiety if serious interruptions and changes affect the routine and behavior of political life. Successions of military coups or continuing collapses of cabinet governments or resignations of presidents create unease and uncertainty. On the other hand, as conditions change—as wars, rebellions, and

Table 8.7 PRODUCTIVITY OF POLITICAL SYSTEMS

Levels of Political Goods	Classes of Goods	Content and Examples
System level	System maintenance	Regularity and predictability of processes in domestic and international politics
	System adaptation	Structural and cultural adaptability in response to environmental change and challenges
Process level	Participation in political inputs	Instrumental to domestic and foreign policy; directly produces a sense of dignity and efficacy, where met with responsiveness
	Compliance and support	Fulfillment of citizens' duty and patriotic service
	Procedural justice	Equitable procedure and equality before the law
Policy level	Welfare	Growth per capita; quantity and quality of health and welfare; distributive equity
	Security	Safety of person and property; public order and national security
	Liberty	Freedom from regulation, protection of privacy, and respect for autonomy of other individuals, groups, and nations

economic disasters occur—or as aspirations change, people turn to the political system for solutions to their problem.

We have been living in a time when the values of change and adaptation are being stressed, but the changes that seem to be called for are limiting the cost, size, and inefficiencies of government after several decades of growth. There have also been periods when order and stability have been at the top of the agenda. The administration of Warren Harding at the end of World War I was such a period. It was called "a return to normalcy." There was a similar withdrawal from mobilization in the aftermath of World War II and the Korean War, during the presidency of Eisenhower. The periods of the New Deal in the 1930s, and the War on Poverty in the 1960s were periods stressing change and adaptation, calling for the extension of governmental powers. But the stress on change and adaptation can be conservative, just as the emphasis on order and stability can be liberal. Contrast the New Deal with the "Republican Contract with America of 1994–95." One counselled large extensions of governmental powers and expenditures; the other urges sharp reductions.

At the process level, we identify such goods as effective, satisfying participation, which most citizens desire if given a choice, and which produces generally positive views of the political system. Participation is not merely valued instrumentally, as a means to force political elites to respond, but for its own sake, because it increases the individual's sense of competence and dignity. Compliance with authority can also be a good, as individuals seek to avoid penalties or to respond to the impulse to serve others, which can be one of humanity's most gratifying experiences. President John F. Kennedy in his inaugural address called on such impulses to serve and sacrifice when he said, "Ask not what your country can do for you, but what you can do for your country." The Peace Corps was an example of this impulse for public service, particularly in the young. Procedural justice (trial by jury, habeas corpus, no cruel and unusual punishment) is another crucial process value, whose deprivation is a severe blow to citizens and without which other goods may be impaired.

At the policy level we come to the values of welfare, its quantity, quality, and equity; personal and national security; and freedom from interference in a life of reasonable privacy. The right to bear arms, protected in the Second Amendment to the U. S. Constitution, has recently become a prominent cause among anti-government advocates. Volunteer militias have been formed in many states, dedicated to providing military training to citizens opposed to government encroachment on personal liberty, and particularly to gun control and the right to own "assault weapons".

We have discussed, indirectly, some of the welfare and security goods, but more must be said about liberty, which is sometimes viewed only as a purely negative good, a freedom from governmental regulation and harassment. Freedom is more than inhibition of government action, because infractions of liberty and privacy may be initiated by private individuals and organizations. In fact, liberty may be fostered by government intervention, when private parties interfere with the liberty of others. Much recent legislation on racial segregation may be understood as impelled by this purpose. Here, of course, different groups and perspectives may come to conflict over liberty, and liberty feeds back into many other goods. Liberty to act, organize, obtain information, and protest is an indispensable part of effective political participation. Nor is it irrelevant to such policy goods as social, political, and economic equality. Prior to the breakdown of Communism in Eastern Europe and the Soviet Union, it was a common view that the Communist countries were trading liberty for equality, by contrast with capitalism which was said to trade off equality for liberty. It will take historians and social scientists a long time to digest and evaluate the Communist experience, but what has come to light in the aftermath of the collapse of Communism in the last decade, is the extent of corruption and privilege in Communist societies, and the relatively low level of productivity of these countries in the last decades. It does not appear to be an exaggeration to say that, while they had surely traded off liberty and had provided a basic security of employment, it was primarily the failure of their economies to enhance productivity and welfare that led to the ideological demoralization.

STRATEGIES FOR PRODUCING POLITICAL GOODS

All political systems embody strategies for producing political goods. The strategies may be oriented to goods on one level or another, or to goods intended for the few or the many. The strategies may be shaped primarily by challenges imposed from the environment, by inheritance from the past, or by the self-conscious efforts of present-day politicians, or some combination. We can in any case think of different kinds of political systems as different sets of institutional choices intended to produce different combinations of political goods. The framers of the U.S. Constitution believed that separation of powers would protect liberty; Karl Marx believed that concentration of power in the "dictatorship of the proletariat" would achieve an equitable and distributive society; Mussolini believed that a single all-powerful leader would increase national power and glory; the Ayatollah Khomeini believed that a state and society modelled after the Koran, and administered by the clergy, would achieve justice on earth, and bring on eternal salvation.

Since the collapse of the Soviet Union, it has seemed as though democracy is "the only game in town." In the earlier decades of the twentieth century there were several political ideologies in competition with political democracy—communism, democratic socialism, fascism, corporative-authoritarianism, and the like. Fascism went down in flames in the Second World War, leaving a wasted and demoralized Europe in its wake. Communism all but collapsed in the late 1980s, drained of credibility by the failure of its promises, and the extent of its corruption. Most of its successor regimes are trying to democratize and establish free markets. The bureaucratic authoritarian regimes of Latin America, discredited by their cruelties, and political-economic failures, in the 1980s and 1990s turned to liberal-democratic alternatives—the market and the democratic polity. The postcolonial regimes of Sub-Saharan Africa, after a brief interlude of populist democracy in the "liberation" enthusiasm of the 1960s, turned to authoritarian regimes of one kind or another, and then in recent years some of them have begun to experiment once again with democracy. Social democracy and democratic corporatism have survived in Western Europe, somewhat tarnished by their association with Marxist macrosocialism.

But although the democratic polity and the free market economy have been the wave of the immediate past, they may very well have crested, and we may be coming into an era in which other strategies become credible once again. In our typology below we spell out what seem to be the major political-economic alternatives in the world today.

The major environmental feature of a political system, which predicts much about it, is its economy, either preindustrial, industrializing, or industrial and "postindustrial." All preindustrial nations face a host of similar problems, growing out of their aspiration to share in the benefits available in the "modern" parts of the world. We usually treat the preindustrial nations as a major category for study, further subdividing them by the political structures and strategies their leaders adopt in their efforts to hold onto power and to move forward. The industrial nations face a different set of problems. One of the major questions they must consider is how to deal with political participation. We saw in Chapters 3, 4, and 5 that socioeconomic development brings increased citizen awareness of and participation in politics. In the industrial nations political input structures must be developed to deal with this potential for citizen participation on a large scale. One major strategy is to introduce a single authoritarian party to contain, direct, and mobilize citizens under government control. The other is to permit competing parties that mobilize citizens behind leaders representing different goods and strategies. We refer to the first of these strategies as authoritarian and to the second as democratic. Within these major classifications, we further classify systems by the conservatism of their policy, the degree to which they limit the role of the political system in relation to the economy. This approach, then, distinguishes the following varieties of political systems:

I. Industrial nations
  A. Democratic
    1. Conservative
    2. Social Democratic
  B. Authoritarian
    1. Conservative
    2. Radical
II. Preindustrial and Industrializing Nations
  A. Authoritarian
    1. Neotraditional
    2. Personal Rule
    3. Clerico-mobilizational
    4. Technocratic-repressive
    5. Technocratic-distributive
    6. Technocratic-mobilizational
  B. Democratic Transitional

Industrialized Democratic Nations

The industrialized democratic nations must reconcile pressures to maintain or increase government services and personal income with the need to accumulate resources for investment in economic growth. In varying degrees all contemporary democratic industrial nations are challenged by unemployment, inflationary tendencies, and relatively slow rates of growth. The classic capital-labor confrontation in these countries has been complicated by the rise of the service economy, and the emergence of the environment, threatened by industrial development, as a salient issue. The service economy complicates the class structure and reduces and transforms the power of trade unions. Industrial pollution of land, air, and water divides nations differently, with a substantial part of the middle classes opposing growth that does not take into careful account environmental consequences, and a substantial part of the working classes favoring growth and employment even at the cost of some environmental danger. These dilemmas—both the old capital and labor issues, and the newer service economy and environmental issues facing all advanced democracies—may be dealt with conservatively as in the Britain of Margaret Thatcher, and the United States of the Reagan-Bush era, or in social democratic fashion as in Norway and Sweden, where social programs have been maintained and the environment largely protected.

But though there are these differences in the policies of the conservative and social democracies, both types of democratic regimes in the last decades, have backed up on taxing, welfare, and regulative activities. The size and cost of government and its inefficiencies, have themselves become major political issues. In the United States both major political parties are embarked on efforts to limit and roll back government—the Republicans leading a campaign to enact a "balanced budget" constitutional amendment; and the Democrats with their program of "reinventing government." The environmental issue tends to divide both conservative and left parties. In some European countries "Green," ecologically oriented parties, have emerged, which typically form coalitions with the social democratic movements.

Industrialized Authoritarian Nations

It is possible to classify industrial authoritarian nations into radical and conservative varieties. Prior to the collapse of Communism in Eastern Europe such regimes as the Soviet Union, the German Democratic Republic, Poland, Czechoslovakia, and Hungary were examples of the radical variety of industrialized authoritarian regime. Poland, Czechoslovakia, and Hungary are now moving in the direction of market economies and democratic polities. If disappointment and failure should undermine their still fragile democratic institutions, it is unlikely that these regimes would return to their socialist pasts. What is more likely is a resort to a *technocratic* authoritarian approach with the containment of popular pressure and protest by repressive means, and the management of investment and distribution in the interest of economic growth.

For Russia and some of the other republics of the former Soviet Union, however, we cannot rule out the possibility that given the continuation of ethnonational disintegration and economic failure, the groups controlling the coercive institutions and organizations may have sufficient vitality to reinstitute repressive politics and preserve much of the command economy of the pre–1989 era. But this is hardly likely to be justified in the rhetoric of Marxism-Leninism. It is more likely that such repression would be justified in ethnonationalist terms. In the Islamic parts of the old Soviet Union clerico-authoritarian trends seem to be on the rise.

Franco Spain (1938–78), the Greece of "the colonels" (1967–74), the Chile of Pinochet (1973–88), and the Brazil of "the generals" (1964–85) are examples of the second, conservative variety of authoritarianism. The military authoritarian regimes of Southern Europe and Latin America of the 1960s and 1970s followed policies of suppressing popular political organization, controlling welfare expenditure, and granting considerable freedom to private enterprise, in the interest of fostering economic growth, though at the expense of increasing inequality of wealth and income.

In general, and across the board without regard to regime type, the credibility of socialism and of high welfare expenditures has declined in the last decades, while that of the market economy has risen. It is still to be seen whether this is the move of a pendulum, or whether the power and penetration of the state reached an historic high point in the 1980s, from which it will retreat in some degree.

The democratization of the Latin American and Eastern European countries may be held hostage to the success of efforts to free and vitalize their economies. Failure in these areas may trigger an authoritarian return. Thus, while the category of the industrialized, authoritarian regime in both its radical and conservative varieties is relatively empty at the moment, it would be a mistake to discard the category as no longer relevant.

Preindustrial Nations

The preindustrial nations face common problems posed by the challenges of modernization. There are some seven strategies of political development followed by preindustrial countries—six of them authoritarian and one democratic.

Authoritarian Regimes

Neotraditional Political Systems   Neotraditional systems emphasize the system good of stability, the maintenance of an established order. The best exemplars of this variety are Saudi Arabia, and the Sheikhdoms of the Persian Gulf. Since these regimes are oil rich, they have so far been able to modernize selectively (for example, the military) and buy off opposition and discontent. But we have to assume that as they develop economically through their oil royalties, and as they provide health, educational, and other amenities to a substantial part of their populations, there is a buildup of opposition and support of some kind and degree of modernization.

Personal Rule   Most of the regimes of Sub-Saharan Africa cannot be assigned to the neotraditional category, though they contain surviving traditional structures such as kingdoms, chiefdoms, and the like. The colonial regimes out of which most of the Sub-Saharan countries emerged were artificial constructs which included several, or many traditional units with different languages, ethnicity, and religions. The formally democratic and parliamentary regimes that were established after independence soon gave way to a variety of versions of what has come to be called "personal rule."[23]

Many of the personal rule regimes in Sub-Saharan Africa are characterized by low growth rates (or even negative ones), low life expectancy, low literacy, low health, and other amenities. Since these regimes are unproductive, they have little legitimacy, and they are susceptible to coups principally from the armed forces. Where these systems stabilize, the rulers maintain control through a system of police suppression, patronage, spoils, and privileges distributed through urban interest groups and ethnic elites. The "personal ruler" is not simply a governor in the limited political sense; he has a "proprietary" relation to the regime, its institutions and agencies, and exploits it for his personal purposes.

Clerico-mobilizational Regimes   In the last decades, and principally in the Islamic countries of the Middle East, a clerico-authoritarian mobilizational ideology and regime has become prominent. This "fundamentalist" religious movement is strongly represented in both branches of Islam—Shia and Sunni. The Shia version is exemplified in Iran, which is an Islamic republic, dominated by clerics and the Koran, as interpreted by Shia scholars, and implemented by Islamic legislators and judges. There are such radical theocratic movements throughout Sunni Islam as well, not only in the Middle East but in Afghanistan, Pakistan, and in the Islamic areas of the former Soviet Union. Movements of this kind are threatening to take power in Algeria and Egypt. The Hamas in Gaza provides powerful resistance to a peace settlement in Palestine, and also favors a clerico-authoritarian regime for Palestine.

It is still unclear what the fate of these new movements will be. In our classification scheme they appear as a new category—clerico-mobilizational. They are antisecular in social matters (in the sense of the status of women and patriarchal family authority), restrictive of civil society as in the censorship of the media, and the suppression of secular opponents. They are authoritarian, neither traditional nor technocratic; they are mobilizational rather than quietistic. They want to control the modern media, use it for their own purposes, clean it of its moral corruption, and bring social relations to the high ethical levels of Islamic scripture. They are ambivalent on the question of economic policy urging control of the market from the point of view of Koranic precepts, but in actual practice they do not favor serious interference with the operation of banks and other economic institutions. They are nationalist and anti-Western. How far these movements can go in mounting an international coalition is still an unanswered question. Nationalism and the sectarian Shia-Sunni split may impede collaboration beyond the tactical level. Collaboration across religious boundaries—between Islamic, Jewish, and Christian fundamentalist movements—is even less likely.

Technocratic Repressive   The technocratic repressive approach has been effective in encouraging economic growth for periods of time in such countries as Brazil, Chile, Indonesia, and the like, where a coalition of military and civilian technocrats and business interests suppressed participation and were able to pursue a growth-oriented investment policy despite growing economic inequality. Such Middle Eastern countries as Iraq, Syria, and Egypt still pursue this strategy. And as we have suggested above, in those countries which have gone democratic, failures of the contemporary experiments with market economics and democratic politics may lead to reversions to technocratic repressive strategies.

Technocratic-distributive   There also is a distributive more egalitarian version of the modernizing authoritarian regime as in South Korea, prior to its recent democratization. South Korea suppressed participation but encouraged some income redistribution along with growth. Early land reforms, rapid development of education, labor-intensive, export-oriented industrialization, and substantial American advice, support, and pressure have marked the Korean experiment. Its economic success seems to have led to effective democratization.

Technocratic-mobilizational   The last category, the authoritarian technocratic-mobilizational strategy, has been exemplified primarily by preindustrial Communist countries, and in a less aggressively mobilizing form in such countries as Taiwan. This approach is distinguished by a single political party mobilizing and involving citizens in the political process. Competitive participation is suppressed or limited. This category has rapidly emptied in the last few years, although we cannot rule out the possibility of its return in the future. It is unlikely to be explicitly Communist or Marxist in ideology, but the reliance on a single mobilizational political party and the pursuit of a technocratic economic growth policy is a combination that might have appeal in the future.

China, Vietnam, North Korea, and Cuba are the last remaining Communist societies, dominated by single mobilizing political parties. China, Vietnam, and even Cuba have opened their socialist economies to market forces. China has been experiencing enormous growth, and there is much speculation about how long it can avoid some political pluralism. North Korea may be on the brink of such a policy shift, and Cuba may be at the point of opening up. It remains to be seen whether the old "social mobilization theory" is ultimately confirmed—that as countries industrialize, educate themselves, and develop the media of communication, they will in due time be unable to resist the introduction of competitive politics.

The non-Communist mobilizational systems vary substantially in success and in their emphasis on growth and distribution. Taiwan has been successful in combining growth and distributive equity under the domination of the Kuomintang (KMT) party. In recent years the monopoly of the KMT party has been successfully challenged, and politics has become increasingly competitive. Mexico has been dominated by the Partido Revolucionario Institucional (PRI) for more than a half-century in an arrangement which incorporated the major interest groups of labor, business, and agriculture into its internal structure. The PRI seemed to be securely in power until the last few years. Confronted by an economic and a political crisis, Mexico in 1995 is on the brink of moving to a genuinely competitive and pluralist system. South Korea and Taiwan, are examples of Third World nations that have achieved the goals of growth and distribution by authoritarian political means and that are now in process of democratizing.

Democratization in Developing Countries

Just as democracy in the last decades has become the "only political game in town," questions having to do with the process of democratization and its consolidation have become the main preoccupations of a sizable proportion of the practicing political scientists in the world today. Journal articles, and entire issues of journals, scholarly books in large numbers, and frequent scholarly conferences deal with such issues as "transition to democracy," "democratic consolidation," the "structural conditions of democratization," the role of "elites and leadership" in democratization, the "crafting" of democratic constitutions, and the like.[24]

The literature dealing with the contemporary patterns of transition to democracy emphasizes the importance of leadership, choice, bargaining, and coalition making, and tends to play down the importance of structural factors such as economic development and social modernization in the transition to democracy. These scholars argue that "transition" to democracy can occur in any kind of sociopolitical setting in which the leaders or elites, influenced by democratization elsewhere, or pressured by western countries, move in the democratic direction. Drawing on a rich database describing these many new experiments in democracy, the recent literature makes the point of the uncertainty and unpredictability of stable and consolidated democratic outcomes very persuasively.[25]

If democratic transition has this uncertain and incompete aspect, and is viewed as a tentative and reversible state of affairs, "democratic consolidation" is defined in contemporary studies as one in which the main elites have accepted democracy (when opposition is loyal), when the limits on democracy which made the transition possible have in some significant part been set aside, and when participatory patterns of behavior have been widely adopted among the general population. From this perspective a great many of the contemporary Third World democracies have to be viewed as not consolidated in both the institutional and cultural sense.[26]

Thus, while the new literature stresses leadership and indeterminacy in the transitional processes leading to democratization, it concludes that the consolidation of democracy requires political and socioeconomic conditions. The conversion of clashing elites into a majority-loyal opposition pattern of political institutions implies the presence of a consensual-competitive pattern of elite political culture. This in turn is associated with the rise of a "civil society" based on free media and a lively associational life. These conditions in turn are associated with widespread literacy and rising economic standards and quality of life. The democratic emergence of Taiwan and South Korea out of economically backward authoritarianism suggest that the old and prematurely discarded "social mobilization theory" still has validity when viewed against the data on the consolidation of democracy. These two countries proceeded as though programmed by Lerner, Lipset, and Deutsch[27] through the "modernization quartet" of industrialization, urbanization, education, and communication exposure to what appears to be a consolidated democratization. But we have learned enough from our earlier failed predictions to avoid assuming that these relations among economic, social, and political developments are more than associations and probabilities. The case of India, a democracy for almost its entire existence since achieving its independence in the late 1940s, demonstrates that a relatively undeveloped country (GNP per capita $310, life expectancy 61 years, and female illiteracy 66 percent), can sustain a democracy indefinitely despite the absence of these economic, social, and political conditions.[28]

TRADE-OFFS AND OPPORTUNITY COSTS

One of the hard facts about political goods is that all are desirable but cannot be pursued simultaneously. A political system has to trade off one value to obtain another. Spending funds on education is giving up the opportunity to spend them on welfare, or to leave them in the hands of consumers for their own use. These *trade-offs* and *opportunity costs* are found not only in simple decisions about giving up education for better health care, but also in complicated decisions about investment for the future as opposed to consumption today. Even more difficult are the trade-offs between security and liberty, or stability and adaptation, where the very concepts imply giving up some of the one for some of the other. The extreme of liberty, wherein each person is totally free to act, would make a highly insecure world where the strong would bully the weak and it would be difficult to arrange collective action. Yet, without some liberty to act, security is of little value, as the prisoner is too well aware. Not only do goods have negative trade-offs, but the trade-offs are not the same under all circumstances. Under some conditions increasing liberty somewhat will also increase security, because riots against censorship will end. Under some conditions investment in education will be paid back many times in health and welfare, because trained citizens can care better for themselves and work more productively.

One of the important tasks of social science is to discover the conditions under which positive and negative trade-offs occur. If a system beset with coups and violence, disease and physical suffering, suppression and arbitrary rule can be replaced with a more stable, more participatory system that makes some progress in economic development, few will doubt that the trade-off is positive. We stress, however, that analogies from economics are no more than analogies. Political science has no way of converting units of liberty into units of safety and welfare. And because politics may involve violence on a large scale, we must acknowledge that we can never calculate the value of a political outcome gained at the cost of human life. People act as though they know how to make such conversions, but political scientists can only point to values that people have emphasized at different times and places, and indicate the range and variety of values considered. The weight given to various goods will vary in different cultures and contexts. The advantage of a clear-cut ideology is that it provides people with logical schemes for telling how much one value should be traded against another, and thus offers orderly sequences of action leading to the outcome that is viewed as best. Such schemes may be invaluable for those pressed to action in the terrible circumstances of war, revolution, and famine. However, there is no ideology, just as there is no political science, that can solve all these problems objectively.

KEY TERMS

central government expenditures

central government revenues

direct taxes

distributive performance

distributive policies

extractive performance

extractive policies

gross domestic product (GDP)

gross national product (GNP)

indirect taxes

neotraditional political system

OECD (Organization for Economic
Cooperation and Development)

opportunity cost

outputs

outcomes

political performance

progressive taxes

public policies

regressive taxes

regulative performance

regulative policies

symbolic performance

taxation

technocratic

trade-off

welfare state

END NOTES

1. See among others, Peter Flora and Arnold Heidenheimer, *The Development of Welfare States in Europe and America* (New Brunswick, NJ: Transaction Books, 1981); Arnold Heidenheimer, Hugh Heclo, and Carolyn Teich Adams, *Comparative Public Policy*, 3d ed. (New York: St. Martin's Press, 1990). See also Francis G. Castles, *The Comparative History of Public Policy* (Cambridge, England: Polity Press, 1989).
2. See, for example, Samuel Brittan, *The Economic Consequences of Democracy* (London: Temple Smith, 1977); Michael Boskin, *The Crisis in Social Security* (San Francisco: Institute for Contemporary Studies, 1978); Mancur Olson, *The Rise and Decline of Nations*, New Haven, CT: Yale Univ. Press, 1982).
3. See, for example, Philippe Schmitter and Gerhard Lehmbruch, eds., *Trends Toward Corporate Intermediation* (Beverly Hills, CA: Sage, 1979); Suzanne Berger, ed., *Organizing Interests in Western Europe* (Cambridge: Cambridge Univ. Press, 1981); John Goldthorpe, ed., *Order and Conflict in Contemporary Capitalism* (Oxford: Clarendon Press, 1984); Peter Katzenstein, *Small States in World Markets* (Ithaca, NY: Cornell Univ. Press, 1985); Heidenheimer et al., *Development of Welfare States*, p. 360.
4. See World Bank, *World Development Report, 1993* (New York: Oxford Univ. Press, 1994), p. 183.
5. Heidenheimer et al., *Development of Welfare States*, pp. 196–97.
6. Ibid., pp. 211–19.
7. Harold Wilensky, *The Welfare State and Equality* (Berkeley, CA: Univ. of California Press, 1975); and Harold Wilensky, Gregory Luebbert, Susan Hahn, and Adrienne

Jameson, *Comparative Social Policy; Theories, Methods, Findings* (Berkeley, CA: Institute of International Studies, 1985).

8. Frederic L. Pryor, *Property and Industrial Organization in Communist and Capitalist Nations* (Bloomington, IN: Indiana Univ. Press, 1973), pp. 46–47.

9. Steven C. Poe and C. Neal Tate, "Repression of Human Rights to Personal Integrity in the 1980s: A Global Analysis," *American Political Science Review*, 88:4, (Dec. 1994), pp. 853–72.

10. For a discussion of regulation in the United States, see James G. Wilson, ed., *The Politics of Regulation in the United States* (New York: Basic Books, 1980).

11. Ruth Leger Sivard, *World Military and Social Expenditures* (Washington, DC: World Priorities, 1993), pp. 42 ff.

12. World Bank, *World Development Report: Infrastructure for Development* (New York: Oxford Univ. Press, 1994), overview, pp. 1 ff.

13. Arnold Heidenheimer, Hugh Heclo, Carolyn Teich Adams, *Comparative Public Policy* (New York: St. Martin's Press, 1990), p. 95.

14. Simon Kuznets, "Economic Growth and Income Equality," *American Economic Review*, 45 (1955), pp. 1–28.

15. Federal Bureau of Investigation, *Uniform Crime Reports 1991*, (Washington, DC: Government Printing Office, 1992); *Izvestia*, October 18, 1994; *The Economist*, July 9, 1994; *Tableaux de L'Economie Francaise 1991–1992* (Paris: Insee, 1993), p. 177.

16. *Izvestia*, Oct. 18, 1994.

17. Charles Taylor and David Jodice, *World Handbook of Political and Social Indicators*, Vol. 1, 3rd ed. (New Haven, CT: Yale Univ. Press, 1983), Chs. 2–4.

18. Such data as there are are reported in George Kurian, *New Book of World Rankings* (New York: Facts on File Publications, 1991), pp. 254 ff.

19. See note 12.

20. Peter Gourevitch, *Politics in Hard Times* (Ithaca, NY: Cornell Univ. Press, 1986).

21. Ruth Leger Sivard, *World Military and Social Indicators* (Washington, DC: World Priorities 1993), p. 20.

22. Ibid. p. 21.

23. See Robert Jackson and Carl Rosberg, *Personal Rule in Black Africa* (Berkeley, CA: Univ. of California Press, 1982).

24. Doh Chull Shin, "On the Third Wave of Democratization: A Synthesis and Evaluation of Recent Theory and Research," *World Politics*, 47, no. 1 (October, 1994), pp. 135–70.

25. See, among others, Guillermo O'Donnell and Philippe C. Schmitter, *Transitions from Authoritarian Rule: Tentative Conclusions About Uncertain Democracies* (Baltimore, MD: Johns Hopkins Univ. Press, 1986); Samuel Huntington, *The Third Wave: Democratization in the Late Twentieth Century* (Norman, OK: Univ. of Oklahoma Press, 1991); Terry Karl, "Dilemmas of Democratization in Latin America," in *Comparative Politics*, October 1990, pp. 1–22; Nancy Bermeo, "Rethinking Regime Change," *Comparative Politics*, 22:3 pp. 359–77; Giuseppe Di Palma, *To Craft Democracies* (Berkeley, CA: Univ. of California Press, 1990; Larry Diamond, "Introduction: Comparing Experiences with Democracy in the Politics in Developing Countries," in Larry Diamond et al., eds., *Democracy in Developing Countries* (Boulder, CO: Lynne Rienner, 1990); Larry Diamond, "Economic Development and Democracy Reconsidered," in Gary Marks and Larry Diamond, eds., *Reexamining Democracy* (Newbury Park, CA: Sage, 1992); Scott Mainwaring and Donald Share, "Transitions Through Treansaction; Democratization in Brazil and Spain," in Wayne Selcher, ed., *Political Liberalization in Brazil and Spain* (Boulder, CO: Westview Press, 1986).

26. Larry Diamond, "Toward Democratic Consolidation," *Journal of Democracy* Vol. 5, No 3, July 1, 1994 pp. 4–17; Lawrence Whitehead, "The Consolidation of Fragile Democ-

racies," in Robert A. Pastor, ed., *Democracy in the Americas* (New York: Holmes and Meier, 1989); Samuel J. Valenzuela, "Democratic Consolidation in Post Transitional Settings," in Mainwaring, O'Donnell, and Valenzuela, *Issues in Democratic Consolidation* (Notre Dame, IN: Univ. of Notre Dame Press, 1992); Scott Mainwaring, "Transition to Democracy and Democratic Consolidation; Theoretical and Comparative Issues," in Mainwaring et al., *Issues;* Terry Karl and Philippe Schmitter, "Modes of Transition in Latin America," *International Social Science Journal;* 138 (May 1991); Larry Diamond, *Political Culture and Democracy in Developing Countries* (Boulder, CO: Lynne Rienner, 1994), Ch. 1; Robert D. Putnam, *Making Democracy Work* (Princeton, NJ: Princeton Univ. Press, 1993).

27. Daniel Lerner, *The Passing of Traditional Society* (Glencoe, IL: Free Press, 1958); Seymour M. Lipset, "Some Social Requisites of Democracy," *American Political Science Review* (Sept. 1959), pp. 69–105; Karl Deutsch, "Social Mobilization and Political Development," *American Political Science Review* (Sept. 1961) pp. 493–514.

28. World Bank, *World Development Report 1994* (New York: Oxford Univ. Press, 1994), Tables 1 ff.

SUGGESTED READINGS

Almond, Gabriel A., and G. Bingham Powell. *Comparative Politics: A Theoretical Approach.* New York: HarperCollins, 1996.

Berger, Suzanne, Ed. *Organizing Interests in Western Europe.* Cambridge, Cambridge University Press, 1981.

Castles, Francis G., Ed. *The Comparative History of Public Policy.* Cambridge, England, Polity Press, 1989.

Dahl, Robert. *Democracy and Its Critics.* New Haven, CT: Yale University Press, 1974.

Di Palma, Giuseppe. *To Craft Democracies.* Berkeley, CA: University of California Press, 1990.

Diamond, Larry, Ed. *Democracy in Developing Countries.* Boulder, Colorado: Lynne Rienner Publishers, 1992.

Flora, Peter, and Arnold Heidenheimer. *The Development of Welfare States in Europe and America.* New Brunswick, NJ: Transaction Books, 1981.

Goldthorpe, John, Ed. *Order and Conflict in Contemporary Capitalism.* Oxford, England: Clarendon Press, 1984

Gourevich, Peter. *Politics in Hard Times.* Ithaca, New York: Cornell University Press, 1986.

Heidenheimer, Arnold, Hugh Heclo, and Carolyn Teich Adams. *Comparative Public Policy,* 3d ed. New York: St. Martin's Press, 1990.

Huntington, Samuel. *The Third Wave: Democratization in The Late Twentieth Century.* Norman, OK: Oklahoma University Press, 1991.

Jackson, Robert, and Carl Rosberg. *Personal Rule in Black Africa.* New Haven, CT: Yale University Press, 1990.

Katzenstein, Peter. *Small States in World Markets.* Ithaca, New York: Cornell University Press, 1985.

Lindblom, Charles E. *Politics and Markets.* New Haven, CT: Yale University Press, 1978.

Marks, Gary, and Larry Diamond, Eds. *Reexamining Democracy.* Newbury Park, CA: Sage Publications, 1992.

Mainwaring, Scott, Guillermo O'Donnell, Arturo Valanzuela. *Issues in Democratic Consolidation.* Notre Dame: University of Notre Dame Press, 1992.

Olson, Mancur. *The Rise and Decline of Nations.* New Haven, CT: Yale University Press, 1982.

Putnam, Robert D. *Making Democracy Work.* Princeton, NJ: Princeton University Press, 1993.

Schmitter, Philippe, and Gerhard Lehmbruch, Eds. *Trends Toward Corporate Intermediation.* Beverly Hills, CA: Sage Publications, 1979.

Wilson, James G. *The Politics of Regulation in The United States.* New York: Basic Books, 1980.

Index

AARP (American Association of Retired Persons), 99
Abachi, Sanni, 65
Adams, Carolyn Teich, 156
Adenauer, Konrad, 144
Adjudication, 33
Afghanistan, 29
Aggregation
  interest. *See* Interest aggregation
  party-electoral, 109
Albania, 4
Algeria, 10
  Islamic fundamentalism in, 53
  migrants from, 14
  terrorism by Algerian French in, 98
Alliance Party (Northern Ireland), 49
Almond, Gabriel A., 57
America. *See* United States
American Association of Retired Persons (AARP), 99
American Medical Association, 69
Angola, 174
Anomic interest groups, 85–86
Area of nations, population and, illustrated, 6
Argentina
  military regime replaced in, 122
  military role in political process in, 120
Aristotle, 26
Armenia, 14
Articles of Confederation (United States), 132
Assemblies, 138–142. *See also* Legislature; *specific bodies*
  differences in structure of, 140–142
  functions of, 139–140
Associational interest groups, 88–89
  interest aggregation and, 106
Athenian Assembly, 164
Austria
  chamber system in, 106
  democratic corporatist interest group systems in, 90
  "Grand Coalition" in, 115
  as member of European Community, 22
  organization of labor movement in, 90
  party systems in, 114
  separation of governmental powers in, 134
  Socialist Party in, 114

taxation in, 156
Authoritarian governments, 135
Authoritarian party systems, 66–68
  competitive party systems versus, 107
  exclusive, 117–118
  inclusive, 118–119
  interest aggregation and, 116
Azerbaijan, 14

Banfield, Edward, 98
Bangladesh, 14
Belarus, citizen participation in politics in, 71
Belgium, 56
  as consensual democracy, 138
  general strikes in, 95
  as member of European Community, 22
  split of traditional party system in, 22
Bicameralism, 141
Bolsheviks (Russia), 146
Bosnia, 15, 50
  political subcultures in, 48
Bosnia-Herzegovina, 14
Brazil, 29
  Afro-Brazilians and, 18
  area of, 6
  domestic welfare outcome in, 166
  economic development of, 12
  economic inequality within, 10
  expenditures by government in, 155
  federal system of, 132
  highly controlled interest groups in, 91
  homicide rate in, 172
  military regime replaced in, 122
  military role in political process in, 119–120
  national income of, 7
  political rights and civil liberties rated in, 162
  population growth in, 5
  technocratic repressive approach in, 183
  trend toward democracy in, 68
Britain. *See* United Kingdom
British Trades Unions Congress (United Kingdom), 90
Buddhists, 19, 54
Bulgaria, 4
Bundestag (Germany), 108
Buraku-min, 18
Bureaucracy(ies)

control of, 149
  functions of, 147–150
  as legitimate access channel, 93–94
  structure of, 146–147
Burundi, 174
Bush, George, 114, 144

Cabinet (United Kingdom), 32
Cambodia, 174
Canada, 3
  electoral system in, 108
  ethnic autonomy movement in, 14
  as pluralistic interest group system, 89
  population growth in, 13
Cárdenas, Lázaro, 118
Carey, John, 135
Carter, Jimmy, 120
Catholics, 5, 16, 19, 49, 53–54, 87, 98
Central Committee of Communist Party (China), 33
Central Committee of Communist Party (Soviet Union), 77
Central Intelligence Agency (United States), 146
Centralization, 6
Ceremonial executive, 142
Channels of political access, legitimate, 91
Chechnya, 18
Chernobyl, 29
Chiapas disorders, 173
Chief executives. *See* Political executive(s)
Chile
  democracy swept away in, 68
  lack of party cooperation in, 115
  military regime replaced in, 122
  military role in political process in, 120
  under Pinochet, 182
  technocratic repressive approach in, 183
China, 29
  agricultural labor force in, 8
  area of, 6
  authoritarian government of, 135
  Communist Party in. *See* Communist Party (China)
  development of political structures in, 68
  domestic welfare outcome in, 166

economic inequality within, 11
elections in, 65
exclusive governing party in, 117
expenditures by government in, 160
Great Proletarian Cultural Revolution of, 77
homicide rate in, 172
Imperial, 58
income distribution in, 10
as member of "Nuclear Club," 176
national income of, 7
National People's Congress of, 32
Politboro of, 33
political executive in, 142
political rights and civil liberties rated in, 162
political structure of, 31–33
political violence in, 173
population of, 5
    growth of, 6, 13
president of, function of, 144
State Council of, 32, 33
taxation in, 74
technocratic-mobilizational strategy and, 184
Tibetans and, 18
unitary system of government in, 132
Christian Democratic Party (Germany), 81
Christian Democratic Party (Italy), 109
Christians, 16, 19, 53–54
Churchill, Sir Winston, 144
Citizens
    as participants, 69–73
    political involvement of, types of, 69
    recruitment of, 68–69
    as subjects, 73–75
Civil society, 20
Class, as agent of political socialization, 54–55
Clerico-mobilization regime, 183
Clinton, Bill, 144
Coercive access channels and tactics, 91–92
Cold War, 14, 15, 23, 27, 131
"Collective action," problems of, 86, 88
Collective executive, 142
Colombia, 174
Commission (European Community), 22
Communication, 20
    media of, 28
    political, 34
Communism, 45, 59, 118, 179
Communist Party(ies)
    contact with government and, 57
    control of interest groups by, 91
    delegation of, in French National Assembly, 77

in Eastern Europe
    fall of, 58
    taxation and, 73–74
    elections and, 79
    as exclusive governing party, 117
    institutional interest groups and, 87, 88
    Marxism-Leninism and, 87, 181
    Roman Catholic Church versus, 87
Communist Party (China), 33, 60
    Central Committee of, 142
    control of associational groups by, 91
    as exclusive governing party, 117
Communist Party (Cuba)
    control of associational groups by, 91
    as exclusive governing party, 117
Communist Party (France)
    control of associational interest groups by, 91
    party systems and, 115
Communist Party (Italy), 109, 115
    control of associational interest groups by, 91
    interest aggregation by, 109
    party systems and, 115
Communist Party (North Korea)
    control of associational groups by, 91
    as exclusive governing party, 117
Communist Party (Poland), 53
Communist Party (Soviet Union), 31, 35, 36, 54, 65
    Central Committee of, 77
    control of associational groups by, 91
    as exclusive governing party, 117
Communist Party (Vietnam)
    control of associational groups by, 91
    as exclusive governing party, 117
Communist Party (Yugoslavia), 118
Comparative advantage, 12
Comparative politics
    concepts in, 26–39
    issues in, 3–23
Comparative Survey of Freedom, The, 162
Competition for offices, 65
Competitive parties
    elections and, 107–111
    in government, 111–113
    interest aggregation by, illustrated, 110
Competitive party system(s)
    authoritarian party systems versus, 107
    classifying, 113–116
    illustrated, 113
    interest aggregation and, 107–116
    parliamentary form of, 78
    presidential form of, 78

Confederal systems of government, 132
Conflictual party system, 114
Conflictual political cultures, 47–50
Confucians, 54
Congress (United States), 112
Congress of People's Deputies (Russia), 79
Consensual party system, 114
Consensual political cultures, 47–50
Conservative Party (United Kingdom), 56
Consociational party system, 114
Constitutional Convention of 1787, 133
Constitutional council, 137
Constitutions, 130–132. See also specific nations
Controlled interest group systems, 91
Convention People's Party (Ghana), 117
Council of Ministers (European Community), 22
Country. See Nation(s)
Crime rates, 171, 172
Cuba
    challenge of United States by, 5
    Communist Party of. See Communist Party (Cuba)
    political executive in, 142
    taxation in, 74
    technocratic-mobilizational strategy and, 184
Czechoslovakia, 4, 28
    move toward market economy and democratic politics in, 181

Dahl, Robert, 27, 75, 76
Daley, Richard F., Sr., 105
de Gaulle, Charles, 144
Decentralization, 21, 22
Decision rules
    defined, 130
    for policymaking, 130–138
Democracy, 21–22
    participant, 75
Democracy in America, 26
Democratic corporatist interest group systems, 89
Democratic Party (United States), 30, 181
    "reinventing government" program of, 56
Democratic presidential regime, 134
Democratic systems, 66–68
Democratic Unionist Party (Northern Ireland), 49
Democratization, 21
    in developing countries, 185–186
    Third Wave of, 68
    trend toward, 59
Deng Xiaoping, 142

Denmark
  constitution of, 138
  democratic corporatist interest
    group systems in, 90
  as member of European
    Community, 22
  organization of labor movement
    in, 90
Deutsch, Karl, 185
Dilemmas, 11–16
Direct contact with governmental
  structures, 57
Direct political socialization, 50
Direct taxes, 156
Disraeli, 54
Distributive performance, 154,
  157–161
Domestic security outcomes,
  171–173
Domestic welfare outcomes,
  164–171

East Germany, 181. *See also*
  Germany; West Germany
  as example of authoritarian
    political structure, 67
  incorporation of, into
    democratic united
    Germany, 68
  trend toward democracy in, 68
EC. *See* European Community
Economic and Social Committee
  (European Community), 23
Economic development of nations,
  11–12, 13
Economic inequality within
  nations, 10–11
Economy and Society, 15
Education, 8
  as agent of political socialization,
    52–53
  government expenditures on,
    158, 160
Effective executive, 142
Egypt, 19, 29, 46
  authoritarian government of,
    135
  development of political
    structures in, 68
  domestic welfare outcome in,
    166
  expenditures by government in,
    155
  homicide rate in, 172
  Islamic fundamentalism in, 53
  life expectancy in, 8
  political rights and civil liberties
    rated in, 162
  political violence in, 173
  population growth of, 5
  taxation in, 155
  technocratic repressive
    approach in, 183
  unitary system of government
    in, 132
Eire. *See* Ireland

Eisenhower, Dwight D., 178
El Salvador, 47
Election(s)
  competition for offices and,
    107–111
  competitive parties and,
    107–111
  laws regarding, 108
  participation in, illustrated, 64
  as political structure, 63–66
Elective office, competition for,
  107–111
Elites
  control of, 80–81
  political recruitment of, 76–80
  selection of, as policymakers,
    77–80
England. *See* United Kingdom
Environmentalism, 20
Estonia, 5
Ethiopia, 174
"Ethnic cleansing," 14, 15
Ethnicity, 16, 18, 56
  resurgence of, 58
European Community (EC), 22
  constitution of, 131
European Parliament (European
  Community), 22–23
Exclusive governing party,
  117–118
Executives. *See* Political
  executive(s)
Extractive performance, 154–157.
  See also Taxation

Falklands, crises in, 145
Family, as agent of political
  socialization, 51–52
Federal Bureau of Investigation
  (United States), 146
Federal Council (Switzerland), 143
Federal systems of government,
  132
Federalist, The, 133
Finland
  as member of European
    Community, 22
  party coalitions in, 112
"First past the post" electoral
  system, 108
Fitzgerald, John F. ("Honey Fitz"),
  105
France, 3
  agricultural labor force in, 8
  anomic behavior in, 85
  bicameralism in, 141
  citizen participation in politics
    in, types of, 70–73
  Communist Party in. *See*
    Communist Party (France)
  conflictual political cultures in,
    48
  constitutions of, 131
  control of associational interest
    groups in, 91
  crime rate in, 171

  development of, 27
  domestic welfare outcome in,
    165
  ethnic autonomy movement in,
    14
  expenditures by government in,
    155
  farmers' demonstrations in, 86
  as former imperialist power, 14
  higher civil service in, 146
  homicide rate in, 172
  "hybrid system" in, 136
  international security outcomes
    in, 174
  judicial review in, 137
  left-wing governments in, 112
  life expectancy in, 8
  as member of European
    Community, 22
  as member of "Nuclear Club,"
    176
  multiparty system in, 114
  National Assembly of, 77, 131
  organization of labor movement
    in, 90
  party coalitions in, 111
  party systems in, 114, 115
  party-electoral aggregation in,
    110
  as pluralistic interest group
    system, 89
  political recruitment of elites in,
    76
  political subcultures in, 48
  political violence in, 173
  president of, 142
  presidential system in, 78
  prime minister in, 78
  prison population in, 173
  protests by doctors in, 94
  radical right and, 18
  revolution in, 73
  Socialist Party in, 115
  strong political party discipline
    in, 93
  taxation in, 154
    evasion and, 74
  "Third Republic," 28
  unitary system of government
    in, 132
  weak political executive and, 145
  wildcat strikes in, 86
Franco, Francisco, 182
Freedom House, 162

GATT (General Agreement on
  Tariffs and Trade), 20
GDP (Gross Domestic Product),
  166
General Agreement on Tariffs and
  Trade (GATT), 20
Georgia, 14
German Democratic Republic. *See*
  East Germany
Germany, 3, 29
  agricultural labor force in, 8

Bundestag of, 108
chancellor of, function of, 143
Christian Democratic Party in, 81
citizen participation in politics in types of, summarized, 70–73
consensual multiparty system in, 114
constitutions of, 131
deaths in international warfare and, 174
democratic corporatist interest group systems in, 90
democratic united, incorporation of East Germany into, 68
electoral system in, 108
emergence of National Socialism in, 174
expenditures by government in, 155
federal system of, 132
ideological spectrum in, 48
industrialization in, 54–55
international security outcomes in, 174
judicial review in, 137
life expectancy in, 8
as member of European Community, 22
multiparty system in, 114
national income of, 7
Nazi, 27
new political arrangements introduced in, after World War II defeat, 131
ombudsman in, 149
parliamentary form of system in, 136
party coalitions in, 111
party-electoral aggregation in, 110
president of, function of, 144
radical right and, 18
Social Democratic Party in, 80–81
taxation in, 155, 156
voter participation in, 63
Weimar, 115
"Wilhelmine," 28
Ghana
Convention People's Party as exclusive governing party in, 117
economic inequality within, 11
military role in political process in, 120
Glasnost, 36
Globalization, 21, 22
GNP. *See* Gross National Product
Gorbachev, Mikhail, 35, 36, 45, 79
Gore, Albert, 148
Gourevitch, Peter, 173
Government(s)
authoritarian, 135
authority of, 132

bureaucracy of. *See* Bureaucracy(ies)
central
expenditures of, 155
revenues of, 154
competitive parties in, 111–113
defined, 28
direct contact with, as agent of political socialization, 57
incumbents and, 56
legitimacy of, 44
military, 119–120
policymaking and, 129–150
power of. *See* Government power(s)
Government power(s)
geographic distribution of, 132
limitations on, 136–138
separation of, 133–136
"Grand Coalition" (Austria), 115
Great Britain. *See* United Kingdom
Great Depression, 164
Great Proletarian Cultural Revolution (China), 77
Greece, 4, 22
Athenian Assembly in, 164
city-states in, 21, 26
conflictual political cultures in, 48
democracy swept away in, 68
left-wing governments in, 112
as member of European Community, 22
polarized cultures in, 124
of "the generals," 182
"Green" parties, 181
Gross Domestic Product (GDP), 166
Gross National Product (GNP), 7, 8
central government expenditures as a percentage of, 155
central government revenues as a percentage of, 154
of selected countries, illustrated, 7
welfare outcomes and, 166
Guatemala, 174
Guinea, military role in political process in, 120
Gurr, Ted Robert, 94

Haiti
American intervention in, 145
military regime replaced in, 122
military role in political process in, 120
Hamilton, Alexander, 133
Harding, Warren, 178
Heclo, Hugh, 156
Heidenheimer, Arnold, 156
Higher civil service, 146
Hindus, 54
Homicide rates, 172
Horowitz, Donald, 135

House of Commons (United Kingdom), 33
House of Lords (United Kingdom), 141
House of Representatives (United States), 130
Hungary
expenditures by government in, 155
move of, toward market economy and democratic politics, 181
taxation in, 156
Huntington, Samuel P., 21–22, 48–49, 59, 68

Ibo, 18
Imperial China, 58
Implementation, 33
Implementation: How Great Expectations in Washington Are Dashed in Oakland, 148
Inclusive governing party, 117
Inclusiveness, evaluating interest group systems in terms of, 99
Income distribution within nations, 10–11
Incumbents, 56
India, 19, 45
agricultural labor force in, 8
anomic behavior in, 85
British withdrawal from, 14
democratic preindustrial system in, 46
development of political structures in, 68
domestic welfare outcome in, 166
economic inequality within, 8
electoral system in, 108
expenditures by government in, 155
federal system of, 132
Hindus and, 18
life expectancy in, 8
as member of "Nuclear Club," 176
national income of, 7
parliamentary form of system in, 136
patron-client networks in, 105
police officers in, 173
political violence in, 173
population growth in, 6
as relatively undeveloped country, 185
religious fundamentalism in, 53
taxation in, 155
war in, 174
Indirect political socialization, 50
Indirect taxes, 156
Individual contactors, 85
Individual executive, 142
Indonesia

authoritarian system in, 46
military role in political process
    in, 120
patron-client networks in, 105
technocratic repressive
    approach in, 183
violent protests in, 95
Industrialized authoritarian
    nations, 181–182
Industrialized democratic nations,
    180–181
Inequalities, 10
Inglehart, Ronald, 98
Inkeles, Alex, 57
Inputs, 29
Institutional interest groups,
    87–88
interest aggregation and,
    106–107
Institutions, political. See Political
    structure(s)
Interest aggregation, 33
by competitive party, illustrated,
    110
competitive party systems and,
    107–116
defined, 104
interest groups and, 105–107
political parties and, 104–124
significance of, 123–124
structures performing,
    summarized, 106
trends in, 121–123
Interest articulation, 33
interest groups and, 98–100
policy perspectives on, 96–98
summarized, 97
Interest groups
access to the influential by,
    91–96
as agent of political socialization,
    55–56
development of, 98–100
interest aggregation and,
    105–107
interest articulation and, 84
systems of, 89–91
    evaluation of, in terms of
        inclusiveness, 99
    labor unions and, 90
types of, 85–91
Internal Revenue Service (United
    States), 74
International Development Fund,
    9
International Monetary Fund, 7
International trade, growth of, 20
Iran, 19
Islamic fundamentalism in, 50,
    53
war in, 174
Iraq
nuclear proliferation and, 176
technocratic repressive
    approach in, 183
war in, 174

Iraq-Kuwait Desert War of 1990,
    175
Ireland. See also Northern Ireland
as member of European
    Community, 22
Islam. See Muslims
Israel, 19
electoral system in, 108
Jewish fundamentalist
    movement in, 53
Jewish population of, 15
as member of "Nuclear Club,"
    176
trade relations of, 29
Italian Bishops' Conference,
    Permanent Council of, 87
Italy, 98
anomic behavior in, 85
Christian Democratic Party in,
    124
Communist Party in. See
    Communist Party (Italy)
conflictual political cultures in,
    48
control of associational interest
    groups in, 91
democracy and, 21
electoral system in, 109
general strikes in, 96
Italian Bishops' Conference in,
    87
labor disorders in, 87
legislature of, 139–140
as member of European
    Community, 22
migration from, 15
new political arrangements
    introduced in, after World
    War II defeat, 131
Parliament of, 47
party coalitions in, 112
party systems in, 115
party-electoral aggregation in,
    110
political subcultures in, 48
president of, 144
Roman Catholic Church as
    institutional interest group
    in, 87
taxation in, 156
weak political executive in, 145
wildcat strikes in, 86
Ivory Coast, 118

Japan, 3, 8, 29
agricultural labor force in, 8
bargaining between parties in,
    112
Buraku-min and, 18
domestic welfare outcome in,
    166
economic inequality within, 10
expenditures by government in,
    155
homicide rate in, 172
legitimate access channels in, 92

Liberal Democratic Party in,
    112
life expectancy in, 8
national income of, 7
new political arrangements
    introduced in, after World
    War II defeat, 131
organization of labor movement
    in, 90
parliamentary form of system in,
    136
patron-client networks in, 105
per GNP product of, 7
as pluralistic interest group
    system, 89
political violence in, 173
taxation in, 154
trade relations of, 29
unitary system of government
    in, 132
Jefferson, Thomas, 130
Jews, 15, 19
Judicial review, 137

Kazakhstan, 16
riots in, 87
Kemal Ataturk, 144
Kennedy, John F., 178
Kenya
long-time president retained in,
    122
one-party system in, 118
Khomeini, Ayatollah Ruholla, 179
Khrushchev, Nikita, 79
King, Martin Luther, Jr., 86
King, Rodney, 95
Kirgizia, 16
Kohl, Helmut, 81, 144
Korea. See North Korea; South
    Korea
Korean War, 178
Kuwait, 175
Kuznets, Simon, 168

Labor unions, 90
Labour Party (United Kingdom),
    56
Länder, 155
Languages, 15
Latvia, 5
Lebanon
civil war in, 47, 50
consociational system in, 115
political subcultures in, 48
religious fundamentalism in, 53
Legislature. See also Assemblies;
    specific bodies
as policymaking institution, 33
as target of interest group
    activities, 93
Legitimacy
defined, 29
of government, 44
Legitimate access channels, 91
Lehmbruch, Gerhard, 134
Lerner, Daniel, 185

Liberal Democratic Party (Japan), 112
Liberal Democratic Party (United Kingdom), 110
Liberalization, 20
Lijphart, Arend, 114, 134, 135, 138
Linz, Juan, 135
Lipset, Seymour M., 185
Literacy, 8
Lithuania, 5
Locke, John, 133
Luxembourg, 5, 22

Madison, James, 133
Major, John, 81, 144
Majoritarian party systems, 113
Malawi, long-time president of, replaced through election, 122
Mao Zedong, 117
March, James G., 132
Marketization, movement toward, 59
Marx, Karl, 179
Marxism-Leninism, 87, 181
Mass media
    as agent of political socialization, 55
    controlled, 57
    as legitimate access channel, 92
Mayans, 18
Media of communication, 28
Mexico, 8, 10
    Chiapas disorders in, 173
    doctors' work stoppages and petitions in, 87
    domestic welfare outcome in, 165
    economic development of, 12
    expenditures by government in, 155
    federal system of, 132
    highly controlled interest groups in, 91
    homicide rate in, 172
    income distribution in, 11
    life expectancy in, 8
    Mayans and, 18
    migrant workers from, 14
    Partido Revolucionario Institucional (PRI) in, 78, 79, 132
        domination of political process by, 118–119
    political rights and civil liberties rated in, 162
    political violence in, 173
    taxation in, 155
    technocratic-mobilizational strategy in, 184
    transitional system in, 135–136
Military
    government expenditures on, 159, 160
    interest aggregation and, 107
    role of, in government, 122–123

Mitterrand, Francois, 144
Mixed presidential-parliamentary regime, 134, 136
Mobutu Sese Seko, 122
Modernization
    interest group development and, 98
    shaping of political cultures by, 58
Moi, Daniel Arap, 118
Moldova, 174
Montesquieu, Baron de, 133
Multiparty systems, 113
Muslims, 14, 53, 122
Mussolini, Benito, 179

Nadel, Mark V., 148
"Nader's Raiders," 149
NAFTA (North American Free Trade Agreement), 20
Napoleonic Wars, 174
Nation(s), 28
    area of, 6
    defined, 3
    economic development of, 5–6
    economic inequality within, 10–11
    formation of, 4
    income distribution within, 11
    labor force of, 8
    language spoken in, 15
    literacy in, 20
    population of, 6
    religion practiced in, 15–20
National Assembly (France), 77
National Institutes of Health (United States), 146
Nation-states, 26
NATO (North Atlantic Treaty Organization), 14, 23, 29, 175
Nazis, 27
Neotraditional political systems, 182
Netherlands
    as consensual democracy, 138
    consociational system in, 115
    democratic corporatist interest group systems in, 90
    domestic welfare outcome in, 165
    electoral system in, 108
    as former imperial power, 14
    as member of European Community, 22
    party coalitions in, 112
    Social and Economic Council in, 106
    taxation in, 154
New Deal (United States), 178
New Zealand
    electoral system in, 108
    majoritarian system in, 138
    as pluralistic interest group system, 89
Nicaragua, 174

Nigeria
    agricultural labor force in, 8
    authoritarian government of, 135
    constitution of, 135
    development of political structures in, 68
    domestic welfare outcome in, 166
    elections in, 64
    expenditures by government in, 160
    Ibo and, 18
    long-time tenure of party in power in, 122
    military role in political process in, 120
    police officers in, 173
    political rights and civil liberties rated in, 162
    political violence in, 173
    population growth of, 5
    recruitment of chief executive in, 79
    religious fundamentalism in, 53
Nixon, Richard, 81, 147
Nkrumah, Kwame, 117–118
Nomenklatura, 80
Nonassociational interest groups, 86–87
Noncompetitive party system; Authoritarian party systems, 107
North, Oliver, 147
North American Free Trade Agreement (NAFTA), 20
North Atlantic Treaty Organization (NATO), 14, 23, 29, 175
North Korea. See also South Korea
    Communist Party of. See Communist Party (North Korea)
    political executive in, 142
    taxation in, 74
    technocratic-mobilizational strategy and, 184
Northern Ireland. See also Ireland; United Kingdom
    civil war in, 47
    homicides in, 96
    lack of party cooperation in, 115
    legitimacy of government in, 45
    political parties in, 49–50
    political subcultures in, 48
    political violence in, 173
    repression in, 43
    voting polarization in, 49
Norway
    consensual multiparty system in, 114
    constitution of, 138
    democratic corporatist interest group systems in, 90
    organization of labor movement in, 90
    separation of governmental powers in, 134

strategies for producing political goods in, 181
taxation in, 154
"Nuclear Club," 176
Nunn, Sam, 120

Occupation, as agent of political socialization, 54–55
OECD (Organization for Economic Cooperation and Development), 156, 157
Office, elective, competition for, 107–111
Olsen, Johann P., 132
Ombudsman, 149
Opportunity costs, 186
Organization for Economic Cooperation and Development (OECD), 156, 157
Outcomes, 35
domestic security, 171–173
domestic welfare, 164–171
in international arena, 173–176
Outputs, 29. *See also* Performance
in international arena, 173–176

Pakistan
British withdrawal from Indian empire and, 14
Islamic fundamentalism in, 50, 53
as member of "Nuclear Club," 176
migration to United States from, 16
military role in political process in, 120
Palestine
migration and, 14
political struggle in, 16
terrorism and, 96
Paraguay, military role in political process in, 120
Parliament (United Kingdom), 32
Parliament Act of 1911 (United Kingdom), 137
Parliamentary form of competitive party system, 78
Parliamentary regime, 134
Parochials, 45
Participant democracy, 75
Participants, 45
activities of, 69–70
citizens as, 75–76
Partido Revolucionario Institucional (PRI) (Mexico), 78, 79, 132
domination of political process by, 118–119
Party coalitions, 111
Party-electoral aggregation, 109
Patron-client networks, 105
Payne, James, 95
Peace Corps, 178
Peer groups, as agent of political socialization, 54

People's Republic of China. *See* China
Perestroika, 36
Performance, 39
distributive, 154, 157–161
extractive, 154–157
in international arena, 173–176
outcomes of. *See* Outcomes
political goods and, 176–186
regulative, 161–163
symbolic, 163–164
Pericles, 164
Perot, Ross, 114
Persian Gulf, crises in, 145, 175
Personal articulation, 69
Personal rule, 182–183
Peru
assassinations by Shining Path guerrillas in, 96
democratic breakdown in, 68
interest group development in, 99
violent demonstrations and riots in, 95
Philippines
development of political structures in, 68
patron-client networks in, 105
people's power movement in, 96
trend toward democracy in, 68
Pinochet, Augusto, 182
Pluralistic interest group systems, 89
Plurality, 108
Poe, Steven C., 162–163
Poland
move of, toward market economy and democratic politics, 181
tension between Communist regime and Catholic Church in, 53
Policy functions, 35
Policy propensities, 47
Policymaking, 33
decision rules for, 130–138
government and, 129–150
interest group access and, 91
selection of elites for, 77–80
Politboro (China), 33
Political communication, 34
Political culture(s)
conflictual, 47–50
consensual, 47–50
contemporary, trends in, 57–60
defined, 43
models of, illustrated, 46
modernization and, 58
policy level of, 47
process level of, 45–47
secularization and, 58
system level of, 44–45
Political executive(s)
functions of, 144–146
policymaking by, 142–146
recruitment of, 142–144

types of, summarized, 143
Political function(s), 28–31
political system and, illustrated, 32
Political goods
opportunity costs and, 186
political productivity and, 176–179
strategies for producing, 179–186
democratization in developing countries and, 185–186
in industrialized authoritarian nations, 181–182
in industrialized democratic nations, 180–181
in preindustrial nations, 182–184
trade-offs and, 186
Political institutions. *See* Political structure(s)
Political parties. *See also specific parties*
as agent of political socialization, 56–57
competitive, 78–80
interest aggregation and, 104–124
as legitimate access channel, 93
noncompetitive, 78, 79
Political performance. *See* Performance
Political problems and world trends, 20–23
illustrated, 21
Political recruitment, 34
of chief executives, 78–80
of citizens, 68–69
elections and, 63–66
of elites, 76–80
of political leaders, 63, 77–80
Political resocialization, 51
Political rights and civil liberties, rating of, 163
Political self, 50
Political socialization, 34
agents of, 51–57
defined, 43
direct, 50
indirect, 50
resocialization and, 51
Political structure(s)
defined, 29
election as, 63–66
Political subcultures, 48
Political system(s)
authoritarian, 66–68
comparative, 26–39
defined, 28
democratic, 66–68
environments and, illustrated, 30
function of, 28–31
neotraditional, 182
outputs of. *See* Performance

performance of. *See*
Performance
political goods and. *See* Political
goods
productivity of, 177
structure of, 28–31
illustrated, 32
Political terror tactics, 96
Politics, 26
Politics, defined, 28
Population
growth of, 5–6
of selected countries, area and,
illustrated, 6
Population Explosion, The, 12
Portugal, 22
constitutional changes in, 131
as former imperial power, 14
as member of European
Community, 22
Powell, Colin, 120
Power(s)
government. *See* Government
power(s)
separation of, 133–136
PPP (Purchasing Power Parity), 7
Preindustrial authoritarian
regimes, 182–184
President. *See* Political executive(s)
Presidential form of competitive
party system, 78
Presidential-parliamentary regime,
136
PRI. *See* Partido Revolucionario
Institucional
Prime Minister. *See* Political
executive(s)
Process functions, illustrated, 32
Process propensities, 45–47
Progressive taxation, 156
Proportional representation, 108
Protest demonstrations, pressure
on government and, 94
Protestants, 16, 49, 53–54
Public policy(ies), 28
performance and, 153–186
political goods and. *See* Political
goods
regulative, 161–163
Purchasing Power Parity (PPP), 7
Putnam, Robert, 98

Radical right, 18
Reagan, Ronald, 60, 144, 147
Recruitment, political. *See* Political
recruitment
Red Brigade terrorism, 115
Redistribution With Growth, 12
Reform Acts of 1832 and 1867
(United Kingdom), 131
Regime(s)
authoritarian, 182–184
defined, 28
democratic presidential, 134
mixed presidential-
parliamentary, 134, 136

parliamentary, 134
presidential-parliamentary, 136
Regionalization, 21, 22
Regressive taxation, 156
Regulative performance, 161–163
Regulative policies, 161–163
Relative deprivation, 94
Religion(s)
as agent of political socialization,
53–54
fundamentalist movements and,
53–54
institutional interest groups and,
87
in nations, 15–20
Republic of Ireland. *See* Ireland
Republican Party (United States),
30, 178
"balanced budget" constitutional
amendment and, 181
Resocialization, political, 51
Riot, as coercive tactic, 95
Roman Catholic Church
control of French and Italian
associational interest
groups by, 91
as institutional interest group in
Italy, 87
Roosevelt, Franklin Delano, 144
Rourke, Francis E., 148
Russia, 29
area of, 5
Bolsheviks and, 146
Chechens and, 18
citizen participation in politics
in, 71
Congress of People's Deputies
of, 79
constitution of, 131
crime rate in, 171
Czarist, 28, 146
deaths in international warfare
and, 174
elections in, 65
federal system of, 132
as former imperial power, 14
"hybrid system" in, 136
as member of "Nuclear Club,"
176
political rights and civil liberties
rated in, 162
political systems of 1987 and
1994 compared, 35–38
return to repressive politics in,
181
role of prime minister in, 78
separation of powers in, 136
Supreme Soviet of, 35, 37
"Tsarist," 28, 146
Russian Federation. *See* Russia
Rwanda, 14, 47

Sartori, Giovanni, 132, 135, 136
Saudi Arabia, 29
neotraditional political system
of, 182

no elections held in, 63
trade relations of, 29
as traditional kingship, 142
Schmidt, Helmut, 81
Schmitter, Philippe, 134
School, as agent of political
socialization, 52–53
Scottish National Party (United
Kingdom), 114
Secularization, 20
shaping of political cultures by,
58
Sen, Amartya, 13, 170
Senate (United States), 137
Senate, as form of assembly, 138
Sendero Luminoso (Shining Path),
96
Separation of powers, 133–136
Serbia, 14
Service economy, rise of, 20
Shining Path (Sendero Luminoso),
96
Shugart, Matthew, 135
Sierra Club, 71
Sierra Leone, 122
Singapore, marketization and, 60
Sinn Fein, 49
Smith, David, 57
Social and Economic Council
(Netherlands), 106
Social Democratic and Labour
Party (SDLP)(Northern
Ireland), 49
Social Democratic Party
(Germany), 81
Social Democratic Party (Sweden),
90
Social Democratic Party (United
Kingdom), 110
Socialist Party (Austria), 114
Socialist Party (France), 115
Socialization, political. *See* Political
socialization
Somalia, 174
South Africa
consociational system in, 115
constitution of, 131
educational system in, 52–53
elections in, 64
interest group development in,
99
political struggle in, 16
repression in, 43
South Korea
democratic emergence of, 185
economic development of, 12
marketization and, 60
technocratic-distributive regime
in, 184
technocratic-mobilizational
strategy in, 184
trade relations of, 29
Soviet Union, 21, 23, 28, 29, 48,
59, 75. *See also* Russia
area of, 5
citizen participation in politics in

types of, summarized, 70–73
Communist Party in. *See* Communist Party (Soviet Union)
controlled mass media in, 57
deaths in international warfare and, 174
economy of, 44–45
elections in, 65
as example of authoritarian political structure, 67
exclusive governing party in, 117
expenditures by government in, 160
for defense, 38–39
former, 38, 148
nomenklatura in, 80
recruitment of chief executive in, 80
riots in, 87
successor countries of, 14, 16, 19
withdrawal of support for authoritarian governments by, 122
Spain
constitutional changes in, 131
ethnic automony movement in, 14
as former imperial power, 14
Franco, 182
highly controlled interest groups in, 91
as member of European Community, 22
trend toward democracy in, 68
Sri Lanka, 16, 19
Stalin, Joseph, 117
State(s). *See also* Government(s); Nation(s)
defined, 28
welfare, 153
State Council (China), 32, 33
Status, as agent of political socialization, 54–55
Strikes
as coercive tactics, 95
pressure on government and, 94
Structural-functional approach, 27
Structure, political. *See* Political structure(s)
Subcultures, political, 48
Subjects, 45
activities of, 69, 73–75
citizens as, 73–75
Sudan
long-time tenure of party in power in, 122
war in, 174
Sukarno, 95
Supreme Court (United States), 81
Supreme Soviet (Russia), 35, 37
Suriname, military regime replaced in, 122
Sweden
consensual multiparty system in, 114

democratic corporatist interest group systems in, 90
domestic welfare outcome in, 165
international security outcomes in, 174
majoritarian system in, 138
as member of European Community, 22
ombudsman in, 149
population growth in, 13
protests by civil servants, 94
separation of governmental powers in, 134
Social Democratic Party in, 90
strategies for producing political goods in, 181
taxation in, 156
unionized nonagricultural work force in, 90
as welfare state, 27
wildcat strikes in, 86
Switzerland
as consensual democracy, 138
constitution of, 138
Federal Council of, 143
Symbolic performance, 163–164
Syria
military role in political process in, 120
technocratic repressive approach in, 183
System, political. *See* Political system(s)
System functions, 35
System propensities, 44–45

Taiwan
democratic emergence of, 185
economic development of, 12
marketization and, 60
technocratic-mobilizational strategy in, 184
Tajikistan
Islamic rebellion in, 174
as member of "Nuclear Club," 176
Tanzania
development of political structures in, 68
expenditures by government in, 155
one-party system in, 118
Tate, C. Neal, 162–163
Taxation. *See specific nations*
Technocratic authoritarian approach, 181
Technocratic repressive regime, 183–184
Technocratic-distributive regime, 184
Technocratic-mobilizational regime, 184
Technology, spread of, 20
Terrorism, 96
Red Brigade, 115

Thailand, patron-client networks in, 105
Thatcher, Margaret, 60, 90, 144
Third Wave, The, 21
Tibet, 18
Tienanmen Square disorders, 173
Tocqueville, Alexis de, 26
Totalitarian party, 116
Trade-offs, 186
Turkey, 4
Tweed, William Marcy ("Boss"), 105

Ukraine
citizen participation in politics in, 71
homicide rate in, 172
as member of "Nuclear Club," 176
as potential hot spot, 16
Ulster, 16
UN. *See* United Nations
Unions, 90
Unitary systems of government, 132
United Kingdom, 3, 6, 29, 133
agricultural labor force in, 8
bureaucracy of, 146
Cabinet of, 32
citizen participation in politics in, types of, 70–73
consensual majoritarian system in, 114
Conservative Party in, 92
constitutional arrangements of, 137
domestic welfare outcome in, 165
electoral system in, 108
as example of democratic political structure, 67
expenditures by government in, 155
farmers' demonstrations in, 86
as former imperialist power, 14
general strikes in, 96
higher civil service in, 146
homicide rate in, 172
House of Commons in, 33
House of Lords, 137
ideological spectrum in, 48
industrialization in, 54–55
international security outcomes in, 174
Labour Party in, 77
Liberal Democratic Party in, 110
life expectancy in, 8
majoritarian system in, 138
as member of European Community, 22
as member of "Nuclear Club," 176
Northern Ireland and, 49
ombudsman in, 149
organization of labor movement in, 90

Parliament of, 47
Parliament Act of 1911 of, 137
parliamentary form of system in, 78, 136
party-electoral aggregation in, 110
as pluralistic interest group system, 89
political parties in, 56
political recruitment of elites in, 76
political structure of, 31–35
political violence in, 173
prime minister of, 143
queen of, 143
Reform Acts of 1832 and 1867 of, 131
Scottish National Party in, 114
Social Democratic Party in, 110
strategies for producing political goods in, 181
strong political party discipline in, 93
taxation in, 154, 156
Trades Unions Congress in, 90
traditional public schools in, 52
unitary system of government in, 132
voter participation in, 63
Welsh Party in, 114
wildcat strikes in, 86
United Nations, 9, 175
General Assembly of, 3
intervention of, in Serbia, 14
peacekeeping and, 23
United Nations Demographic Year-book for 1994, The, 172
United States, 3, 4, 133
Afro-Americans and, 18
anomic behavior in, 85
area of, 6
under Articles of Confederation, 132
bargaining between parties in, 112
Central Intelligence Agency of, 146
Christian fundamentalism in, 53
citizen participation in politics in, 70
types of, summarized, 69, 70–73
Congress of, 112
consensual majoritarian system in, 114
Constitution of, 132
amending of, 137–138
contact with government in, 57
crime rate in, 171
decentralized political party organizations in, 93
Democratic Party in. *See* Democratic Party (United States)

disillusionment with Vietnam War in, 55
domestic welfare outcome in, 165
economic inequality within, 10
electoral system in, 108
ethnicity in, 16, 18
expenditures by government in, 155
for defense, 38–39
Federal Bureau of Investigation of, 146
federal system of, 130
higher civil service in, 146
House of Representatives of, 130
ideological spectrum in, 48
interest aggregation in, 123, 124
interest group development in, 99
Internal Revenue Service of, 146
international security outcomes in, 174
judicial review in, 137
labor force in, 29–30
agricultural, 8
life expectancy in, 8
majoritarian party system in, 113
as member of "Nuclear Club," 176
military intervention of, in Serbia, 14
National Institutes of Health of, 146
national party conventions in, 109
National Security Council of, 142
New Deal in, 178
organization of labor movement in, 90
Peace Corps of, 178
as pluralistic interest group system, 89
police officers in, 173
political action committees in, 93
political culture in, 59
political recruitment of elites in, 76
political rights and civil liberties rated in, 162
political subcultures in, 48
population growth in, 13
president of, 143
presidential system in, 78
prison population in, 173
protests by "gray panthers" in, 94
Republican Party in. *See* Republican Party (United States)
revolution in, precipitated by efforts to raise taxes, 73
Senate of, 137
strategies for producing political goods in, 181

Supreme Court of, 81
taxation in, 74, 154
voter participation in, 63
War on Poverty in, 178
Urbanization, 20
Uruguay
democracy swept away in, 68
military regime replaced in, 122
USSR. *See* Soviet Union

Vatican City, 5
Verba, Sidney, 57
Vietnam
Communist Party of. *See* Communist Party (Vietnam)
taxation in, 74
technocratic-mobilizational strategy and, 184
Vietnam War, 29
demonstrations against, 94

War on Poverty (United States), 178
Weber, Max, 15
Weimar Republic. *See* Germany
Welfare outcomes, 164–171
Welfare state, 27
Welsh Party, 114
West Germany. *See also* East Germany; Germany
domestic welfare outcome in, 165
environmental movement in, 100
homicide rate in, 172
organization of labor movement in, 90
parliamentary form of system in, 78
Wildavsky, Aaron, 148
Wilensky, Harold, 160
Wilhelmine Germany, 28
Wilner, Ann, 95
World Bank, 9, 12
World Development Report, 6, 8
World trends and political problems, 20–23
illustrated, 21
World War I, 18, 59, 68, 130, 178
World War II, 5, 19, 21, 22, 23, 29, 59, 68, 114, 115, 119, 130, 131, 133, 164, 166, 174, 179

Yeltsin, Boris, 35, 37, 65
Yes, Minister, 149
Yugoslavia, 4, 5
breakup of, 28, 48
civil war in, 47
Communist Party in, 118
"ethnic cleansing" in, 14
legitimacy of system in, 45

Zaire, 122
Zambia, 122
Zimbabwe, 135